Conversations with
George Saunders

Literary Conversations Series

Monika Gehlawat
General Editor

Conversations with George Saunders

Edited by Michael O'Connell

University Press of Mississippi / Jackson

The University Press of Mississippi is the scholarly publishing agency of
the Mississippi Institutions of Higher Learning: Alcorn State University,
Delta State University, Jackson State University, Mississippi State University,
Mississippi University for Women, Mississippi Valley State University,
University of Mississippi, and University of Southern Mississippi.

www.upress.state.ms.us

The University Press of Mississippi is a member
of the Association of University Presses.

First printing 2022
∞

Library of Congress Cataloging-in-Publication Data

Names: O'Connell, Michael J., 1980– editor.
Title: Conversations with George Saunders / Michael O'Connell.
Other titles: Literary conversations series.
Description: Jackson : University Press of Mississippi, 2022. |
    Series: Literary conversations series | Includes index.
Identifiers: LCCN 2022004944 (print) | LCCN 2022004945 (ebook) |
    ISBN 9781496840295 (hardback) | ISBN 9781496840301 (trade paperback) |
    ISBN 9781496840318 (epub) | ISBN 9781496840325 (epub) |
    ISBN 9781496840332 (pdf) | ISBN 9781496840349 (pdf)
Subjects: LCSH: Saunders, George, 1958—Interviews. | Authors, American—
    20th century—Interviews. | Authors, American—21st century—Interviews.
Classification: LCC PS3569.A7897 Z46 2022 (print) | LCC PS3569.A7897 (ebook) |
    DDC 813/.54 [B]—dc23/eng/20220415
LC record available at https://lccn.loc.gov/2022004944
LC ebook record available at https://lccn.loc.gov/2022004945

British Library Cataloging-in-Publication Data available

Books by George Saunders

Major Works

CivilWarLand in Bad Decline (1996)—short story collection
Pastoralia (2000)—short story collection
In Persuasion Nation (2006)—short story collection
The Braindead Megaphone (2007)—collected essays
Tenth of December (2013)—short story collection
Lincoln in the Bardo (2017)—novel
A Swim in a Pond in the Rain: In Which Four Russians Give a Master Class on Writing, Reading, and Life (2021)—essays

Other Book Publications

The Very Persistent Gappers of Frip (2000)—illustrated children's book
The Brief and Frightening Reign of Phil (2005)—novella
A Bee Stung Me So I Killed All the Fish (2006)—chapbook of essays and humor pieces
Congratulations, by the way: Some Thoughts on Kindness (2014)—gift book edition
Fox 8 (2018)—illustrated short story

Contents

Introduction: "Why Not Try?"

When I first emailed George Saunders about putting together an edited collection of his interviews, he wrote back, "I've often felt that I've done some of my best 'work' in interviews—there's something about the spontaneity and the lifting of the burden of being heavy that helps me tell the truth, sometimes." This assertion that some of his best work is done via interviews sets an extremely high bar for this volume, considering the accolades his other work has garnered, including the Man Booker Prize, for his novel *Lincoln in the Bardo*, and the Folio Prize and the Story Prize, for his short story collection *Tenth of December*. But I think readers of this collection, whether they are longtime readers of his work or newcomers to it, will understand why Saunders makes this claim. The interviews in this volume are funny, insightful, wise, surprisingly moving—the same traits that define his fiction and his essays.

Saunders is one of America's most popular and celebrated writers. He is the author of four short story collections and one novel, as well as two essay collections, a children's book, and one novella (see the attached list of the author's major works). He has been awarded both MacArthur and Guggenheim fellowships, along with the PEN/Malamud Prize for excellence in the short story. He is a member of the American Academy of Arts and Sciences, and, in 2013, was named one of *Time*'s "100 Most Influential People in the World." His short stories and essays are regularly published in the *New Yorker*, *GQ*, and *Harper's*, and subsequently make frequent appearances in the various *Best American* anthologies. His books regularly appear on the *New York Times* bestseller list. His popularity is such that even his commencement address at Syracuse University was reprinted in gift book form, as *Congratulations, by the way: Some Thoughts on Kindness*, and became a bestseller.

Alongside this mainstream appeal, Saunders's work is the focus of expanding critical attention. *George Saunders: Critical Essays*, the first book-length consideration of Saunders's work, came out in 2017. The newly established George Saunders Society has sponsored panels on his work at recent American Language Association conferences, and his work has been featured in panels at the Modern Language Association conference as well. In recent years, essays on his work have appeared in a number of scholarly journals, including *Critique: Studies in Contemporary Fiction*; the *European Journal of American Studies*; *Contemporary Literature*; and *Studies in American Humor*. As this critical conversation continues to expand and develop, the presence of this volume will provide important insights into Saunders's writing process. In these interviews, he provides numerous insights into how he thinks fiction works and what he wants his own work to accomplish, and as such I think it will be an invaluable resource for scholars.

Besides his popular and critical appeal, one reason I was excited to work on this project is that Saunders is truly an excellent interview subject. Over the nearly twenty years of interviews that are represented in this volume, he provides detailed insight into his own writing process and craft, interpretations of his own work, reflections on common themes that recur throughout his oeuvre, and commentary on his relationships with other writers, both living and dead. These interviews also cover aspects of his biography, including his childhood, his experiences as both a student and teacher in MFA programs, how parenthood affected his writing, the role of religious belief and practice in his work, and how he has dealt with his growing popularity and fame. In these interviews we see him in conversation with former students, other writers, mainstream critics, and literary scholars, and in each instance it is clear that he is actively engaged in the back and forth dialogue. As he told me, via email, "I've always enjoyed doing interviews. I was a big fan of *The Dick Cavett Show* as a little kid and the idea got into my head that an intense, respectful conversation was, really, an art form—an exploration of sorts." Readers of this volume will have the pleasure of joining him in this process of exploration.

As the editor of this volume, I found the principal challenge to be one of selection. How does one choose which interviews to include, when there are literally hundreds of worthwhile options to select from? I wanted to include interviews that spanned the length of Saunders's career, so that readers can see how these conversations evolve over time as his fame has grown and his own understanding of his craft has developed. To represent the early years, the selection process was relatively straightforward; there were only a handful of substantive interviews that came out around each publication (though it was still difficult to choose just one or two to represent them all). But with the success of *Tenth of December* and *Lincoln in the Bardo*, the number increased exponentially. Invariably, some of these interviews become repetitive, as interviewers ask similar questions to each other, or cover ground that was discussed in depth in earlier interviews. When I asked him about this experience, he wrote back, "I never did that many interviews until *Tenth of December* came out and then I did so many, so quickly, that I ran into this timeless dilemma: if, through trial and error, you've discovered the optimal (most honest and effective) answer to a question, do you just . . . keep giving that answer? (Often, at book-tour pace, you don't have the time or energy to really dig deep—and/or you're getting the same group of questions over and over.) Someone once gave me some good advice on this, which was to remember that the answer is new to the person asking the question, so repeating your optimal answer with good cheer (and, of course, being open to variants and new discoveries) might even be seen as a form of generosity."

Perhaps fittingly, he gave a similar answer to Roy Kesey in his 2005 maud newton.com interview (chapter 4 in this volume): "One of the weird things about being interviewed is that, if you've been interviewed before, and had one of those enviable moments where you answer sensibly, and actually come up with exactly the right thing to express what you're trying to express, then you're in a pickle: next time you're asked that question or one similar, do you use the example you thought of before, or not? . . . You get to a certain point where these things start following you around—you start sounding like: 'Ah, you're asking about PLOT. Allow me to invoke Chestnut #9!'" In selecting these particular interviews for this volume, I tried to avoid having too many moments where Saunders resorts to the same chestnuts, or where the interviews cover the same ground (though, as the index will show, Saunders does repeatedly invoke certain authors, particularly Chekhov and O'Connor, and both make frequent appearances in these conversations).

I also opted to include interviews that appeared in print, rather than transcripts of podcasts or public conversations. In part, this was because Saunders told me, "My preference is for email interviews, simply because I literally think better when typing." Some of the interviews included here were conducted via email; some have been distilled down by the interviewers themselves from longer conversations (for the most part, the headnotes to each interview explain the format or process for the interview). One can easily find YouTube videos of Saunders's in-person interviews, or appearances on late night shows, and these are worth seeking out; his warmth and generosity of spirit clearly come through in these venues. But I find something is often lost in the transcription of these conversations; the in-print interviews tend to have a coherence and depth of focus that I wanted to maintain throughout this volume.

For the most part, I also have avoided selecting interviews that focus primarily just on one particular publication (whether a full book or an individual story). There are certainly places in the following interviews where he discusses the themes of a given story or book, but I thought that readers and scholars interested in one particular work will have the ability to seek out Saunders's views on them without much trouble. The one exception is the interview with Deborah Treisman of the *New Yorker*, which I have included because it is representative of a series of interviews published on the magazine's website, where Saunders discusses a story that appears in that week's print version of the magazine. I chose this particular interview to represent the series both because it is about a significant story in Saunders's oeuvre ("Escape from Spiderhead"), and because it captures Saunders's thoughts on going into detail about individual stories. He tells Treisman, "I am not very good on questions of intentionality, i.e., questions of the 'Why did you do that?' variety. I think the writer's main job is to provide a wild ride for the reader. So most of what I'm doing on a given day is just trying to ensure that the wild ride happens, trusting and hopeful that the thematics will take care of themselves" (58).

Though he is not particularly keen on discussing intentionality, throughout this volume readers will find Saunders and the interviewers engaged in real, substantive conversations about the style and subject matter of his work, and of art in general. Saunders is quick to acknowledge that "the really vexing questions of life don't really have answers" (125), but the interviews I have selected do tend to circle them anyway. These conversations often touch on the moral and ethical responsibility of fiction, as well as how his work engages with issues of social and political commentary, even while acknowledging—as he told me via email—that often "the interesting part of art takes place in a zone that can't really be articulated or reduced. So what are we really talking about? I like to give myself permission in this way: thinking that any interview only approximates the truth about the process of writing a story, but that's okay. We're not attempting a scientific proof. We're goofing around, on the periphery of the actual act, and sometimes that goofing around can become a beautifully shaped or insightful or surprising or inspiring little work of its own—a sort of two-person dance that has the effect, hopefully, of conveying some good energy to one or both of them, and to the reader. Why not? We're only here for a short time. Why not try?"

As I worked on this collection, I spent a fair amount of time thinking about why readers would pick up a collection of interviews. Presumably they are looking for insights into the author's process, craft, interests, and/or biography. But another joy of this reading experience is being able to witness this "dance": being a fly on the wall for truly excellent conversations, and picking up some of this "good energy" that Saunders describes. Saunders repeatedly states that he believes deep, thoughtful engagement with literature can benefit both the writer and the audience. I spent a great portion of the COVID-19 pandemic reading through countless interviews with Saunders, and in a time marked by mandatory quarantines and social distancing, his warmth and wit and kindness have been a source of consolation amidst the isolation and darkness. In a similar vein, Linn Ullman closed her podcast interview with Saunders, which was recorded in the midst of the pandemic, by stating, "I feel a little more hopeful."[1] It is my hope that readers of these interviews will leave the book feeling a bit more hopeful as well.

In close, I wish to extend my deepest gratitude to all of the people who have helped shepherd this project to completion. I am so pleased to have worked with the wonderful editorial staff at University Press of Mississippi, particularly Mary Heath. I first had the pleasure of meeting George Saunders during a day conference hosted by the Hank Center for the Catholic Intellectual Heritage at Loyola University Chicago, and I am deeply indebted to Michael Murphy, the director of the Hank Center, for inviting me to take part in that conference, and his support over the years. I would also like to express my thanks to my colleagues and the administration at Siena Heights University; I spent part of my sabbatical working on putting this book together, and am grateful for the support the university has provided me.

This project would not be possible without the graciousness of the interviewers and editors who granted me permission to republish their work. Unfortunately, for reasons of space, I was not able to include every interview that I had initially identified as a potential piece, and I am grateful to those individuals who granted me permission even if the piece did not ultimately become part of the final project.

I am also, of course, grateful to George Saunders. Getting to correspond regularly with Saunders has been a great professional pleasure. While compiling these interviews, one pleasant aspect of the process was not just people's willingness to be involved, but their enthusiasm about the project, and their eagerness to share stories of how memorable their encounter with Saunders was. Many of the participants went out of their way to tell me how kind and gracious Saunders was with his time, and I have found this to be true as well. I had to send countless emails in the process of putting this book together, and few people were faster to respond than Saunders himself, and none were as thoughtful.

Finally, thank you to my wife, Lauren, and my boys, Owen, Timothy, and Henry. During a period of social distancing and general social isolation, it has been such a joy to spend my working, and nonworking, hours surrounded by you all. We'll all keep trying, together.

Note

1. Linn Ullman, "Episode 4: George Saunders," *How to Proceed*, podcast audio, October 11, 2020.

Chronology

1958   Born on December 2, in Amarillo, Texas. Shortly thereafter, his family moves to the Gage Park neighborhood on the South Side of Chicago, where his father works for Petersen Coal. In 1964, the family moves to the south suburb of Oak Forest, Illinois. Saunders attends St. Damian Catholic School. During high school, Saunders works as a delivery driver for his father's restaurant, Chicken Unlimited.

1977   Graduates from Oak Forest High School. During his senior year of high school, Saunders plays guitar in a band but, after reading *Atlas Shrugged* on a ski trip to Wisconsin, decides to quit the band and pursue a college degree.

1981   Graduates with a BS in Geophysical Engineering from the Colorado School of Mines, in Golden, Colorado. After graduation, he works for a time on an oil exploration geophysics crew in the oil fields of Sumatra, Indonesia. Upon returning to America, he bounces around, working at a variety of jobs, including as a knuckle-puller at a slaughterhouse in Amarillo, Texas, a roofer, a convenience store clerk, and a groundsman at an apartment complex.

1986   While living in Amarillo, attending West Texas State University part-time, and playing in a country bar band called Rick Acton and the Good Times Band, publishes his first short story, "A Lack of Order in the Floating Object Room," in *Northwest Review*. On the strength of this story, he's accepted into the Syracuse MFA program, where he studies with Tobias Wolff and Douglas Unger.

1987   Marries Paula Redick, a fellow student in the Syracuse University MFA program. They become engaged just three weeks into the relationship.

1988   Earns his MA in English, with an emphasis in Creative Writing (Fiction), from Syracuse University. The couple's first daughter, Caitlin, is born.

1989   The family moves to Rochester, New York, where Saunders begins work as a technical writer for the Radian Corporation, where he works until 1997.

1990   Their second daughter, Alena, is born.

1992   Publishes "Offloading for Mrs. Schwartz" in the October 5 issue of the *New Yorker*, the start of a long, fruitful relationship with the magazine.

1994   Wins the National Magazine Award for Fiction for "The 400-Pound CEO" (published in *Harper's*).

1995   In April, he publishes the novella "Bounty" in *Harper's*; the story wins the 1996 National Magazine Award for Fiction.

1996   He publishes his first short story collection, *CivilWarLand in Bad Decline: Stories and a Novella*, with Random House. The book is a finalist for the 1996 PEN/Hemingway Award.

1997   He joins the faculty of the Syracuse University Creative Writing Program. His story "The Falls" (*New Yorker*) wins second place in the O. Henry Awards and is included in *O. Henry Prize Stories 1997*.

1998   His story "Winky" (*New Yorker*) is included in the *O. Henry Prize Stories 1998* anthology.

1999   Saunders is chosen as one of the "Top Twenty Writers Under Forty" by the *New Yorker* in its Summer Fiction Issue ("20 Writers for the 21st Century: The Future of American Fiction"). His story "Sea Oak" (*New Yorker*) is included in the *O. Henry Prize Stories 1999* collection. Sometime in the late 1990s, he begins to practice Buddhism.

2000   In May, he publishes his second short story collection, *Pastoralia*, with Riverhead Books. In August, he publishes an illustrated children's book, *The Very Persistent Gappers of Frip*, with illustrations by Lane Smith, with Random House. He wins the 2000 National Magazine Award for Fiction for the story "The Barber's Unhappiness" (*New Yorker*).

2001   He receives the Lannan Literary Fellowship for Fiction from the Lannan Foundation. He is also named one of *Entertainment Weekly*'s "100 Most Creative People in Entertainment," in their July 2001 "It" Issue. His story "Pastoralia" (*New Yorker*) is included in the *O. Henry Prize Stories 2001* anthology.

2002   From 2002–2004, Saunders works on screenplays for both "CivilWarLand in Bad Decline," for actor/director Ben Stiller and his company, Red Hour Films, and "Sea Oak," in conjunction with director Keir McFarlane. Eventually, in 2017, "Sea Oak" makes it to the pilot stage with Amazon Studios.

2003 "Jon" (*New Yorker*) is selected for inclusion in *Science Fiction: The Best of 2003* anthology.

2004 He wins the National Magazine Award for Fiction, for a fourth time, for "The Red Bow" (*Esquire*). "The Red Bow" is also selected for inclusion in *The Year's Best Fantasy and Horror 2004: Seventeenth Annual Collection*.

2005 Publishes the novella-length fable *The Brief and Frightening Reign of Phil*, with Riverhead Books. The story "Bohemians" (*New Yorker*) is selected for both *Best American Short Stories 2005* and *Best American Nonrequired Reading 2005*. His political humor piece "Manifesto: A Press Release from PRKA" (*Slate*) is also included in this *Best American Nonrequired Reading 2005* anthology.

2006 Publishes his third collection of short stories, *In Persuasion Nation*, with Riverhead Books; the book is a finalist for the 2007 Story Prize. A chapbook of nonfiction essays and humor pieces, *A Bee Stung Me So I Killed All the Fish*, was published in a limited edition alongside *In Persuasion Nation*. He receives a MacArthur Fellowship and a Guggenheim Fellowship. He also wins the World Fantasy Award for Best Short Story for the story "CommComm" (published in the *New Yorker* in 2005). From September 2006 through November 2008, he writes a weekly humor/commentary column for *The Guardian* (UK). His essay "The New Mecca" (*GQ*) is selected for both the *Best American Travel Writing 2006* and *Best American Nonrequired Reading 2006* anthologies.

2007 Publishes his first nonfiction collection, *The Braindead Megaphone*, with Riverhead Books. His essay "Buddha Boy" (*GQ*) is selected for *Best American Travel Writing 2007*.

2008 The story "Puppy" (*New Yorker*) is selected for *Best American Short Stories 2008*. His essay "Bill Clinton, Private Citizen" (*GQ*) is selected for *Best American Nonrequired Reading 2008*.

2009 Receives an Academy Award in Literature from the American Academy of Arts and Letters.

2010 His essay "Tent City, USA" (*GQ*) is selected for *Best American Nonrequired Reading 2010*.

2011 His story "Escape from Spiderhead" (*New Yorker*) is selected for *Best American Short Stories 2011*.

2012   His story "Tenth of December" (*New Yorker*) is selected for both *Best American Short Stories 2012* and *Best American Nonrequired Reading 2012*.

2013   Publishes his fourth collection of short stories, *Tenth of December: Stories*, with Random House. The book goes on to win the 2013 Story Prize, the inaugural Folio Prize (2014), and is a finalist for the National Book Award. This year, Saunders also wins the PEN/ Malamud Award for Excellence in the Short Story, and is named one of *Time* magazine's "100 most influential people in the world." The story "The Semplica Girl Diaries" (*New Yorker*) is selected for *Best American Short Stories 2013*.

2014   Saunders is elected to the American Academy of Arts and Sciences. Publishes *Congratulations, by the way: Some Thoughts on Kindness*, a reprint of his 2013 commencement address at Syracuse University, with Random House.

2017   Publishes his first novel, *Lincoln in the Bardo*, with Random House. The novel wins the 2017 Man Booker Prize. The audiobook version of the novel, which features a cast of 166 actors, wins the 2018 Audie Award for best audiobook. The pilot episode of "Sea Oak," which Saunders wrote and co-executive produced, airs on Amazon, but is not picked up. His essay "Who Are All These Trump Supporters" (*New Yorker*) is selected for *Best American Nonrequired Reading 2017* and receives the Sigma Delta Chi Award and Bronze Medallion from the Society of Professional Journalists.

2018   Publishes *Fox 8: A Story*, with Random House. He is inducted as a member of the American Academy of Arts and Letters.

2019   George and Paula move to Santa Cruz, California, though he still teaches short intensive courses at Syracuse.

2021   Publishes *A Swim in a Pond in the Rain: In Which Four Russians Give a Master Class on Writing, Reading, and Life*, with Random House.

**Conversations with
George Saunders**

George Saunders

The Very Persistent Mapper of Happenstance

Kevin Larimer / 2000

Poets and Writers Magazine, July/ August 2000, pp. 34–40. Reprinted by permission of the author and Poets & Writers, Inc., pw.org.

Don't tell George Saunders you can't get there from here. En route to an enviable writing career, he traveled from a working-class childhood in south Chicago to the oil fields of Indonesia, a slaughterhouse in Amarillo, Texas, and the stuffy office of an environmental company in Rochester, New York. Along the way he collected an MA in creative writing from Syracuse University, where he studied with Tobias Wolff, and a degree in geophysical engineering from the Colorado School of Mines.

Saunders readily admits he didn't chart his course, and he approaches the writing of fiction the same way—with no particular destination in mind. As a result, his stories end up in some unexpected places: a prehistoric theme park; a future world where citizens belong to two classes: "Normal" or "Flawed"; and a self-help seminar where participants learn to identify who has been "crapping in your oatmeal." Ask him why his stories, at once hilarious and macabre, are littered with severed hands, dead aunts, see-through cows, and Civil War ghosts and he'll share your curiosity. "Where does this shit come from? I don't have an answer."

Today Saunders teaches creative writing in the graduate program at Syracuse University. He lives with his wife of thirteen years and his two daughters, ages nine and twelve. His first collection of short stories, *CivilWarLand in Bad Decline*, was published in 1996 by Riverhead Books. In May, Riverhead published his second collection, *Pastoralia*. Villard will publish his modern fairy tale "for adults and future adults," *The Very Persistent Gappers of Frip*, illustrated by Lane Smith, in August.

Recently I visited Saunders in Syracuse. During lunch at Erawan Restaurant and over coffee in his sunny Victorian home, he revealed two qualities that make him so popular among his students—a friendliness and a generosity one wouldn't necessarily expect to find in someone at this stage of a successful writing career. He also displayed a quality one would expect to find in the author of such stories as "The 400-Pound CEO" and "Downtrodden Mary's Failed Campaign of Terror"—an uncanny ability to find humor in improbable places.

Kevin Larimer: One of the things that's immediately intriguing about you as a writer is your sort of nontraditional background.

George Saunders: That's a nice way to put it . . .

KL: Well, it doesn't seem like you've been stagnating in some university setting.

GS: No, that started up here. It was kind of an inadvertent path. When I look back I'm always a little bit embarrassed because it's not like I had any sense. I had such a malformed sense of the world at each point that I ended up making some stupid decisions without really realizing what the options were. I grew up in Chicago in a pretty working-class neighborhood, so writing wasn't something . . . well, I didn't really know who did it. It never occurred to me that I might do it. But I never even read a whole lot. I remember reading *Johnny Tremain*—that was a big watershed. I got a degree in geophysical engineering from the Colorado School of Mines. This was at the height of the oil boom, so I went over to Sumatra and worked for a couple years in the oil fields. After that was a period of just bombing around with no real sense of what was going on. I worked in a slaughterhouse for a while in Amarillo, Texas. I was probably twenty-four or twenty-five. In that town, if you wanted to get some money quick that's where you went, and they would hire anybody and you could stay for as short as you wanted.

KL: What did you do at the slaughterhouse?

GS: I was a knuckle-puller. It's a leg thing. It would come in on a hook. It would look like a big chicken leg. There was this complicated series of cuts. You had a hook in one hand and a knife in the other. The cuts were very surgical, some of them. When that was done you just sort of heaved it across onto this conveyor belt. It was like this big Rube Goldberg thing and it would go somewhere else. At one point I got demoted because I was too slow and I went to this place where all the stuff that was left over at the end came by on this big belt and you had to separate it. There was one box that was for bone and one was for fat and one for miscellaneous. The story was that the bone went to make pizza toppings, and fat was for marshmallows. It wasn't too good.

KL: So you were de-knuckling the leg. Of what animal? Cows?

GS: Oh, cows, yeah. It was hard to tell. It could've been brontosaurus for all I know.

KL: You're a vegetarian now.

GS: Yeah, but that's pretty recent. One wasn't a result of the other.

KL: How did these kinds of experiences inform your work?

GS: I always wanted to write but had never read anything contemporary. When I was in Asia, there were all these great things to write about during the oil boom, but I didn't have the vocabulary. I found myself drifting and not knowing how to put the stuff that was happening into the work because I had never seen it done before. But then I read that story "Hot Ice" by Stuart Dybek and that was basically my neighborhood where I grew up. To see that in prose . . . I couldn't pretend that only Hemingway mattered after that. Dybek was a big breakthrough because I could for the first time see what you had to do to reality to make it literature, because I knew the neighborhood and I knew the people and I could see what he'd done to it.

KL: You played guitar in a bar band in Texas.

GS: A really bad bar band. We were called—it's really embarrassing—we were called Rick Active and the Good Times Band. It was along Route 66 in Amarillo, where they had these drunk palaces where you'd go to drink and they'd pay us each fifty dollars a night and we'd play the same set six times over and over again, never practice, no original songs. This was 1986. I should've known better then. In a way it's like half of your mind is saying, "It's okay, I'm just slumming, I'll write about this someday," and the other half is just that there weren't a whole lot of other options.

KL: Were there any other early influences?

GS: *Monty Python* was a huge influence—the way that they would get at something archetypal through a side door was always really interesting. We just turned our kids on to that recently. The argument sketch. Do you remember that one? "I'm here for an argument." "No you're not."

I remember watching *Monty Python* with my father. He was really busy, and we didn't do a lot together, but every Sunday night we'd watch that. In our neighborhood, a very working-class neighborhood, jokes were really a currency. If you could tell a joke or even if you could imitate somebody it was a really big deal. Junot Díaz, who teaches here at Syracuse, has this great theory that writers come out of any kind of situation where language equals power. So in his case, in the Dominican Republic, English was clearly a meal ticket. And I think that's true. So that combined with just sitting there with my father roaring at *Monty Python* . . . somehow humor became validated. But for years, like a lot of working-class people, writing was that thing which I could not do. It had to be just beyond my grasp or it didn't count, right? So it was only when that sort of dropped that I could really have fun with it. But that was relatively recently.

KL: Humor is obviously a very big part of your writing—humor combined with sentiment. I'm thinking of the ending of the short story "Isabelle" in *CivilWarLand in Bad Decline*. It's heartbreaking.

GS: I'm increasingly happy to be a funny writer. What I find really funny is the straight faces that people keep in spite of the fact that life is so full of suffering. I think of the poses people strike, and the hatred that they develop in spite of the fact that in fifty years we are all going to be dust. We have to occupy those places so that's really funny to me. Whenever I try to write hard and earnestly it always comes out like that. I have to sort of trust it. I can't write anything that isn't comic—I don't know about funny, but comic. Earnestness is my enemy.

KL: You've written short stories and a novella. Have you ever tried to write a novel?

GS: Most of those stories started out as novels. I've tried and I just recently got to the point where I'm not going to try anymore. If it happens it'll happen organically. I'm not going to sweat it because in the past when I tried to write a novel I thought, "I'll have to do something fundamentally different, I'll have to stretch things out." But if I have any gift it's for compression. At forty-one I'm like, "Well, it's nice that I can do something. I don't have to do everything." We'll see what happens.

When I was working as an engineer at the environmental company there was just no way that a novel was going to happen. When I was in that job I was desperately trying to figure out another way because not only was it not a lot of money, but not a lot of time with the kids. There's that great quote by Terry Eagleton: "Capitalism plunders the sensuality of the body." That was such a beautiful lesson because you come home half-despising yourself because you've done such stupid things with your day. You've groveled and you've not even groveled efficiently. Then you come home and you're exhausted and you're not capable of generosity and I find it really sad.

KL: A lot of your stories, like "Pastoralia" and "CivilWar Land in Bad Decline," take place in this bureaucratic, artificial universe, Disneyland gone wrong.

GS: I think it's mostly that job I worked at the environmental company. It was a provincial office of a medium-sized company that was based in Texas, so it had all the rigidity with none of the brilliance. There were probably thirty people there and they were all pretty anxious and by the time I got there they were shrinking the place down. It wasn't huge enough that it was faceless. We all knew each other. There was quite a bit of inside space where there was no natural light. My own ego, my youthful arrogance, and my own high expectations of myself were put suddenly in conflict with this because, you know, by then I had two kids. I was maybe thirty-three or thirty-four and nothing was going as planned. I hadn't won the Nobel Prize yet and Hollywood wasn't calling because I hadn't published anything, so there was something about that that made it seem absurd. It was a pretty petty place and there were a lot of rules. I mean at one point I was sending stories out and I got a nice rejection from the *New Yorker* and I was so excited because an actual person had responded and in a fit of madness I mentioned this to my supervisor at the end of the day. And he got this stricken look on his face and he said, "Well actually, George, it's come to our attention that you are using corporate resources to produce your 'writing' so we'd like you to discontinue that." And this was a guy who knew me and he knew my kids. So that wasn't too good.

KL: How are you able to negotiate some of the awful things that happen in your stories—death, dismemberment—with humor?

GS: That's a South Side of Chicago thing because our whole world— communicating anything emotional—was to be sarcastic. If you wanted to say you loved somebody you'd punch him in the crotch. My impulses are always very sentimental—I mean mawkishly, sitcomishly so. So in some ways I think it's a cloaking mechanism. If you have in one scene a kid getting his hand cut off, I think in some funny way you're more willing to accept a sentimental scene. I don't know if you're more willing to accept it, but maybe the juxtaposition of those two things is more interesting. As a writer I'm really aware of my defects and how much I have to find other things to substitute, so humor helps. It's got its own inherent energy so if you can sustain funniness you almost always have to sustain something else. Pure funny you see sometimes in humor columnists who are just funny, but in fiction to keep funny going you almost always dredge something else up. I think.

KL: For some reason I think of Charlie Chaplin.

GS: Yeah, *The Great Dictator*. I think partly it's ritualized humility. If you think of the great evils: when China invades Tibet they're not funny, they're not self-doubting. There's no trace of humor in what they're doing. And Hitler: not a guy who's at all prone to see funniness in himself. One of the great things about fiction is that if I write an asshole into a story it has to be me. I can't generate him. And it's always funny in the reviews they say my stories are full of losers. I know where I got all those things. I didn't just make them up. I think it's ritualized humility.

KL: In your stories, one thing that continually strikes me is guilt. I'm thinking of "Winky" in *Pastoralia*, and just about every story in *CivilWarLand in Bad Decline*.

GS: Well, I think it's the Catholic background. The binary that got set up was that you were either doing good or you were doing evil, and you were never doing good. If you actually appeared to be doing good there was probably something wrong with your intentions. I think if you have any moral tension, guilt is part of it. If people can feel guilt they are at least cognizant of a moral interplay. It's a powerful emotion—one, because it implies you've done wrong, and two, that you know you've done wrong.

When I was a kid in Chicago, the big thing was to go to a Bears game because it was expensive and people didn't really do it. But this family that lived two doors down from us—they were maybe ten years off the boat from Poland and they didn't have much money and they lived in a house that was completely bare, no furniture. It always smelled like noodles and they were always kind of barking at each other. One day the kid came over and said, "I got Bears tickets." It was like someone in the poorest neighborhood saying they had a house in the Hamptons. So I said, "Great, we're going to go." It was his father, his uncle, Greg, and me. It was a big journey with trains and buses, and we stopped at other Polish relatives and there was a lot of cheek-pinching. But I was going to endure it all to see Gale Sayers and Dick Butkus. So we finally got to Wrigley Field and just before we go in the father says, "All right, boys, we've got a little problem which is that we only got two tickets, but don't worry about it we got it figured out. The Andy Frain guys they never look up when they take your ticket." So they picked each one of us up—we were maybe ten or eleven—picked us up and put us on their shoulders. And in those days they were still wearing those big overcoats, and they had us put our feet down their overcoat and they buttoned it up. And so the plan was that they were going to walk in and they would take our tickets and not look up. Now I was the all-time Goody Two-shoes, straight A, never had an evil thought. And I was just appalled to be cheating, and cheating publicly. Then the father says, "Now if they do look up, all you got to do is look retarded." And he was serious. The idea was that if they thought you were retarded they would let you in for free. So he says, "Now let's see how you're gonna do it." So we had to practice. And we started in. What I was really deeply ashamed of afterward is how willing I was. I was not going to get caught. If they busted us, I was going to go into the retarded thing, I was going to do what he said.

Something of that is in my writing too. When I'm getting ready to send something out, I get really intensely self-critical. To my credit, I get really fanatical about revising, but sometimes that can bleed over to just lock-up.

KL: I think sometimes you can find yourself frightened of what you're going to find if you look at it too closely too soon. I finish something and I think it's good and I don't want to go back to it too early. How many times do you wake up the next morning and say, "That's trash," you know?

GS: I think you're right. Part of being a writer is to know when to trust yourself. I know I'm going to have a cycle. I'm going to love it more than it should be loved at first, hate it more than it should be hated later. You let your ecstatic side have it for a while, then you let your neurotic, self-doubting side. For me it was a breakthrough to realize that that wasn't abnormal, that you weren't right or wrong in either of those two, that you were right in both and wrong in both, and you just had to let it have a long shelf life and then it would start to make sense. Part of it, too, is knowing when to quit.

When I start to write a story I always have a simple design that would make it sort of classic and beautiful, but I can't do it. I have some kind of weird thing that twists it, but the twist isn't meaningless. Somehow the distortion that always happens if I work hard is useful. It's like having this dog and going out in the field and saying, "Bring me back a pheasant." That dog is your talent, and it runs out and it comes back with the lower half of a Barbie doll. But if every time it brings back the lower half of a Barbie doll, you put those things together and you think, "That's kinda good." I don't fight it anymore.

KL: You write on a computer. You also said you revise a lot. How do you trust your ecstatic instinct electronically?

GS: The kind of writing I do I wouldn't be able to do without a computer. Until I get to the end part of a story I work on the screen almost exclusively. Anytime something strikes me I just put it in or cut it or whatever. If there is anything significant that happens I'll save it. But the main thing I do is to try to keep it really free. Nothing is ever lost. I can always go back to it. It's like those fast motion pictures of trees growing. I don't know if it's true with trees or not but let's pretend it is. You sort of see this thing accreting and parts disappear and come back in but in the long run it's working in a general direction. I couldn't do that on hard copy.

For me, writing has become—it sounds a little pretentious but sort of true—a spiritual practice. If you're open to whatever the story presents with no attachments to what you did yesterday or any attachments to what you want the thing to be or how you want to be perceived, but just open to the needs of the story, that's kind of ecstatic. It's really beautiful to say, "What I did yesterday or for the last twenty years might be shit but that's okay." It's interesting to see how the artistic form teaches you. It instructs you on your own shortcomings as a person. I love that writing can really help me turn back the spiraling neurosis. It can help me be a little bit less stupid, less judgmental and unkind.

KL: You said it is important to be there when you're writing, not thinking about yesterday or tomorrow. Is that harder for you now that you have a couple books?

GS: It was really hard after the first book because I just thought I had squeaked through a door. "The Falls" was the first story of the new book that I wrote and it was a real lucky sort of breakthrough because it was so different from the other book. And I remember writing it and thinking, "No, I shouldn't send it out because it's not like the other ones." But when the *New Yorker* took it I thought maybe whatever it is I have to offer is not totally manifest in that book, it's something different, and that was a nice feeling to think it's not really about style but something else you have to offer.

And maybe you don't even know what it is yet, and maybe you never will. Maybe you'll be eighty and you just keep cranking stuff out and you're good enough and then you die. When you're young you think, "I want my work to last," and then you see that nothing lasts. Shakespeare doesn't last, nothing does. The moment of doing it is really all there is. Everything else is all delusion. It's hard to remember, especially now when books are coming out.

KL: Tell me a little about *The Very Persistent Gappers of Frip*.

GS: I have two daughters, and I would tell them these made-up stories about this little girl and they were funny and in some ways they were funnier than anything else. They were freer and not so programmatic. And I wrote it. It's basically a short story really. And I liked it. There was something *Monty Python*-esque about it. I didn't have to worry about any realism and I had a really good time working on it and I sent it to Daniel Menaker at Random House and he bought it. As kind of an extra bonus he sent it to Lane Smith and Lane had read *CivilWarLand in Bad Decline* and said, "Yeah, I'll do it." So that instantly became more of an important book than it was. That was really a thrill. I'd go down to his studio in New York and there would be a whole wall of sketches. Not only were they true to my work, they were twice as good as I could've ever dreamed of. One, he understood that the book is an exaggeration, but two, he understood the flavor of the exaggeration. It was really a thrill for someone who is not a bit visual. It was a good lesson for me because he is the least neurotic person I've ever met. He goes into the studio every day habitually and gets it done. I'm sort of a Catholic, "I think it's good but it probably isn't." The Eeyore School of Literature.

KL: Are you currently working on more stories?

GS: I've got one that Lane Smith and I might do if I can get it to be good enough. It used to be a novella. It seems to be pretty funny. It started to be a kids' story and then it extended to be about genocide. So unless there's a big need for a child's guide to genocide it won't be that. I'm sure this summer I'll be working. I don't really make too many plans. I just sort of see what develops.

An Interview with George Saunders

J. J. Wylie / 2001

From *Missouri Review* 24, no. 2 (2001): 53–68. Reprinted by permission of the author.

J. J. Wylie: Douglas Unger has called your admission to the Syracuse Creative Writing Program a "grand experiment" that he and Tobias Wolff "had to fight for," one that has obviously paid off. Given your nonliterary educational background, did you feel out of place as a student there?

George Saunders: I was always aware that I didn't have quite the intellectual guns that a lot of the other students had. But at the same time the atmosphere was open enough with Doug and Toby that I felt it didn't matter all that much. They encouraged me to get up to speed with whichever writers worked for me without worrying about being comprehensive in my catching up.

JW: Were you aware at the time that you were a "grand experiment"?

GS: No. I felt more like a "clerical error." I didn't know that Doug and Toby had had trouble getting me in, though I was aware that many of the other students were from Ivy League English departments, whereas my undergraduate degree was in geophysics, from the Colorado School of Mines. So while the other students knew all about Shelley and Keats, I knew about Alfred Wegener, the father of plate tectonics, whom we affectionately used to call "Big Al." But fiction is open to whoever comes in the door, as long as you come in energetically, and so I had a feeling there was room for me.

JW: Vonnegut wrote something about the best education for a writer not being in English literature. Would you agree?

GS: It depends on the writer. There's Flannery O'Connor, who got an English degree and who I think went into an MFA program directly after graduation. Nobody has ever suggested that her work might have been stronger had she gone out and worked on a shrimper. My background was unconventional in that I'd been educated at an engineering school and had worked in the oil fields and so on and wasn't well read in any comprehensive way. The working experience was invaluable because it gave me a low-level rage, or at least a sense that there was injustice in the world and that this injustice was playing out every day on the bodies and minds of the people toward the bottom of the heap. All that work and travel gave me a moral stance that eventually evolved into a certain prose style and set of thematic concerns. Also, those years gave me confidence to invent things, to exaggerate, to make some claims about our culture. On the other hand, almost all of the work I've done in fiction has been to compensate for my shortcomings, some of which, I'm sure, have to do with how restricted my reading experience is and how late in life I did much of that reading.

For me it might have been a good thing to have come from a non-traditional background because I'm not exactly an intellectual giant. I suspect that if I'd had a more extensive background in English before I started to write, I might have ended up just badly parroting other writers. But because I hadn't read enough to even know whom to parrot, the experiences of my own life were what drove me to fiction. Then the task became to find a style that would do justice to these experiences and wouldn't require too many big words or complicated flashbacks.

JW: Your work is consistently characterized as satirical. Yet you said in an interview once that for you writing is an exercise in compassion. Don't you think that satire and compassion are mutually exclusive impulses?

GS: No. I think they're manifestations of the same impulse. By compassion I mean plain sight. If you see something plainly, without attachment to your own preconceptions of it and without any aversion to what you see, that's compassion because you're minimizing the distinction between subject and object. Then whatever needs to be done, you can do it quickly and efficiently, to address whatever the suffering is in that situation. Satire, for me, is a way of encouraging clear sight. Teasing is a way of encouraging clear sight. The only problem I see in it is that some satirical modes preclude getting into certain spaces. For example, I have two kids and a wife, whom I love like crazy, and my life is very, very good right now. But I'm not sure how to write that.

But it's not fiction's job to be photographically representative of reality. If I want to make a fictional world where there's no kindness, this doesn't mean I believe there's no kindness in the real world. In fact, what it may mean is that I very much value kindness. Like if you make a painting in which only greens are allowed, it wouldn't mean you don't believe in blue. You're just saying: Wow, look at green. I've heard it said that comedy is the indirect praise of perfection. So if you make a world in which compassion is absent, you are, via its absence, praising compassion.

JW: Are there limits to how far a writer can depart from this world?

GS: My sense is that if you go far enough in any stylistic direction, you can make a beautiful and complex representation of reality, although that representation may not be linear. God knows we've got enough linearity in our representations of our world. We've tremendously overvalued analytical knowledge, rationality, etc. To me, the process of writing is just reading what I've written and—like running your hand over one of those mod glass stovetops to find where the heat is—looking for where the energy is in the prose, then going in the direction of that. It's an exercise in being open to whatever is there.

JW: Do you ever get the itch to test your chops at a more conventional realism?

GS: Unfortunately, yes, which is how I spent the years from 1987 to 1990. It started when I got to Syracuse. I had written this crazy story to get into the program. Then I thought I'd be a "real" writer and write nice, realistic stuff. But what I eventually found out was that in realist mode the life went out of my writing. I had about three or four years of this, where nothing was really working for me. This was my Hemingway-if-Hemingway-had-never-been-to-a-war-and-was-working-as-a-tech-writer-and-was-actually-sort-of-a-wimp phase. All these stories had titles like "In Parking Lot K," "A Hard Rain Is Coming," or "In the Employee Cafeteria, Across from Employee Relations." It was about the time our second daughter was born, and I was getting a little desperate for some power. In that desperate mode, all of my South Side of Chicago impulses came back, and I started simply trying to be funny.

JW: And it worked. You haven't looked back, it seems.

GS: I still have this dilemma, this Funny versus Earnest polarity. I love, for example, Chekhov, but I know by now that if I'm going to honor human beings in the way he does, in their weirdness and sweetness, I have to drop the realist convention and go down a wackier avenue. In my work, and in my psyche, there's this very sentimental, traditional, conventional side that's always in argument with a more radical, sarcastic side. Some of my stories are really sentimental, but they're layered over with weird, satirical stuff. For example, "Sea Oak" is a very straightforward story about the haves and the have-nots, about one of the have-nots saying, "Why didn't I get anything?" To get away with what could be a saccharine, sentimental arc, I cover it with all this dark, perverse stuff that makes the reader mistake me for a scatological cynic.

JW: Where does the dark, perverse stuff come from?

GS: You know, in my old neighborhood, the people were very passionate and sentimental, very loving. But they would never say, "Gosh, Cal, you are certainly very important in my life." Instead they say, "Cal, you son of a bitch, come over here so I can kick your red head up your ass, you jack-off." But you understood that this was code and that they were crazy about you. There's a little of that in my work. On one level, I am a total softie, sort of depressed and afraid of losing the people I love or failing them. To disguise that, there's all this harsh, poop-centric, external swagger, full of nastiness. It's a cloaking device.

JW: In a piece you authored for *Feed* magazine, you wrote about a particular corner in Los Angeles where you realized the significance of Terry Eagleton's statement, "Capitalism plunders the sensuality of the body." It seems to me that this idea underpins all of your work, from *CivilWarLand in Bad Decline* through *The Very Persistent Gappers of Frip*. Has this always been a conscious agenda of yours?

GS: No. In fact, when the jacket copy came back for *CivilWarLand in Bad Decline*, Dan Menaker had written very wonderfully about fin de siècle capitalism and all that, and of course I was thrilled to hear that I had written about that, but it honestly hadn't occurred to me that I had. In the reviews there was all this talk about down-and-out American dystopic losers, and I was like: I did that? That was just what my life was at that time, although most of us down-and-out American dystopic losers didn't actually describe ourselves in those exact words. Because of the way my life has been, which is that I've been working since I was fifteen, most of the decisions I've made along the way have been saturated with issues of money or scarcity, or the fear of scarcity. I was looking at some old letters recently, actually from that LA period, which I remember as being sort of free and romantic and Kerouacian. Every other paragraph is about scrounging up fifty dollars to pay for this, putting together enough to get the car going again so I could drive to some nebulous interview dressed in exactly the wrong clothes, which I'd had to borrow. Lately it's really struck me how much of our energy in America, especially if you're from a working background, is spent just keeping your head above water. It really saps your grace and your strength.

JW: How did that background help form you?

GS: My dad is a wildly intelligent guy, a genius, really. When I was a kid, he hadn't finished college yet. He later went back and finished, but at that time—the mid-1960s—he was working long hours for a coal company in Chicago. Anyway, he would bring home books like Machiavelli's *The Prince* or Michael Harrington's *The Other Side of America* or *The Jungle* by Upton Sinclair, and he would just leave them on my bed, saying, "I think you should take a look at this." Because it was coming from my dad, whom I really looked up to, I was all over the stuff. My dad was very interested in the politics of Chicago, the wild energy of it, the comic side. I'd sit up with him late at night as he interpreted the life of the city for me. This was the time of Daley and the Democratic Convention; Jesse Jackson was around town; Mike Royko was writing in the *Tribune*.

Politics got into my head as a noble way to approach things, something adults talked about and cared about. Understanding politics was a way, in our extended family, of getting respect—politics and humor. We'd have these big Sunday dinners and everybody would be sitting around arguing about Nixon or Vietnam. If you could handle the politics or if you were funny, nobody blinked. You were welcome to sit there and participate. I thought that was very cool. You know, I was a nerd. Dick Cavett was my big personal hero. I got very giddy at the idea that I was participating in an Intellectual Discussion. I actually had this recurring fantasy in which somehow Dick Cavett got wind of this very bright little political wunderkind on the South Side of Chicago and flew me out to New York and made me his permanent sidekick, à la Ed McMahon, except I was in fourth grade at the time.

In terms of fiction writing, I think that if you set out to write a political story, then that is what you will get: merely a political story. Your story will be confined by your ability to conceptualize it. Our conceptual mind is much less subtle and perceptive and joyful than our non-conceptual mind.

JW: You've praised Douglas Unger for helping you become a writer and for being such a generous and committed teacher. You're now a teacher at the very program where he helped get you admitted. If you ever reached a point where you could quit teaching to write full time, would you?

GS: This is like when they ask the first-term senator if he would ever run for president. No, no, of course not, never in a billion years. I intend to teach and continue writing letters of recommendation from beyond the grave. In truth, I could see cutting back some, but at this point I honestly think I would keep teaching. I have, at Syracuse, really amazing students. They are talented, but they are also real mensches, terrific people. I get a lot of energy from them. They are like really good friends—if those friends were fifteen years younger than you and much more talented and better looking, and yet you still were sort of the boss of them. The only problem I have with teaching is that it is located in the Land of Analysis. Unless you're really careful and energetic, it's very easy to forget that writing, the writing process, is nearly impossible to talk about. That's what you do when you teach; you talk about writing. When things are going well, I find it easy enough to be honest, to say very often that the process is mysterious, etc., etc. But at other times the pull to dogma is very strong. It's much easier to resort to cant and theory and the language of science, of rationalism. Your responsibility is to undercut that at every opportunity. If things are going well, you can teach in this really sensitive way that is more akin to mentoring or coaching. But toward the end of the semester, when you're a little overloaded, you fall into this dogmatic mode where you're just basically barking, "Show, don't tell!" or "I'd like to know more about the mother!"

JW: So when things are going well you tell them . . .

GS: I think the best way to teach writing is to bombard the student with alternative approaches, in the hope that something you say will resonate with their own intuitive approach and hasten things along. I constantly ask my students to remind me that we can't really talk directly about writing. We can allude to it; we can catalyze it and get wheels turning. But we really can't talk about the actual doing of it. Any mastery you can achieve in writing is totally personal and incredibly nuanced. It's a sort of anti-mastery, feeling comfortable with being unsure. After fifteen years of doing this, what I know about writing is nothing I could actually say to you. It's like boxing, maybe. A good boxer could tell you, "Always keep your hands up," or "It's important to be a good counterpuncher." But the reason the boxer is a good boxer is not that he can articulate those things but because he can do them instantaneously—and also of course because he has great abs and can jump rope for three hours straight.

Being a teacher of creative writing is like being a teacher of personality. I'm trying to coax out of my students the most raw and real energy that they have, which is not going to be the same kind of energy that I have. Luckily, we have such great students that it's a pretty low-risk deal. If we gave them three years on an island with computers and replaced ourselves with parrots, they'd still produce great writing and learn very quickly.

JW: Did you begin *The Very Persistent Gappers of Frip* with the idea that it would be an illustrated children's book?

GS: Yes, I did. I've always wanted to do an illustrated book. I had tried and failed a few other times, primarily because I had that common idea that the difference between kids' books and adult books is that when writing a kids' book, you could be stupid and sloppy. So I wrote "Tommy the Miffed Pink Bunny" or some nonsense like that, and even my own kids were rolling their eyes. When I started this one, I tried to approach it pretty much the same way as I did the other two books, using as complex a diction as I liked and trying to be dark and funny and satirical, the only difference being that in this book I saw myself talking consolingly to someone, maybe a kid, who really needed to be consoled. My normal approach is more to talk chidingly to some adult who needs to be chided. When I tell my daughters stories, they prefer the ones that are wise-assed and dark, with many fart jokes and talking body parts that march off in the dead of night to become stars on Broadway, only to realize the error of their ways after the first time they see themselves in a partial leotard. That sort of thing.

JW: So you've read the book to them?

GS: Actually, when we first got finished copies their favorite babysitter read it to them. And they really enjoyed it. I had this great moment when I got home and they came running down the stairs saying, "Daddy, you wrote a good book!" That was a nice moment.

JW: You've published two collections of short stories and a children's book. Do you feel any pressure to produce a novel?

GS: One of the wonderful benefits of energetically pursuing a writing career is that I've come to understand the staggering limitations of my abilities. If there are Three Hundred Things That May Be Done in the writing kingdom, I can do three, and when I try to do any of the other 297, readers start dozing off, but dozing off in a state of mild irritation. So one way I cope with this humbling state of affairs is via a little mantra: if I just stay fully engaged in whatever has presented itself, things will be fine. That is, I try not to think about things like: next, I begin MY NOVEL!

JW: What does the rest of your family think of your work? Do you ever get their input while you're writing?

GS: My wife is a great reader for me. She reads everything and always sets me straight. She knows when I'm slacking off or being Johnny Denial, trying to sugarcoat something. She's very smart and knows me very well, which is a dangerous combo if you're trying to get away with something. We met in the Syracuse Creative Writing Program, as students way back when, and got engaged in three weeks, so our connection is very, very deep, and I trust her completely, even when she is pointing out that the last three months' work has been a total waste of time.

JW: Your work is seen as very dark. I'm thinking of that section at the end of "The 400-Pound CEO." Does that darkness signal any real pessimism or misanthropy on your part?

GS: Well, a story like "The 400-Pound CEO" doesn't say, I don't think, that life is always shit, though it does say that some people's lives are sometimes shit. It says that a shit-life is a possibility. I think that's true and important. It's important to remember, if happy, that our current happiness is not permanent and is not due to any intrinsic "goodness" on our part. American society is uncomfortable with the idea that some people's lives are difficult past the point of sanity and that they aren't necessarily to blame. There's no way you can argue that everyone has a difficult life. This is an incredible culture; the majority of people live in amazing comfort, with real dignity, maybe more comfort and dignity than any other culture in the history of the world. We live relatively safe and sane lives, which, if you've ever loved anybody and therefore feared for them, is a wonderful thing. But part of our moral responsibility is to keep in our minds those whose lives are unsafe and insane. In this way, fiction can be like a meditation, a way of saying: Though things are this way for me right now, they could be different later and are different for others this very moment.

JW: We're not all equally privileged.

GS: Exactly. Let's say that in some hospital somewhere, Baby One and Baby Two are born side by side. Baby One has intelligent and loving parents, is healthy and without defects, smart and beautiful. Baby Two has abusive parents, is missing a leg, is stupid and ugly and has an obnoxious personality. If you extrapolate from that point, then Baby One, no matter what you throw at it, is going to have more reserves and more good fortune, while statistically Baby Two is going to come up short. Whatever troubles are thrown his or her way, they are going to cost Baby Two more than the same troubles would cost Baby One. So who is to blame? At what point did Baby Two screw up? When he or she came out of the womb? A month before? Three years after? Of course, it's absurd. Seen this way, Baby Two is the inevitable flowering of a chain of events that literally goes back to the beginning of time. Therefore, the order of the day is compassion, and I think that fiction has a part to play in urging us, as a species, toward compassion.

JW: The typical fiction workshop model is that one or more students posts their work and the class then critiques it. This classroom critique is supplemented with individual meetings with the instructors. How are your own workshops different?

GS: We basically work within that model. The only thing I try to do is to constantly be reminding my students (and myself) that this whole workshop thing is really just an economic construct. Historically, it was (and is) a great way to get older writers paid to teach and younger writers paid to write. And this method can severely affect the fiction; there's that committee tendency. So we try to constantly deconstruct the process itself. The other thing I've been playing with is the idea of getting away from the traditional let's-all-crap-on-Hal's-story approach and instead using exercises and close readings of very short passages of text and so on to open things up a bit. What I find myself doing more and more is approaching a story as a manifestation of energy and trying not to say what's good or bad about it but focusing on where and how a story is attempting to manifest itself. That is, I try to look at how the strengths and weaknesses of a story are intimately bound up together.

Ultimately workshops aren't something you're supposed to do your whole life. I think of it as two or three years of shock therapy that you won't ever repeat again. Sometimes I think the whole point of workshops is to humiliate you and frustrate you until you come to the realization that you are the only one who can figure this writing thing out for yourself. That's how it was for me. After two years of workshops, I was totally convinced that I was going to have to do it myself and that I was never going to negotiate with someone about my stories again.

JW: So much of your fiction is charged with social import. Given our recent political upheavals, have you ever thought of writing overt political satire?

GS: I'm not very interested in that kind of satire because it works on the assumption that They Are Assholes. Fiction works on the assumption that They Are Us, on a Different Day.

JW: Do you think being funny can be taught?

GS: No. But you can take someone's innate funniness and show it to them, which almost always involves compression. You can say: This is funny. And you can show them how their humor is actually their ticket to a deep, interesting, sophisticated place in their work. Most funny writers long to be serious. I know I did. I distrusted humor because it came easily and because all my writing heroes were the big serious brooding guys. The best thing anyone ever did for me—and Toby and Doug both did this for me—was to steer me toward funny writers who did big moral things with their humor: Gogol, West, Kafka.

You can also help someone learn to discipline themselves so they know how to cut out all but the funniest bits. Bill Buford at the *New Yorker*, for example, is great at showing me the things in my stories that are practice runs for funnier parts. For instance, in "Sea Oak" there's a reference to a TV show called *The Worst That Could Happen*, which is these computer simulations of tragedies that haven't yet occurred but theoretically could. Well, I'd originally included a couple of other similar TV shows, which were essentially rough drafts of that show. But I left them in because I liked them. And Bill pointed out that those other shows were just lame versions of the first TV show and that by cutting them I could make that first show even funnier. So you can show a writer what her 5.6 (on a scale of 10) looks like and what her 8.9 looks like, and encourage her to get rid of anything that's not at least a 9, which strengthens the whole piece and makes her seem more intelligent and likeable.

JW: "The Falls" is a story that has a very open ending. John Barth asserts that it is the function of fiction writers not to create worldviews but to create worlds. I was wondering how complete the world of that particular story is. Do you, as the author of "The Falls," know what happens to Morse and those little girls after the story ends?

GS: I don't know. What was important about that ending for me was the fact that he jumped. It really doesn't matter if he saves them—that depends on wind and water currents and that sort of thing, which in the world of the story are just random elements. What matters—what we feel matters—is if he's going to be able to extrapolate from his own son to those two nearly dead girls, and transcend himself. At least that's how I felt about it when I stumbled on that ending. Here's an interesting thing about endings: I was teaching my students the Vonnegut story "Harrison Bergeron," and I'd gotten a copy of it out of an anthology and given it to my students. But when I actually sat down to read what I'd passed out, I realized that the version in the anthology was truncated by about three pages. So as an exercise, I told them about the truncation and had them write a new ending. And the amazing thing is that every kid in that class wrote a decent ending, even the kids who really couldn't write. My point is, the ending of "The Falls"—of any story—is just a kind of flourish. It's the first two-thirds of the story that really matters; to use a lame juggling analogy, it's the throwing of the balls into the air that matters. If there are the right number of balls and they're sufficiently interesting, it almost doesn't matter in which order they come down, or whether one of them gets stuck up on the roof beam.

JW: Has your publishing success affected your relationship with other writers?

GS: I don't think so. I hope not. It's a pretty mild success, really. Most of the writers I'm friends with now were friends from long before anything happened for any of us, so those friendships are pretty deep and immune to dopiness on either side. Success is nice because then you don't have to worry so much about having been unfairly robbed of your very richly deserved success. Success is bad because momentary good fortune can temporarily hide the fact that you are still, despite your success, full of shit. One of the great blessings I've had was the period while I was writing the stories in *CivilWarLand*, when I had given up all hope of publishing anything and was just going to my job and typing a few paragraphs a day, then riding my bike home from work to my wife and kids. It was an amazingly happy time, even though nothing was going right career-wise, maybe even because nothing was going right career-wise. I couldn't have felt any dorkier or more foolish running my little photocopier in too-tight brown corduroys, writing Environmental Health and Safety Assessment Plans, but even so, life was all around and it was good and I was enjoying it. And so when things started to heat up, and stories started to sell and so on, I pretty much knew what was what.

An Interview with George Saunders

Ben Marcus / 2004

From *The Believer*, no. 11 (March 1, 2004). Reprinted by permission of the author.

"That, to me, is art's highest aspiration: to show that nothing is true and everything is true."

He was born George Saunders and has kept the same name his entire life. Sometimes he moves through the streets beneath a great coat designed to keep himself from being killed. Otherwise he is fearless, naked in the evenings, a family man. There has been a moustache, a beard, a bald face. The area locale where he has chosen to live is brutal and cold and produces a large share of lonely people. He sleeps and eats and functions as any person might. But there the similarities end.

For part of each day, Saunders is a hero. He would never agree to this designation. But his modesty, his generosity, his expansive imagination, and his fully developed tenderness-generating technique are a large part of his heroism. His heroism is fitted with a blind spot that keeps Mr. Saunders from knowing about, or being able to acknowledge, the ways that he has beautifully scoured and remade—through artisan-quality writing—the people in many countries. His writing appears in books and magazines and quickly subsumes them, explaining the appearance of horizon fires in the far Northeast. The books of fiction are called *CivilWarLand in Bad Decline* and *Pastoralia*. The Suits call his writing "stories," but they are really soft bodies to wear for a larger experience of life, hollowcore person-shapes that one can slip on in order to attain amazement. Saunders writes bodies, and his readers wear them. Some of these readers are probably in your house. If they are glowing or trembling, now you know why.

The following conversation took place on an old Toshiba calculator.

—Ben Marcus

I. "Pay Attention to Everything as if This Was Your Last Moment on Earth."

Ben Marcus: When I visited your city of Syracuse, New York, I was kept awake all night by crows, who raised such a terrible noise in my motel room that I thought I might get killed. I later heard from other overnight visitors that this had happened to them also. Explain.

George Saunders: It's true, we have a lot of crows up here. It's part of a Municipal Program to become the West Nile Virus Capital of the Northeast. We actually "recruit" crows from all over the United States—bring them here on special Crow Interview Trips, construct special "GlamorNests" for them all over town, screen weekend-long Heckle & Jeckle fests at our local movie houses. And they are loud. We had one in particular around our house who used to sound exactly like he was calling my wife's name ("PauLA! PauLA!") until finally—in connection with the Crow Recruitment Program—we had a translator over, who informed us that what the crow was actually saying was, "I could sure use some freaking grapes! I could sure use some freaking grapes! If I don't get some freaking grapes, I'm going back to Cleveland."

BM: Where does the name George Saunders come from?

GS: It actually comes from the fact that my great grandfather, who emigrated from Greece, was catching a lot of crap for his last name, Vlahakis, and his accent. I think he was working as a fruit seller at the time. So he went for something very British. The accent he couldn't do anything about. He was kind of a wildcard—left my great-grandmother and their sons for two years to go back to Greece and fight the Turks. And then as soon as he came home, he ran off with a waitress, to Napa Valley.

BM: Rather than ask who your ideal reader is, since I have met your ideal reader and he hurt me physically, I wanted to ask you how aware you are of entertainment, as a specific gift to a reader, and whether or not there's ever a tension for you between what you feel you ought to do as a writer, and what you actually do. This is not a question about capitulation to a generic sense of what a reader might want, but rather a question of a potential discrepancy between what might please you and what you feel will please others.

GS: This question rattles me, because it makes me realize that I make no distinction between what pleases me and what might please a reader. That is, if I feel the reader will be pleased by a thing, I simply want to do that thing. Period. My feeling is something like this: the basis for literature is the fact that all of our brains are essentially, structurally, identical. First love in 1830, in Russia, beneath swaying pines, is neurologically identical to first love in 1975, back of a Camaro, Foghat blaring. That's why that wonderful crossfiring occurs when we read. It is not the case, as we sometimes feel, that the writer is making us feel what she felt. It is, rather, that the writer is poking that part of our brain that already felt (or knew, or sensed) what the writer felt (or knew, or sensed). Without getting too *Star Trekkie*, there really is, I believe, one universal mind, but the basis for the existence of that universal mind is the structural similarity of all those individual minds. Because the brain is a machine, and all those individual minds are just slightly different versions of that machine, only so many mind-states exist, and therefore you can know what I think, because it is what you thought, roughly. So, when I'm writing, I am trying to move myself, or impress myself, or prevent myself from getting bored and walking away—in the faith that, if I succeed in this, the writing will have some equivalent effect on the reader. On every reader? No. On every reader, to some extent? I think so. I hope so. Anyway, that's what I assume. That, to me, is the really magical thing about writing: if I write toward my own best nature, I am also writing toward the best nature of others. It sort of doesn't make sense, and even feels a little fascist, but I think it's true. Here I have to confess that I also believe that certain effects have more power in prose than others, and that this tendency is, at least in part, universal. I believe in efficiency, action, clarity, velocity. I think these qualities are responsible for the feeling of being "drawn into" a piece of prose. Also, maybe paradoxically, I think that constructing this hierarchy of preferred effects is what style is all about. If one writer prefers some other suite of effects, and energetically tries to construct a prose-world based on the preeminence of those effects, style will result. I will also confess that, for complex reasons of background, etc., I really don't care much about anything but being entertaining—with entertainment, I hope, being defined as "ultimately interesting." Ideally, I aspire to write stuff that takes into account the fact that we are all dying. So there's no time to be bloatedly intellectual, no time to be Merely Clever, no time to be stupid, or programmatic, or cloying. That's the hope, anyway. And as for that ideal reader of mine, sorry about that. "Max" is basically a good guy, but he doesn't get out much, and, for him, his fists are his most expressive part. That is, what you construe as "punching" is, for Max, sort of like kissing might be for most people.

BM: Your theory of a universal mind suggests that Buddhism plays a role in how you think about fiction.

GS: You bet. I find Buddhism inspiring in that it says: Everything matters. Suffering is real. Death is imminent. Pay attention to everything as if this was your last moment on earth. And then I see writing as part of an ongoing attempt to really, viscerally, believe that everything matters, suffering is real, and death is imminent. Chekhov said that art prepares us for tenderness, and I think this is also what spiritual practice can do. On a practical level there are also parallels. Buddhism emphasizes honesty and openness, non-attachment. So if you thought your story was going to be a biting satire of a nail-biting patriarchal brutalizer, but then, on page three, a street vendor comes in and makes a really interesting speech about his lifelong love of broccoli, and that speech has more energy in it than anything that came before—openness means admitting to yourself that your story needs to follow that vendor out into the street. That sort of thing.

BM: A cross old man once announced to me that it was impossible to teach writing. I replied, just as crossly, that he meant *he* couldn't teach writing. Nevertheless, non-teachers of writing seem to love to declare its impossibility, to call writing programs scams and money-wasters, and just to generally deride the whole enterprise. Book reviews frequently resort to a shorthand critique, citing "workshop" stories, and a recent *Village Voice* article claimed that Jonathan Safran Foer's originality stemmed, at least in part, from his outsider status, since he did not attend an MFA program. I was thinking of you and a few other writers—namely Charles Baxter and Aimee Bender—who have a reputation for being extraordinary teachers of writing, not to mention obviously original and productive writers. I'd be curious to hear your take on teaching, what its value might be, and why writing-instruction, unlike other artistic studies—painting or theater or music—seems so susceptible to criticism.

GS: I suspect that what your Cross Old Man was trying to say was: only one young writer in a thousand ever gets a book out, and of those books, only one in a thousand lasts in even the slightest way, so why are you writing-program teachers holding out hope to so many young people, when you know and I know that only one out of a thousand out of an original thousand have any hope of writing an enduring work of literature? And basically, I would agree with that. The chances of a person breaking through their own habits and sloth and limited mind to actually write something that gets out there and matters to people are slim. But I also suspect that your Cross Old Man is too narrowly careerist. Because he seems to be neglecting the fact that, even for those thousands of young people who don't get something out there, the process is still a noble one—the process of trying to say something, of working through the craft issues, and the worldview issues, and the ego issues—all of this is character-building, and God forbid everything we do should have to have Concrete Career Results. I've seen, time and time again, the way that the process of trying to say something that matters dignifies and improves a person. I've seen it in my own failures, in writing and otherwise. I think it comes down to the motivation of the individual student. If the student writer wants to get over, become famous, dominate others with his talent—then no matter what, he's going to lose. On the other hand, if he wants to go deeply into himself, subjugate his own pettiness, discover some big truths about life—there's no way he can lose. And the thing is, we all have both of those motivations within us, every second that we're writing. So it's an ongoing, lifelong battle to write for the right reasons. There's a sort of instant karma always working, if you see what I mean.

Having said that, I do think it's possible to "teach writing," in the sense that an older, like-minded person can certainly speed some younger person's progress along that younger person's personal arc. I imagine it this way: the younger writer is racing through some snowy woods, wearing ice skates. The MFA experience, ideally, is a frozen lake that suddenly appears. The writer just gets sped up. The way is easier. The trajectory is roughly the same, but the velocity is higher. The danger of a workshop environment is a kind of groupthink that can creep into even the most enlightened gathering. Since ultimately what we are trying to do as writers (let's admit it) is be iconic and undeniable and breathtaking, setting up a group whose function is to Thoughtfully Regard, then Rationally Critique, may be problematic. But then, I also think it's possible to take that into account—to undercut that tendency, to keep knocking the legs out from under it, so to speak. Finally: I think the success of the MFA experience is proportional to how closely such a program resembles a salon, or a group of friends. So I think small numbers are important, a longer residence time, financial support. I find that the best teaching moments happen when I know my students well enough, personally and artistically, to make certain intuitive leaps with them, leaps that aren't strictly dictated by the work sitting in front of me. By the way, it may interest you to know that the Cross Old Man lives next door to Max, my ideal reader. Because of the Cross Old Man's impertinence to you, I have just sent Max over to "kiss" the Cross Old Man. I'll let you know how it turns out!

Can I do a follow-up, to you? Because what I am wondering about, in reference to the workshop questions, is what your experience was as a student in a workshop. Did you workshop anything that later became *The Age of Wire and String*, and, if so, how was it received? If you had put some of those stories up, and they'd gotten resistance—would it have mattered? I guess I'm asking because of the extreme originality of that book, and the fact that one of its many charms is that it keeps insisting on abiding by its own new paradigm.

BM: The closest I got to workshopping pieces from that book was in a class that Robert Coover taught called "Ancient Fictions." He assigned us to write new mythologies, or creation myths, and a few of the earliest pieces in *The Age of Wire and String* were written in response. It was more of a literature class, with some fiction writing options instead of critical papers. But it was by far the best course I ever took having anything to do with fiction writing. The pieces we wrote weren't really discussed. I think we read them aloud and all nodded thoughtfully.

The workshop situation I was in with other teachers tended to err on the side of permissiveness, and actual teaching was more or less absent. It seems strange to say this, but in my own teaching I've tried to reverse almost everything I experienced as a student. Students now also seem to expect far more than I or my classmates ever did: extensive line editing and lengthy written critiques, follow-up conferences, and then extra critiques of whatever revisions they've done. We were lucky if our teacher showed up or said much at all. At the time, the teacher's silence or reticence seemed like blinding intelligence, but I'm not so sure now.

II. "It's Not a Dramatic Arc So Much as a Dramatic Vector: Straight Down into the Mud."

BM: Even in your wilder stories, a current of deep ethics seems to run through your characters, an immense desire to do good, and it is this desire, the conflicts it creates, that seems to generate story for you. Big moments of grief seem to result, and these serve as epiphanies, revelations, or just incredible finales. Is this connected to a belief you have about character, or does it derive more from your sense of what might propel a story? Or neither?

GS: I like the kind of story where the reader comes away loving the character, feeling strongly identified with the character. And I think the way to make that happen is to make a character who is as good as the reader. That is, the reader feels the character is doing everything just as he or she would, if put in the same situation. So for the writer this means no slumming, no puppeteering—by which I mean, no manipulating your character to prove a point or illustrate something you believe or service some prejudice you have or fulfill some secret hope for the story. Don't make the character stupider or blinder or meaner than yourself. That is, credit the character with the same basic nature as you, albeit tempered or complicated by whatever is happening to him, or has happened in the past, that makes the character "you," but in a parallel universe. Even if your main character is Hitler, believe that there is some part of yourself that could swell into Hitleresque proportions. Another way of saying this is: believe that there but for the grace of God, go you. So, in part, this ethical tendency you note is just a strategy to get more warmth into the story.

But to be another degree more honest, I think that's just the way I see the world—in fairly simple ethical terms. I always have. As a kid I was interested in philosophy and religion, and came to reading and thinking via Catholicism, had amazing early experiences in the Church, glimpses into what ideas such as compassion and self-sacrifice might mean at a visceral level, got the sense that life was big and painful and that the purpose of an individual life was to aid other beings in trouble, which runs counter to our instinct, which is protect our own ass. And then that beautiful heroic narrative of Christ sacrificing himself to save everybody, even when he didn't want to. I found that very moving. That naïve big-question sensibility ("What are we doing here? How should we behave?") stayed at the heart of my ludicrous, spotty reading life through college. Years later, when I was first working on *CivilWarLand*, I felt like I turned an important corner in my artistic life by letting that sensibility back in, that feeling that things matter, and that literature exists to help us examine the big questions. That there are such things as power, as abuse, as bad luck, and it definitely matters which side of the fence you're on. It matters whether we're hungry, whether your love is returned or rejected, whether we walk into the room with a fireplace and the cheering crowd or are locked out of the room and have to stand out in the cold with wet sneakers, etc. I guess what I'm saying is when it comes to writing stories, I don't know any other way to proceed. As soon as I start writing, things start to unfold around some central moral vector, and that's that. So, sometimes to my frustration, my stories tend to be "problem" stories: will he or won't he do the right thing? And they also tend to be fables, although I didn't realize that until recently. So the tendency you mention is both a blessing and a curse: I have something to write about, but there is a sort of an implicit ceiling, a kind of limit of subtlety I can't get past. The dangers of this approach are oversimplicity, preachiness, and, eventually, fascism.

Can I ask about your relation to this ethical stuff? I feel your work as extremely "ethical," in the sense that I always feel opened up when I'm reading it. I am, in the Chekhovian sense mentioned above, prepared for tenderness. Is this part of your intent?

BM: I'm not sure that in attempting sympathy in fiction I can claim a connection to ethics. It's hard for me to link writing with good deeds, since most of what I wrote for so long was character-free, and then when characters did show up they were interested in killing or at least harming the other characters. Not very ethical. A kind of coldness used to appeal to me. Behavior, if present at all, was mechanized and described the way a tree might be: sort of the stubborn opposite of giving human properties to inanimate things. But if I ever do get lucky and spill out some people-like pieces of writing, they are inevitably cruel or pitiful, take your pick. Unfortunately it yields only minimal drama. The cruel people act cruel to the pitiful people, who become more pitiful. It's not a dramatic arc so much as a dramatic vector: straight down into the mud. I'm sure most people get over this narrative paradigm in third grade, but it's about all I can manage so far.

I'm interested in the trace fantastical elements that appear in your stories, as well as the occasional ghost. So much of your stories seem wedded to an emotional realism, yet your settings—the landscapes—are often, if not fantastical, then exceedingly odd or improbable, leading to real emotions in an unreal world. And then your stories, sometimes very slightly, leave the realm of physical possibility entirely (the dead awaken, for instance). Are these three distinct writing-spaces to you? Do you see a difference between "realism" and fantastical writing?

GS: I guess it's strategic on one level: if you're going to have some really crazy things happening, you have a better chance of being believed if you jump off from some believable ground. It maybe comes from a sales instinct: if I'm trying to hustle ten bucks from you, and I've invented a wild story to support my hustle, it's probably best not to sing that story in an operatic voice. Better if I tell it in my normal voice, eyes downcast, acknowledging all your doubts about the veracity of my story. That's how I see the realist touches. I think the fantastical elements are there as my lamebrained attempt to mimic the real strangeness and mystery of even the most ordinary day. Realism is nonsense, when you think of it. I mean, there is no such thing. Nobody writes realism, if realism is defined as "fiction that is objective and real and not distorted, but is just, you know, normal." But I think that's what "realistic" has come to mean. The nature of all fiction is distortion, exaggeration, and compression. So what we call realism is just distorting, exaggerating, and compressing with the intention of alluding to, or hand-waving at—taking advantage of our fondness for—what I've heard called "consensus reality"—the sort of lazy, agreed-upon "way things are." Which, of course, is not at all how they actually are. How they actually are is: we are walking corpses. Ideas people die for fade within ten years. Murderers walk. The dead don't really die because they can sometimes continue to affect the actions of the living just as much as if they were still around. Et cetera. So realism, as beautifully practiced by Zola, Chekhov, Carver, et al, is a strategy—a strategy to elicit our emotional loyalty by doing some sleight of hand to make the distorted, exaggerated, compressed thing they've made remind us of consensus reality. Why? Power of effect. They want to make a powerful effect. What I find exciting is the idea that no work of fiction will ever, ever come close to "documenting" life. So then, the purpose of it must be otherwise. It's supposed to do something to us to make it easier (or more fun, or less painful) for us to live. Then all questions of form and so on become subjugated to this higher thing. We're not slaves any more to ideas of "the real" or, for that matter, to ideas of "the experimental"—we're just trying to make something happen to the reader in his or her deepest places. And that thing that happens will always be due to some juxtaposition of the life the reader is living and the words on the page, no matter how unconventional or conventional the representation of those events is—the heart will either rise, or it won't. I think it's interesting, though, that some writers of our approximate generation have a sort of queasiness around this issue of realism. I know I do. There's something about the normal approach ("Bob, age forty-three, pale blond hair—a senior-level accountant—felt good about his marriage. He got into his tan Lexus, thinking of Maribeth") that makes me scared and sick. I am always trying to avoid it. You've written two radically unconventional books. Do you ever feel that pull toward what we're calling realism? If so, what's stopping you? What do you think that pull is about? That is, what do you fear you're missing by not doing "realism?" What concessions/changes would you have to make to be "more realistic?"

BM: I do feel a pull toward realism, but there's always a hand waiting to smack me down off it. From afar, where I definitely am, realism looks like a place of readability, which I very much desire, by which I mean that inscrutability is not something I value. But I can almost watch my fiction turn generic as I attempt realism, and then the trade-off leads to work that is punishingly dull. So what stops me is a total lack of ability. For probably good although unfathomable reasons, a narrative framework, a skin of storytelling—which I equate with a writerly promise that time will pass and that people will move around in a made-up space—seems to justify many kinds of conceptual or innovative approaches to fiction, but I find that, in itself, a kind of fantastical notion. I've seen a few writers I hugely admire, such as Joe Wenderoth or David Markson, become marginalized or called "experimental" because they have forgone the typical narrative skins and pursued more conceptual or subversively informational fiction. Yet their realism is, for me, extremely high.

There are these soporific, safe phrases like "once upon a time" that make non-realist writing much more OK, and so I'm at the point where I'm wondering if that's a good thing worth pursuing or if it's a capitulation.

III. "Have We Sufficiently Described the Wonders of Living in Our Time?"

BM: Several less narrative pieces of yours ("Four Institutional Monologues," which was in *McSweeney's*, and "I Can Speak!" which was in the *New Yorker*) did not make it into *Pastoralia*. What was the process of selecting work for that book? The above pieces were far less story-driven. Did that play a role in your decision?

GS: If I remember right, "I Can Speak!" was written after the manuscript was finished. So I had all these story-driven pieces and the one monologue, and it didn't seem to fit. But both stories you mention, plus another monologue ("A Survey of the Literature") will be in the next collection. The monologue-like pieces feel different for me—easier, in some way. They don't depend on surprising myself as much as the more story-driven pieces. But I like them, and my thought for this next book is that they might add a little something—maybe offer a political or institutional angle on stuff that is covered more emotionally by the stories. I can picture a sort of a "spine" of these types of nonnarrative pieces running through the book. I like the way books like *In Our Time* or *The Coast of Chicago* use little spacer pieces that are different in tone and intent than the longer, more narrative pieces.

My usual approach so far has just been to put everything together that feels like it came out of the same aesthetic suite of ideas, which usually corresponds to a certain three-to-four-year time period—and then weed out the weaker links, or the anomalous ones. I usually have two or three pieces I start and don't finish, and another two or three that I finish but am not happy with, and then another couple that I'm happy enough with, but don't seem to fit with the rest. They make a sort of goiter on an otherwise smooth shape. And then I figure that, if each of the pieces represents an intense move in some direction, a move that I played out aesthetically, then if I put them all together, with attention to the order—the book should be more than the sum of its parts. That's the theory, anyway. For this next book, there is a pretty strong nonnarrative presence and also, I think, a stronger political (or overtly political) feeling. This wasn't planned but was maybe a product of the time during which the book was written.

BM: There is a word sometimes used in connection to fiction—moral— that can scare the bread out of me because I use it too, and then must secretly admit that I don't really understand it, or what it means, yet it seems to me to be a word that is reached for when something called "serious fiction" is discussed, a word we'd like to assign to the fiction we care about. Does "moral" fiction mean something to you that you can articulate?

GS: The short answer is: all good fiction is moral, in that it is imbued with the world, and powered by our real concerns: love, death, how-should-I-live. This is true, I think, of all great writers, regardless of their approach: Sterne, Chekhov, Barthelme, Morrison, Gogol, Bellow—whomever. But I think that word has taken on additional overtones since the Gardner-Gass debates of the 1980s, where the binary was: (1) fictional effects are effects of language versus, (2) fictional effects are effects of represented experience. My guess is, most of us who have ever tried to write a sentence in a story know that both (1) and (2) are simultaneously true. If I write, "The cow, ducklike, made a ducklike cow sound, then disappeared down the Shaughnessy Chute,"— we recognize that there is a pure-sound quality to that, but also that cows and ducks and chutes are somehow "appearing" in our reading-mind. So it's the confluence of these two effects that makes the heart-rise I mentioned above (or doesn't, in this case). But somehow, at that time, there was this sense that the purpose of fiction was "moral" in the sense of "instructive." That I reject. I mean, it is instructive, it feels that way, but instructive in a deep way, and in a way that does not flow from a writer's desire to instruct, if you see what I mean. Rather, it flows from the writer's confusion in the process of writing, or at least the writer's sense of exploration. Writing can be a formal way of enacting Thomas More's great plea: "For the love of God, man, think it possible you may be mistaken." When a writer does that, then I think the result is moral, in the sense of "accounting for all complexities." I think you leave the work of art not instructed, but baffled, baffled in a way that humbles you and makes you move more carefully (but fully) through your life, at least until the effect wears off. For writers of our generation (and of course, using that expression means I am really talking about me), that phrase "moral fiction" seems to signify something else, though, some deeper fear, a fear that the assumptions "we" have made about writing are self-limiting, especially around the issues of being ironic/edgy/experimental—a feeling that maybe our approach is preventing us from reaching into the more profound aspects of our experience, especially as we get older and less jaded and the checks start rolling in and the grandkids have grandkids and we see that life is not so angsty after all, at least not all the time. That is, the fear that our approach may be omitting significant aspects of our actual experience. I sense a real feeling of discontent hovering over American fiction right now and maybe all American art forms, post-9/11, that has at its core questions like (and please excuse the *USA Today* "we" in what follows): Does what we are doing matter? Are we writing as big as we need to write? Are we just spoiled-brat sneering aesthetes who are masturbating while looking away from the big questions of our age? Have we sufficiently described the wonders of living in our time? Are we properly accounting for the good and the beautiful and the enjoyable? But also: Are we properly accounting for the fact that evil exists, and exploring the difference between this and not-evil? How much of the irony and cleverness of our experimental writing—and for that matter, how much of the earnest and uplifting We-reinforcement of our realist writing—is just knee-jerk and ultimately reactionary? In other words, life came brutally knocking at our door, and now we are reconsidering the venture. And I'm not saying everyone should get busy on their Kosovo novel—I think there is a way in which even the most domestic story (or wild experimental story) can take into account the larger world. But one could argue that American fiction has ghettoized itself by insisting on a self-reifying view (humanist/materialist?) in which all answers are known, the political binary is carved in stone, we all have swallowed whole certain orthodoxies, and the purpose of the fiction is just to reinforce these. At the heart of this lies a selfish agenda that has (one could argue) really ceased seeing the world as a unity, and has begun aggressively internalizing certain capitalist dogmas that say: of course you are the most important thing, of course you exist separate from the rest of the world. I'm not sure I actually believe all of the above—but I do find myself thinking about these kinds of things a lot lately. Does this make any sense? Do you feel any of this? It may just be that I am saying: I really, really hope to, in the future, write better. By the way, I just came back from the Cross Old Man's house, and am happy to report that, after many many "kisses" from Max, the Cross Old Man has at last admitted that writing can be taught.

BM: I worry that if you smother an old man with kisses, crank up his sexual heat or whatever, he'll admit to anything. These lonely people are just waiting to tell us what we want to hear.

IV. "That Voice of Hemingway's Can't Function in a Wal-Mart, on Christmas Eve, When You Have an STD . . ."

BM: You have a film project underway. Can you tell me about it?

GS: Back in 1997, Ben Stiller optioned *CivilWarLand* and so for the last year or so I've been working with him on a script. It's been interesting in that film writing is so much about structure and so little about language. You can just say, "Tens of thousands of chimps emerge from mobile phone booths, speaking French," and that's it. There are the chimps. In other words, you don't have to do what we usually do, which is convince with language. You can just make these little structural units, which will be de facto "convincing" because the viewer will be seeing them. So it changes the nature of the challenge, writing-wise. It forced me to use a different part of my brain; the part that says, if I put A, then B, then C—trusting that each of these will be done well—then I've made resulting Meaning D. Which is not how I think when I'm writing fiction—then, I tend to concentrate on the individual line, trusting that some worthwhile effect will come out in the end, but I don't necessarily know what it is. It's also been interesting anthropologically—getting some idea of how movies get made, how the larger mass culture might get accessed, how finances play into the whole thing, etc. So much of our storytelling now takes place within this quasi-corporate framework, and so it's interesting to see if there is a sort of de facto editing effect working, and if so, what the flavor of it is. Also it's been interesting for me to think about broad appeal—is it possible/desirable for somebody like me? What is the difference between "literary" and "popular?" I've been especially interested to see, in myself, a sort of knee-jerk tendency toward the dark, the negative, the nihilistic—somehow, film writing made this tendency more noticeable. When I do this knee-jerk thing, it's more apparent, feels more like flinching. In film, it seems like because there are actual people up there, somehow my urge to credit the noble, the good, the simply decent is more easily managed than in stories. I'm not sure what to think of all that, but I've noticed it, and am sort of mulling it over. It goes back to something we talked about earlier: how much of the brooding cynical nature of our art-fiction is meaningful (i.e., is telling a deep truth) and how much of it is just limited technical ability and/or sloth? I think there are deep truths about our time that are dark and scary—but I also think that not every dark/scary move that is accomplishable via fiction necessarily has a real-life corollary. Sometimes they're just easier—as Tolstoy said: "Happiness writes white."

BM: You've had two amazing and critically lauded collections of short stories. Do you feel pressure to write a novel?

GS: I sometimes do. I just finished reading *Appointment in Samarra* and *Revolutionary Road* and those really made me want to write a novel—they're such beautiful, complicated books, and they show America in so much wonderful detail. My main problem is a very small intersection-set between (1) the abilities it takes to write a novel, and (2) the abilities I actually have. Working on a story, I have very strong and intuitive opinions. With novels, I have mostly Ideas, which, in my case, are deadly. I seem decent at compressing, but not so good at elaborating. So for now, I'm just allowing myself to do what I love, which is write stories. The one thing I would love to do in a novel is show the world as a big, stunning, contradiction: to show Truth A in all its glory, then show Truth B (which contradicts Truth A) in all its glory. There's a beautiful story, which sounds like a joke, because it starts: "Once Tolstoy and Gorky were walking down the street." As Gorky described it (in a memoir piece he wrote about Tolstoy) this mob of hussars comes walking up the street, and Tolstoy launches into this brilliant bit of polemic about how that sort of young man—brutal, cocksure, militaristic—represents everything that is wrong with Russia. And Gorky was convinced. Then, as the hussars passed in a cloud of tobacco smoke and cologne and leather, etc., Tolstoy spun on his heel and delivered an equal-but-opposite dissertation on why that sort of young man—fully alive, masculine, passionate, spontaneous—was the hope of Russia's future. And again, Gorky was convinced. That, to me, is art's highest aspiration: to show that nothing is true and everything is true. To work as a kind of ritual humility, and ritual celebration, of all that is.

BM: Like Raymond Carver and Denis Johnson before you, your stories have served as an ideal model—an inspiration—for legions of newcomers. This may be an awkward question, but does being so widely emulated by younger writers change the way you approach what you're doing?

GS: I don't really see that. Every so often, someone will send me a story full of funny franchise names, or composed completely of acronyms. But to the extent that it's true, I'm honored. And it's funny how, as you get older, and look back at your own work—it seems young. In a good way, but . . .

young. And you remember whom you were channeling or admiring at the time. So I say, anything that gets us going. I remember basically rewriting *Red Cavalry* by setting it in an oil camp in Indonesia, where I'd once worked. And also rewriting *In Our Time*, but set in Amarillo, Texas, and Nick had not just come home from war, but was on spring break. And what I felt most acutely, doing those little knockoffs, was how inappropriate and uncomfortable someone else's stylistic tics were, superimposed on my life. In other words, those imitations helped me realize that there is no Real Life—there is no objective reality. There is just your version of it, and that version has to be in your language. I thought: that voice of Hemingway's can't function in a Wal-Mart, on Christmas Eve, when you have an STD and your uncle is drunk and trying to buy an O-Jays record to give to his new girlfriend, a speed-freak waitress. Hence the constant necessity for new voices.

Roy Kesey Interviews
George Saunders

Roy Kesey / 2005

From maudnewton.com, September 7, 2005. http://maudnewton.com/blog/roy-kesey
-interviews-george-saunders/. Reprinted by permission of the author and maudnewton.com.

Says Mr. Kesey: This interview was conducted over the course of five days, between the 19th and the 23rd of August 2005. Throughout the interview, Mr. Saunders wore a brownish cowboy hat with a python-skin band, a sheer black cocktail dress of scalloped Thai chiffon, and yellow flip-flops. Actually, that may or may not be true. This interview was conducted via email. We have no idea what he was wearing.

Also, please note that the entire interview, if translated into Cantonese, would form a phonemic anagram. That was entirely coincidental.

Roy Kesey: Good evening, Mr. Saunders. According to my sources, you have a new book out, a novella called *The Brief and Frightening Reign of Phil*. Word on the street, and behind the Shop-n-Save, and on the porch, and in many of Beijing's top-drawer massage parlors, is that it's a political fable. Any truth to that?

George Saunders: I'm not really sure what to call it. It started out as a kids' book, but then suddenly became about genocide. So much for the marketing tie-ins! But I'm glad they're talking about it in the massage parlors. It just goes to show you that phone marketing really does work.

The way I usually work is to try and find some little thing—a concept or a bit of dialogue or whatever—and then let a story grow from there, with as little preconception as possible. In this case, Lane Smith, who illustrated a previous book (*The Very Persistent Gappers of Frip*) suggested I try to write a story where all the characters were abstract shapes. So I tried that. At some point—I can't exactly remember when—this line came out about there being a country that was so small, only one of its citizens could live there at a time. And this raised certain questions. So that's how a story like this proceeds, for me.

RK: Oh, no question about it—if you've got the masseuses on your side, the battle is won.

I want to get back to the new book in a minute, but just now I'm fascinated with this business of "with as little preconception as possible." That gets right to the heart of the mystery, doesn't it? I've seen you mention Barthelme's essay "Not Knowing" elsewhere, heard you talk about how not knowing where a story is headed is actually a prerequisite for getting it on its way. Do you have a favorite metaphor for the way things build or accrete in spite of your not knowing? Magnetism, maybe? Gravity? Dust-bunnies? And a quick follow-up: you've also said elsewhere (again with the elsewheres!) that you know a story is working when it manifests a "complexity that results from (1) truth, and (2) accretion." Could you explore the dark side of that coin for us?

How do you know when things are building in the "wrong" direction, and what would "wrong" mean in that context?

GS: Wow, okay. Excellent. I can see this is going to be fun.

I do have a favorite metaphor for this—but before I get to it, a disclaimer or apology of sorts. One of the weird things about being interviewed is that, if you've been interviewed before, and had one of those enviable moments where you answer sensibly, and actually come up with exactly the right thing to express what you're trying to express, then you're in a pickle: next time you're asked that question or one similar, do you use the example you thought of before, or not? If you're trying to be truthful and accurate and precise, you probably should—it came to you in a moment of revelation. But then you get to a certain point where these things start following you around—you start sounding like: "Ah, you're asking about PLOT. Allow me to invoke Chestnut #9!"

So this is just to say that if I repeat myself relative to something I've said before, somewhere else, I'm not being cynical or lazy but am trying to be truthful and concise.

Okay. So my favorite metaphor for the thing you're talking about is the seed-crystal metaphor. Like in high school biology: you put the thing in water and it starts growing. The key, for me, is that the crystal is not trying to grow in a certain direction, or to make a certain pattern, or because it wants to be a certain kind of Big Crystal when it's done. It is, I suppose, following some sort of path of least resistance. That is what it feels like, in the best case. I am not trying to do anything in particular, except stumble on something. I don't know what. Funny is good, tight is good, clever is good—something that, once you've put it down, you go: "Well, okay, whatever else happens, I'm pretty sure that's staying there." Or another way to say this: You feel like the events described in that little bit of prose have just gone from Typing to Something That Happened. It gives off a feeling of undeniability, if you see what I mean. You don't feel like negotiating at least that little bit of story.

As for how it feels when it goes wrong, I was just about, of course, to fire off a definitive answer. But maybe I should first say that a good percentage of the time, if there is such a diagnostic, I miss it. I spend a lot of time writing things that don't get used. At the time they feel very much like what I described above.

So maybe the truth is, this process is incremental and repetitive. I am familiar with this feeling: what felt right yesterday suddenly is obviously wrong. And: what you cut two weeks ago suddenly is absolutely needed, and right.

In some ways, I suppose, all of these very good questions about writing, that I suspect every writer asks and answers in his or her head as he or she wanders around the kitchen late at night, as if being interviewed by some Charlie Rose-like figure—and the idea that there might BE an answer—mostly just serve to reassure us. When you consider something you've written that you like, think of how many rules you broke, or forgot to honor. Think of how uninterested you were in the generality of the approach you were using, the repeatability of it, etc. You were just in there feeling good.

The set of "skills" that add up to Becoming Better are split-second skills, irreducible skills, skills that build up over many years in the same ineffable complex way that, say, our ability to fall in love and sustain relationships builds up. In a sense what I'm saying is: We don't have to worry. Whatever is going to sustain us is happening every time we write, whether we are aware of it or not.

But: one way I know things are going wrong is when I get indecisive and start thinking too much, having little working models of "how the story works" and/or political rationales and/or pages of notes and/or elaborate rationales of how this or that section is going to work, rationales which have nothing to do with the process of a real live person, just home from work, picking the thing up and reading for pleasure.

When it's working, it feels simple, is viscerally pleasurable to read, and I feel very decisive—I know just what to do, what is needed.

But that state—I'm in that state very infrequently. It happens at two places: once at the beginning, when the story isn't bearing any weight yet (and hasn't even gotten to the point of being a riddle) and once towards the end, when the feeling is one of pleasantly painting yourself into a corner. At the end, the story now means something, something specific, and your choices are fewer; and this in itself is fun, because every choice has the potential to throw light through the story and make it exponentially bigger than it was in the last draft.

Long answer, because the question was so good.

RK: Well, not to worry—as soon as we need to start varying lengths and tempos, I'll move to the "If you could choose one writer, living or dead, and hit that writer over the head with a shovel, what kind of shovel would it be?" type questions. But as long as we're talking shop, let me hit you with a few more story-geek questions, and then we'll move on.

In *Pastoralia*, you did a bold thing with the sequencing, starting off with the novella, by far the longest piece in the book. It works really well, but I'm wondering how you came up with the idea, what the reasons were behind it, how you see/saw it affecting the dynamic of the book as a whole . . .

GS: Your timing is interesting—I just spent the last week trying to figure out the order for this new collection that's coming out in May. Arghh. Index cards everywhere.

What I've tried to do in both collections is come up with an order that (1) takes the reader pretty strongly from one story to the next, just in terms of quality and stylistic variation and staving off boredom, and (2) tells a kind of uber-story.

What I mean by (1) is, I try to set it up like a Dream Date. From one good thing to another, and that second thing is in a slightly different flavor, followed by some third thing you weren't expecting, after which there's a killer dessert. So I guess at that level I'm trying to find an order that helps me avoid feeling repetitive, etc. And in *Pastoralia*, there was something about the length of the novella and the humor that made me think putting it first wouldn't lose me any readers, whereas later, it might. (I tend to think that way—a little defensively.) Or, to put it more positively, I thought the piece was funny enough and odd enough that, having read it, a reader might at least say: Huh. Okay. I'll read one more.

I also have an idea you should put the stories with the most gravitas towards the end of the book, to avoid a feeling of letdown. The thing is, I basically take five-to-six years to accrue enough stories for a book. So the idea of maintaining a plan, or control, during that time—well, I couldn't do it. But what does happen is that each story is a puzzle. You solve it and it leads you to the next, more complex, puzzle. You don't solve each puzzle in an equally elegant way but at the end you've enacted a kind of subconscious pattern. So then the table of contents step involves recognizing and honoring that pattern.

It's actually kind of wonderful to see how non-random the pattern is—the pattern of the stories you started and didn't throw out, etc., etc.

As for 2), in the first book, I was aware that I basically had eight or whatever stories that were very similar in tone and action and ethos, etc. All were basically: guy in the shit gets pushed deeper into the shit. But what distinguished one from the next was what the guy did after the pushing. In some he just despaired, in others he fought back and lost, in one at least he fought back and kind of won. So I ordered them from least hopeful (i.e., most passive) to most hopeful (most involved/active).

In *Pastoralia* the thinking was similar. In the novella, he ends up taking on the identity of this person he's just helped to fire. Things are looking very bad, and we've already established that he doesn't have many options. So that's a bummer. By the end of the book, "The Falls," the main character is giving his life for someone else. So, even though I absolutely didn't write them in that order, or with that progression in mind, my hope was that the reader would feel the progression, if only subliminally: there is a Bad Thing (oppressive capitalism, say, or crippling passivity); there is also a way out.

So for me the key is to go deeply into the stories again at publication time, and in this way get re-sensitized to them, and then trust my instincts, and my index cards.

RK: And again (again!) with the follow-ups: the stories in *Pastoralia* seemed to—how to say?—to allow the reader slightly more breathing space than the stories in *CivilWarLand in Bad Decline*. This might be a function simply of them being, on average, a bit longer, but I have a sense there's something else at work here. Could you comment on the motives behind, the mechanics involved in, and/or the repercussions of this trend toward lengthierliness, if in fact it is one, or, alternatively, assure me that it's all in my head?

GS: No, I think you're right. But whatever it is, it wasn't conscious. I think it was organic. The stories in *Pastoralia* were, at least at first ("The Falls" was written first) a reaction against that very laconic first-person in *CivilWarLand*. So I was trying to see if there was anything else I could do. And so the longer sentences, and the kind of neurotic internal monologues, do make the stories a little more—I dunno what. Spacious? Inefficient? Spaciously inefficient?

One thing I've noticed about my stories—when I'm working on them individually, I am really big on compression. I tend to cut out the physical descriptions and have an aversion to what I consider "normalizing" prose. I like Style. I like to sound odd and, hopefully, unique. This of course has a cost. When I get the stories together—well, I wish I could put a disclaimer at the front: Please read no more than one or two a day. Otherwise it feels to me like the contours that I put in there (when I was working on just that story) get lost in the reading process.

So that's something I'm trying to figure out, that tradeoff between a certain amount of flash and compression, and the real pleasures of a story told in a natural voice.

RK: It's interesting, this question of maintaining uniqueness (uniquity? That can't be a word, but I like it much better) in terms of voice, thematic concerns, dynamics, what have you, but in a way that allows you to evolve, to avoid repetition. I've been thinking about this a lot lately, because as I was reading "CommComm," the story of yours that appeared a few weeks ago in the *New Yorker*, I had the sense that it was maybe a story you've spent years getting ready for. So many of the themes and tropes and tics that have appeared elsewhere in your stories—in "The 400-Pound CEO" and "Sea Oak" in particular, but in others as well—seem to have peaked—to have gone forth and multiplied and come back to chat about it—in this new piece. And as a result, the story reaches a whole 'nother plane of grace, or so it seems from here on the outside, looking in. And so I ask you: as you finished it, did it feel at all to you like some sort of culmination?

GS: It did.

It was maybe the feeling of . . . well, this may not be the best example. But you know when you're playing a complex video game and get killed, you can go pretty quickly through the game back to that point, and then the real work begins? It felt something like that. I would feel a certain thematic thing or ethical thing coming up and would be dimly aware that I'd been here before, and now was a chance for complication—to stand on the back of what I had done already and reach a little higher. A nice feeling.

I've also been more aware lately of certain automatic tics—usually towards darkening a piece or a character. And so I have started questioning these more actively. As in: Is there possibly more to this guy? Am I being fair to him? Is change possible? I don't mean that I'm thinking about these outside the story, but kind of viscerally, as I write it—I'm less content with a stock character. This was the case with that guy Giff in the story.

And the truth is, the only knowledge that matters about stories is the knowledge we have in real time, as we write or re-read what we've written. Hemingway used to say he tried never to think about a story when he wasn't working on it, actually working on it. I've found that advice true and liberating—you don't have to do a lot of strategizing all day. Just trust that the motor is running all the time—your subconscious is always working on the story.

RK: Giff, exactly—great name, by the way—and even Rimney gets his moment of light near the end as the narrator sees "that even now all [Rimney's] thoughts are of Val, desperate loving frightened thoughts of how best to keep her safe."

I'd like now to loop back slightly to what you were saying before about the "real pleasures of a story told in a natural voice," and to the slightly lengthier stories that such a voice implies, or facilitates, or encourages, or something. Do you think you will ever follow that natural-voice+length urge to one of several possible logical conclusions, and actually write a (and you knew the question was coming, the way it always does, not because we interviewers get our jollies out of making you repeat yourself, though that is kind of fun, but in the hope that this time the answer will be "Yes!") novel? I mean, don't you realize that ever since we first discovered *CivilWarLand* in, no joke, the history section of our local bookstore, we've just been sitting around waiting for you to write a novel, so that we could enjoy, for much longer stretches at a time, the (as you once said, paraphrasing Barthelme—again with the Barthelme! Again with the agains!) "record of the imaginative journey of a particular mind," in this case, specifically, yours? I mean, we just sit here and stare at things—the wall, the unmoving ceiling fan, the dust in the air—and say, out loud, "Novel novel novel novel novel novel novel novel," like turkeys with speech impediments. What have we ever done to you that makes you want to see us suffer like that? Why do you hate us so much?

GS: Well, a novel would be nice. I'm just waiting to grow enough that it feels really enjoyable and natural. I think the time will come. But I've made the mistake often enough of mistaking a slightly sloppy, early phase story for The Big One. And then I spend months adding unnecessary padding, then months taking the padding back off.

I have a feeling that even though a novel and a short story collection seem very closely related, they are, at the origin, very different. Like, say, a fox and a wolf. The mindset may be completely different, even from the first line.

I've had intimations of this—I recently reread Gogol's *Dead Souls* and was struck by the fact that, in a novel, the whole point is the little constructions along the way . . . a chance to describe a certain household, or a certain while-traveling phenomenon, etc. And the plot is just a way to link these together and, in a sense, "justify" them. In the end, at least in that book, the plot is sort of a red herring. Whereas, in a story, the progression of the plot is what the whole machine is ultimately judged against. You can do the other things—description, dialogue, etc.—but any piece that is inessential to the plot-machine (to the sense that this thing is moving forward, and along a certain thematic track) is felt as extraneous. And I am very firmly in the latter mindset, having more or less trained myself to it over these many years of reading and writing stories.

So I guess the answer is, we'll see. My approach to writing so far has been colored by having not enough time, too many responsibilities, and too little talent. I take what I can get. If an idea seems interesting, I rush off in that direction, trusting that if I pay attention to something, it will eventually come to have some of me in it, and won't be a total waste of time.

RK: Fair enough. And speaking of differences between art forms, according to this thing I just found, your story "The End of FIRPO in the World" was at one point turned into a ballet. Is that right? Or a modern dance piece? Or something? Which was then performed in Austin, New York City and Chicago? Did you have any input on that? Did you see it? Any thoughts?

GS: It was modern dance—as I remember it, one or two performers, performing over just the read text. And I liked it very much. I never saw it in person, just on video. It was done by a very talented choreographer at UT Austin whose name is Holly Williams. I didn't have (and didn't want) any input, since what I know about dance is: Don't Fall. If You Do, Get Up Quick, Look Casual.

RK: See now, that's the same strategy I use when crossing the street.

Shifting gears a bit, in an essay you wrote for the *Guardian* back in March of this year, you said, "Specificity, precision, and brevity, applied in language, drive us towards compassion." Which reminded me of another thing, from what I think was the last piece of prose Raymond Carver ever wrote, called "Meditation on a Line from Saint Teresa." The line of hers that he quotes there is "Words lead to deeds . . . They prepare the soul, make it ready, and move it to tenderness." Carver then discusses two beautiful scenes from Chekhov's "Ward No. 6," the first describing a man who "has picked up the habit of a certain kind of tenderness," and the second involving a character who ends a bit of dialogue with, "Oh, I think to myself: 'Old fogey, it is time you were dead!' But there is a little voice in my soul that says: 'Don't believe it; you won't die.'"

And then Carver says, "The scene ends but the words linger as deeds." It's his use of the word "as" that really gets me—as if words, chosen so carefully as to have the very palpability and irrefutability of deeds, actually become deeds in a certain sense. He's saying, I think, that just as good writing drives writers to compassion, good reading of good writing drives readers to tenderness.

When I first started thinking about bringing this up with you, I didn't actually have a question about it—and was going to say as much. It was just something I really liked thinking about. But now I wonder: Is this drive toward compassion or tenderness something that a writer can—or should—be thinking about as a given story is in the course of taking shape? Or is it maybe the kind of thing—the kind of responsibility, really—that could almost become paralyzing in its size and weight? I don't mean to ask you to speak for all writers, but is this drive something that you keep front and center as you work? Or is it more a question of coming to this conclusion about the importance and validity of the drive just once, and then keeping it in the background, even the subconscious if possible, and repeating the mantra (maybe in the form of an acronym, SPBALDUTC?) only when necessary, and otherwise keeping your focus tighter, locked into language and character and arc and so forth?

GS: Well. A beautiful question, beautifully put. I'm tempted to just answer: Yup, for sure.

But one thing your question makes me think: This talk about compassion and tenderness. I think in writing, as in all things, saying to yourself: Be Compassionate! only goes so far. I think it might tend to make us saccharine—just as untruthful as being bitter, but in the other direction.

I think we can make this desire to be compassionate and tender more practical. It seems to me that if a writer (1) pays attention and (2) tries to keep the mind free of preconceptions about what he wants the story to be about (or wants a character to do, etc.)—then he will automatically move towards a story which is richer, more full-hearted, etc. In this model, compassion just means keeping yourself open to the possibilities of the story, which, in turn, means keeping oneself open to the possibilities of the world—what's actually there, rather than what you want to be there.

Let's say you start out to write a story about an Evil Radical Republican, because it happens that you are a liberal and are sick of all this shit that's been going on. Well, if you write with attention and open-mindedness (and these are, or can be, craft-based things—more on this in a minute) then you will soon find there is no such thing as an Evil Radical Republican. There are people we may call that, or who may call themselves that, but once you leave the superficial plane, no—no such thing. Or, another way of saying this: leaving your character as just that is going to make a very boring story. So you look deeper. And you find that this guy you thought was an ERR, is actually, you know, "Hal." Hal has hobbies. He used to have a stutter, maybe. He has amorous fantasies about a Swiss girl in braids who, as he imagines her, shyly plays with one braid while they walk down, inexplicably, Hal's street in Des Moines. You find, in other words—as you must, that Hal is— crikey!—a manifestation of You. Where else could he come from? Which leads to another realization: You and Hal are not—cannot—be that different. He is not unimaginable. You could get to Hal from where you are. That, to me, is compassion in a nutshell.

Now, as for the craft: I think it's about sentences. You write: "Hal, as usual, was talking a lot of right-wing bullshit that made no sense." Okay, fair enough. But now, in revision, you feel that the sentence lacks specificity. Forget about politics, truth, fairness, all that—it's dull because it's vague. The question is: What does he say, exactly? And what does his face look like as he says it? And who is he saying it to? And what do they think? And what is Hal thinking as they look at him? Does he feel he's being judged? Is his stutter getting worse, filling him with rage? Is the father of the Swiss girl there, looking appalled at Hal's stutter? Is the Swiss girl playing nervously with her braid, suddenly ashamed of Hal? So you have to cross out "talking a lot of right-wing bullshit" and give Hal something to say, in a specific voice. And now suddenly you're really paying attention to Hal, which means you're being compassionate. You're actually curious about what Hal is all about, instead of pre-knowing what he's about.

What I'm saying is, all moral concerns in fiction reduce to technical concerns. And technical concerns drive us towards specificity and detail and truth.

RK: And there I was, trying desperately to come up with a natural-seeming segue from craft to politics, and you lob one in over the plate. Much obliged.

It seems that most species of fiction, for reasons you just touched on, and other reasons as well, are better suited to raising certain kinds of questions—political, social, philosophical—than to answering them in any sort of categorical way. But interviews on the other hand! So. To take one specific example: in *The Very Persistent Gappers of Frip*, Capable's father says, "There have always been gappers, and exhausted children brushing them off." In the course of the story, Capable finds a way to deal with the plague of gappers—a way that requires great courage, let it be said, since it entails resisting all sorts of powerful pressures—economic, historical, political, and societal just for starters—and her world becomes a better place. Do you believe that such a move—"selling the goats," as it were—is feasible in our own current politico-social real-world brand of Frip? If so, what would that move consist of? And if not, is there something inherently honorable and heroic about continuing exhaustedly to brush gappers off our goats each day? Or should we all just kill ourselves now and get it over with?

GS: I think the trick has to do with scale—with the scale of the perceived problem and the scale of the proposed solution. I think one reason for cynicism is that, early on, we have a too large idea of how perfect life can be made. "Life is suffering," the Buddha said, and Christ said, "The poor will be with us always." There is, in other words, a limit to our influence. So the "goat we sell" might be a relatively small thing—you can't cure cancer but you can be a mindful friend of someone with cancer, can't cure hunger but can send some small amount to work against hunger. The trick, I think, is to recognize a small good thing as just that. A small but GOOD thing. It's not so easy to do small good things. More often than not, we're overlooking those opportunities.

I'm not sure if this is answering the question. I agree with what you say about fiction—Chekhov said the same thing: "Art doesn't answer questions, it only helps us formulate them correctly." But art also reminds us that life is complicated, so complicated that its first demand on us is humility. Not to get too big for one's britches is an admirable life goal, I think. And art also adjusts our gaze, so that we are seeing life's very real cruelties—and the very small but real chances to salve these—on the scale on which they really exist—not hoping for too much influence, but also not underestimating what we can actually do.

I've known people who started out wanting to fix the world, and when they find out the world can't be fixed (because in fact it's not broken) they retreat to a sort of cynical stance. When you think about it, that's all ego: the world refused to be fixed by me, the center of the universe; therefore I hate the world.

There's a complicated Buddhist idea that I haven't even come close to really getting yet, but it has to do with the idea of all of this mad life-energy as being a kind of display. You try to see it in a nonjudgmental way: just "things-as-they-are." What makes good and evil come into existence is our insistence on seeing ourselves at the center of it, as permanent entities, and then judging everything according to how it affects us. Of course, this is entirely natural—but also entirely delusional. So I think writing can help in this—by examining small phenomena from multiple perspectives, reminding us that what looks like some kind of fixed, still point at the center of things (Us) is every bit as transitory and negotiable and impermanent as every other thing.

Well, I'm answering this question late at night and any moment will burst into a rousing chorus of "Desiderata"—so I will go to bed and check in again tomorrow, when I'm feeling more awake and less Ethereal.

RK: No no no, Ethereal is good—it's the one rope we have, I think, leading up from the cubicle, the ditch, the seat we reserved months ago as part of the live studio audience. And this business of art reminding us that our best first response to life's intricacy is humility, and calling our attention to both life's cruelties and our limited but not insignificant opportunities to assuage them, brings us at long last back to your new book, *The Brief and Frightening Reign of Phil*, to a place and time where cruelty abounds but assuagement too can be found.

I'm curious as to what sort of research went into the novella. Phil himself seems to incorporate elements from any number of genocidal nationalists from the past—a bit of Hitler, a bit of Pol Pot, a bit of Andrew Jackson. Did you look into any historical figures in particular, searching for actions or excuses or even specific bits of language to incorporate?

GS: I didn't do any research as such. I tend to read a lot of history and then trust that it will filter down into whatever I'm writing. So a certain historical referent would present itself and as soon as I recognized it I'd try to move on to another. I'd feel a certain Holocaust metaphor creeping in and then try to first finish that riff well and then shake it off, move to something else. In other words, I didn't want to do a point-for-point metaphor for some particular thing, but rather, through this technique, try and develop a kind of composite portrait of the human tendency to tyranny. Asking: What, if anything, do these various tyrants have in common? I did this once before in a novella called "Bounty," where I was using slave narratives and sci-fi riffs, etc., but trying to mix it up and confuse myself as to the referents— and then, with all of the easy referents confounded, some other thing is being referred to—hopefully some new thing, some new way of looking at a familiar phenomena.

In the Phil book, I had in mind, at various times, Rwanda, Bosnia, Hitler (especially the way he took over power in Germany), and then bits and pieces from the post-9/11 world—Phil has a touch of Bin Laden about him, but also some Abu Ghraib, and he's got this tendency to inefficient language that Orwell talked about being the sure sign of a despot. Basically he became kind of a lab test for the question: What does it look like when someone goes genocidal—by which I mean, when they negate the humanity of their opposition, so as to more easily kill them—and how do they defend it to themselves?

But really—in the actual doing of it, it was about trying to make the narrative viable—creating intense characters and good transitions and trying to make the story seem inevitable, even though at heart it was so silly and odd.

(By the way—I feel strongly that whenever a writer talks about a particular technical approach, all he's really saying is: Given my particular flawed talent, here's how I tend to [or have to] do it. I'm not sure how useful one writer's approach is to another writer. Maybe hearing about it is good, just so we remind ourselves about how many valid and different approaches there are, and thus feel better about making up our own.)

RK: You mentioned that the idea for Phil began when Lane Smith dared you to write a story where all the characters were abstract shapes, and in the end, most of the characters are sort of amalgamations—part human, part machine, part plant. A quick chicken versus egg question: given the seed-crystal approach you've discussed, the organic sense in which everything develops in response to everything else, with highest attention paid at the sentence-level and a trust that everything will work itself out as a result, did you, in general, "flesh out" the shapes and then allow them to develop personalities that were in some sense correlative, or did you let the personalities form first and then sort out specific biological/mechanical/botanical accoutrements to match? Or both? Or neither?

GS: As I remember it, both things were going on. For example, there's a president that Phil ends up overthrowing, and I described him as having a bunch of bellies and mustaches. Then as I started to have him talk, it turned out he was repeating himself, which led to the idea that he had a special kind of senility, wherein he is getting more and more forgetful every minute, and then suddenly he was sprouting additional mustaches and bellies, which became sort of connected to the increased memory loss—but it was all done in the heat of the moment, just trying to make the prose funny and quick. I really try hard not to strategize when I'm not actually typing.

Or then later, I had this vague notion to put some media figures in there—guys with the press—and I remember I just ran my mind over in that direction to see what they'd look like. And I'd recently done a talk where I'd described television as this big dumb guy with a massive megaphone growing out of his chest—and so I made these media guys look like that. Then, when I had them talk, they of course talked very loudly, and (thinking of that big guy, dominating a party with his banalities) I made them say really trivial things, really loudly—so it's not a conscious thing, but the image and the personality playing off one another in real time. (Otherwise, planned, it gets too neat.)

Or there are these guys called Phil's Special Friends—these very stupid enforcers. I was thinking about who the Brown Shirts were—what would make them so loyal and brutal? So these guys were, of course, huge, but also, as I was writing them, it turned out they were also very emotionally needy. I asked myself why—and it turned out they had been mistreated and neglected as kids—so when Phil shows them the slightest attention, he wins their loyalty completely. And then, when the time came to describe them, I gave them red shirts, without really recognizing the connection to the brown shirts. But again, all of this happened quick, in one draft, in one or two afternoons. Later there was a bunch of refining and editing and cleaning it up. But the basic seeds of who they were came out right away, in one or two sittings. I think the subconscious blurt-out can be very wise, and there are times when it occurs with such authority and joy that you just kind of trust it.

So I guess I would say it was a process of coming up with one thing—an image or a voice—and then quickly coming up with the rest of the package, playing off that first thing. It was more playful than deliberate and I hoped that the cross-firing between image and voice would be complex—not just straight-line metaphorical.

RK: Borges once wrote, "Time is the substance I am made of. Time is a river which sweeps me along, but I am the river; it is a tiger that devours me, but I am the tiger; it is a fire that consumes me, but I am the fire." I'd like to end here by asking you about time, about its relation to the content and form of your work, about the way you talk it into sort of folding in on itself. It seems—particularly in *The Brief and Frightening Reign of Phil*, but in other stories of yours as well—that one of your central interests (or artistic strategies? or subconscious urges?) is in creating something like futuristic ancient folktales that are happening right this moment. Okay, there's got to be a better way to put that. How about: would it be fair to say that part of the process involves taking the silliest, least promising, least attractive aspects of how and when and where we currently live, and pushing them into the future, and thinking of them as though they were past, and then dredging them for anything that might still be human and useful, even beautiful, even true? And if that would be unfair to say, what would be fairer?

GS: I think the way I'd put it is that I'm trying to take the real life, and distort it in some way, and, in this way, find out more about the essence of that real life. If you had a movie where everyone was incredibly grouchy, the movie would actually be about kindness. If there was a painting of a forest and all green had been omitted, you would suddenly value green, and be really aware of it. Somebody once said: Satire is the indirect praise of perfection. That seems right to me.

Or here's another way I look at it: let's say that you were given the job of writing a story about two talking, sentient rubber bands on a desk. Within those confines, I'd say, the story could become about the entire cosmos, because the generating agency—your mind—is infinite. Even with this dumb constraint, your story would strain to be about Everything, because your mind is always straining to accommodate Everything. The rubber bands would talk, fight, fall in love—whatever. (The paper clips a few feet away would come to represent something to the rubber bands—and then you're off to the races.) And in this way, the whole world could find its way into that story. And maybe—because the writer of that story wouldn't be distracted by things like "describing the trees accurately" or "recreating the 1960s" he or she might cut to the chase—what's the real essence of this life, when this life is shorn of all its distracting surface? I think this is what Beckett was doing.

So, to date, my stories have started out with some version of this rubber-band constraint. Why? Well, partly it's limited talent. I think about a grand all-encompassing novel and I get nervous. But also—there's something about looking at us when we're at our worst, or our most stressed—when we're occupying some kind of end condition—that tells us about us at our best. What's the bottom-line in this life? I'm not sure the answer lies in looking at the happy and honest and well-fed. I mean, it might be, for a great writer like Tolstoy or somebody. But for me . . . I think there's value in looking at human beings at the point of fracture. Put six people in a boat with one hot dog and no water, and you'll find out a lot about human nature very quickly—and some of it will be ugly, but some of it will be wonderful.

My real feeling is that we don't have to do too much thinking about what stories should do, or can do, or much time defending them or anything like that—I have this faith that, if we train ourselves to the task and then go at it with all the energy we have, then that process is a noble and worthy thing in itself—just looking at the world, through the construct of language, and trying to understand the world, and to love it better.

RK: Thanks very much, George, for this and for what is to come.

George Saunders Land in
Its Heady Prime

Dave Weich / 2007

From powells.com, March 20, 2007. https://www.powells.com/post/interviews/george -saunders-land-in-its-heady-prime. Reprinted by permission of Powells.

If you've ever read a George Saunders story, here's something vaguely unsettling to consider: he's one of the most down-to-earth guys you're ever likely to meet. Which means what? Every average Joe is walking around with crazy shit like this in his head?

Saunders has won three National Magazine Awards; four times his stories have appeared in O. Henry Awards anthologies. Realism, however, is not his shtick. "If I try to write a sensitive story about a recently divorced couple living in Syracuse, it's going to be lame. I don't have the chops to make it interesting," he claims. "The energy of the prose goes down."

Three volumes of stories, a political fable, a captivating children's book, and an essay collection on the way—quite an output for the one-time geologist whose literary debut landed just over ten years ago. "Mr. Saunders's satiric vision of America is dark and demented," Michiko Kakutani announced in 1996. "It is also ferocious and very funny."

And still the prose goes deeper than that, beyond uproarious humor and biting social commentary. What sets Saunders's work apart is the wonderfully twisted path he blazes, yes, but also its destination, a compassionate and deeply vulnerable heart.

Dave Weich: Have you ever participated in a re-enactment?

George Saunders: No, but I play the guitar, and many years ago I played at a friend's wedding at the Genesee Country Museum in Rochester. Unlike the place in the book, it's really cool—they fastidiously restored nineteenth-century houses. We went early for the rehearsal. We had the whole church to ourselves for the day. I've taken my daughters back there a couple times to look around.

DW: I wondered whether after writing about several of these places you'd be invited to visit one.

GS: One time somebody had contacted me to go to Disneyland and write about that, but no.

There's something about those theme parks. If I stick to one of those I tend to write more interesting prose than if I'm trying to write about something more quotidian. If I try to write realism, the energy of the prose goes down.

It might be that if literature is a kind of scale model, then a scale model inside a scale model can be fun. To say: Literature is a theme park where we rarify the air and leave things out and cut to the chase, basically, in the hopes of giving ourselves pleasure, in the same way that theme parks do.

DW: So here's a theory, developing now for all of thirty-six hours: reality TV is not unlike a theme park modeled after contemporary life. It shows how we live *now*.

GS: Right.

DW: And one reason it's so popular is because Americans are too narcissistic to care about other cultures and too lazy to seek them out.

GS: That's probably true, but for me it's more technical or functional. Having done a few theme park stories, suddenly you have a bag of tricks. You don't want to use a bag of tricks, so your mind looks around for something similar. Reality TV is at hand. It allows the same kind of linguistic bypass that I first discovered through theme parks.

To me, what's scariest is the blank page. Most authors go for whatever will flood in there easily. If you know ballet, you go right to ballet. If you're Turgenev, you know the Russian countryside and you talk about that. Somehow, the pop culture stuff, I have a lot of it, and I know what to do with it. If I'm writing a story made all of commercials, I won't be able to trip myself up with my fake-Hemingway impulses. Thematic elements arise, but at the point of starting out it's more of a survival tactic.

If I try to write a sensitive story about a recently divorced couple living in Syracuse, it's going to be lame. I don't have the chops to make it interesting. But if I write about a recently divorced couple that happens to work at a Siberian Gulag theme park, I'm going to get to the same emotional stuff and I'm going to have more surface material to work with. It comes from not wanting to fail. You do the thing that has energy.

DW: It's hard to talk about humor. Comedy is tragedy plus time, according to Alan Alda's character in *Crimes and Misdemeanors*. What do you think? How does humor work?

GS: To me, it's just the truth told faster. The truth told without the normalizing bumpers we normally put on.

You and I, we don't know each other, but we're talking nicely. One truth is that in x number of years we're both going to be corpses in a box—not the same box, unless something happens. But that's weird. If you wrote about it in a purple tone, it wouldn't be funny, but if you state the truth abruptly in an unexpected way, we laugh.

I do write some pieces that are just trying to be funny—I'm writing for the *Guardian* now, and those pieces are mostly trying to be funny in 500 words—but usually I'm trying to trim out the normalizing bullshit, the literary ticks. *Frank, an attractive man in his mid-thirties, very interested in the insurance business, made his way up Bushberry Road.* Uch. Who's saying that? As you start cutting it, you end up getting into some realm of higher truth.

I'm not sure, but for me humor is a byproduct of some other factor, maybe a sense of urgency or an unusual vector through the material. Humor is a side product.

DW: So much of your writing sets the mundane and the absurd, extremes, side by side. In "Bounty," for instance: "Tanner's is a brothel in a former Safeway." And another great passage in the same story—it's actually a single word that amplifies the conflict:

> *What was I supposed to do, contradict Dad in front of Mack? To tell you the truth, Dad scares me. I wouldn't be surprised if someday he didn't hold me down and burn a hole in my neck. Gosh, we probably shouldn't be going on like this.*

Gosh. Innocence and horror in the same passage.

GS: When people talk about writing, I always imagine a telescope. There are two ends. One is the end you look in when you're reading, and it tends to be more analytical and conceptual. The other end is the one you look in when you're actually writing. At the moment that sentence ended, about burning a hole in his neck, my mind is looking for a next line. Why does it go to "gosh"? Complicated.

I think it's because I'm aware that the previous line was so stark. And I'm vaguely aware that the literary convention would be for the character to be some scowling brute of a man. Eh. Boring. We know that one. So your mind veers a little and asks, "Can I counterbalance that?" *Gosh.* It's that quick.

It's more or less a hustler's instinct. I was raised Catholic in Chicago. As kids, we were constantly trying to stay out of the way of nuns, but once you got busted there was always a way to spin yourself out of trouble. It wasn't exactly a lie; it was a tonal lie. "Sister, I'm really sorry about that. I didn't mean to push Father Jim down the well."

I'm writing, you're reading, and if you sense some big fat Moral with a capital M coming, and I sense that you sense that, I can undercut it with a line. In such a subtle way. It's not conceptual. Suddenly you're back on my side again. Really, a whole story is just that: an elaborate, real-time dance. I think that's actually the answer to almost every question about craft.

You give your reader credit. You don't say, "Let me teach you something. I know a little something you don't." Instead, you say, "Wow, isn't this life weird that we're in together? You're in a different place, but still we have this in common." Talking frankly, in a way that you would talk to yourself. Then you get that beautiful experience, like a sidecar: I'm leaning left, and you're with me.

Whether it's Nabokov or Shakespeare or Toni Morrison, any of the great writers, you feel that they credited you a hundred percent and they always knew where you were. It's part of that great literary game, the reader thinking, *I'm going to close this fucker if you don't pick it up, I'm going to close this book.* The author is playing that game: *Give me another line.* To me, that's the whole experience.

DW: There's so much texture in your stories. You describe in such vivid specifics. More than once, I was reminded of Amy Hempel's writing. There's very little slack in the prose. But at the same time the voices you use, especially in dialogue, create a slack tone because they're colloquial, they're not highly educated. It made me wonder how much you refine and edit.

GS: A lot. 80 percent of the work is that. And actually, Amy teaches at Syracuse now.

DW: I didn't know that.

GS: I love her work, for the same reason. You can feel the power of her deliberation. She reads those short pieces, and you can see that none of it is there on accident, even if it sounds colloquial or if it sounds as if it just flows out. We've talked about it. She's a reviser. I love that level of revision.

You know what, though? You develop a shtick. My shtick has always been, "Yes, I revise fanatically." And I do. But also, the truth is, as you get older you get more confident. I'm at the point that if by chance a really good paragraph drops out, I know better than to fuck with it. I'll take it as a gift.

The complex truth is that I rely on revision to give me the leeway to not lock up. If I were going to write something, I certainly couldn't know it was going to be any good, but I would know that I could shape it later. That shaping might mean cutting it entirely, but that freedom gives you a power to write. For me, the most colloquial things are the hardest. I learned this from Isaac Babel, the Russian writer. I don't know exactly how he wrote, but I suspect he did a lot of redlining.

Most of what our mind creates is banal. Most of what any mind creates is going to be the same as other minds create. It's like the Bell Curve. If you say, "Write a story about a guy standing on a dock," most of us are going to write, "The choppy waves . . ." There's going to be a list of eight or nine things that everyone will think of first. The trick, or part of it, is to wait yourself out. Of course the choppy waves, of course the seagulls. That's all fine. But is there one thing in that list that maybe you and I would think of differently? That's what revision does.

Jim walked into the midsize apartment and sat down on the couch, waiting for Valerie.

Fine. It's grammatically correct. But then you think: *midsize apartment.* Do I really need that? Does a reader care that it's not big or small? What is midsize? Cut that. Now: *sat down on the couch.* Do you have to sit down on a couch? No. Cross out the word *down. Jim sat on the couch waiting for Valerie.* Okay. Does he have to sit? Is the sitting essential to what is going to happen? Probably not. Interesting. *Jim waited for Valerie.* If the next line is, "Valerie walked in," we don't need that *sit.* In cutting that, you've eliminated a banal line. You have nothing now—you have zero words so far—but at least you're not full of shit yet.

That's the thing about cutting: you can take your own banal mind and let it settle down. Then you look: is there anything in this vast field of banality that might not be banal? Select that, move it over, and start again.

DW: You've started writing nonfiction. Essays.

GS: I wrote some pieces for *GQ.* They sent me to Dubai first, and then to Nepal to see this little kid who'd been meditating seven months without food or water. I drove the whole Mexican border for a piece last summer.

Those have been really fun. Twelve thousand nonfiction words. It's been a great midlife thing to do. As you get older, at least for me, your mind starts staying on the side of the pool a little bit. *Oh, I know about that. I have an idea about that.* So it's been amazing to go to those places and in each case to have my conceptual mind, have its ass kicked, if that's not too mixed of a metaphor.

That book [*The Braindead Megaphone*] is coming out next year with Riverhead. I'd never done reporting at all. Andy Ward at GQ was so great about saying, "Trust yourself. Come back with ten thousand literary words."

DW: Why you, do you think? What do you bring to the task?

GS: Andy and Jim Nelson, the executive editor, had read my fiction, and the first assignment they thought of was Dubai, which is very theme-parky, and also it's got a crazy class divide where there's a handful of rich people hiring a bunch of very poor people to build this paradise. So I think that was their first thought. And their instincts were good. It was weirder than anything I'd ever written.

The first one was sort of a trial. It worked, and they knew I was Buddhist, so they thought maybe Nepal would be good. But Jim, when he was younger he worked for *Harper's*. He was there when they ran my first couple stories. He remembered that.

It was fun to have to describe a room. In my fiction I don't usually do that. But you have to describe the hotel. You have to do it, so you do it the best you can, and you find out that you actually have some gifts you didn't know about, or you can come up with a way to do it.

DW: Do you find yourself having to resist taking off a little bit, fictionalizing?

GS: A little bit. But something about writing short stories, your long practice with language, and what will and won't sell in a fictional world— that really helps when you're reporting because there are things that don't feel like stories, but as a fiction writer you know that they can be. I'll give you an example.

In Dubai, the community got together and made snow in an exhibition hall. It's a hundred thirty degrees out, the kids have never seen snow, so they super-refrigerate this room and make a little tiny pile of snow. It's almost as if you took a frozen parking lot in Syracuse and chopped it up, not really snow but big ice chunks. But there's a big long line, a thousand people waiting to get in.

I'm in line, and I know I'm going to write about it. And just at that moment, inexplicably, there's this guy dressed up as a goose, this really dirty, cheesy, Disney costume of a goose, but with a long tail. Kind of like a cross between a dinosaur and a goose. And there's a guy following him around whose job it is to make sure he doesn't run into anything. It's not the story, but the guy who was minding him seemed to be in love with him. He'd pick up the tail and stroke it, and he was always whispering things to the goose. As a fiction writer, I knew there would be funny sentences in that somehow, whereas if you were stricter I don't think that would necessarily occur to you.

On the Mexico trip, I spent a night with these minutemen, these guys who are "guarding" the border, quote. We went on a morning "recon" with them, recon again in quotes. They got hopelessly lost in a space about the size of this room. All lost. It was so funny. They're doing all this military talk: "Attention all units. We've got a body of water in front of us, possibly one foot deep. Let's try to circumscribe that thing."

I was with a couple of AP reporters, and I'm practically peeing myself. I can't wait to get back and report this. They were like, "We can't use it." There was no story. But the fiction writer in me said, "Oh, no. This is writable. I know how to make a scene out of this."

Also, you learn. I've learned a lot about structure. If you set a nominal outline for yourself and fill it in—that's probably how you do a novel, which never has occurred to me before, somehow. Knowing that I had 12,000 words and eight things I wanted to write about—well, okay, let's take some index cards, put those in . . . Lifting your eyes up from the line to look at the bigger structure was really educational for me.

DW: And working on a deadline.

GS: Right. Saying it can't be perfect, but can it not be sucky?

DW: "93990" is so different from the rest of *In Persuasion Nation*. It feels like nonfiction. There's no accessorizing of the scientific report. There's no dialogue. What set you off to write that?

GS: I worked for a pharmaceutical company before I wrote my first book. It was an old fashioned place, a horseshoe-shaped building around a nice courtyard—the upstairs was offices, and downstairs were the animal labs. When you'd go to your car, you'd go down through the labs.

My job was to take 300-page studies and condense them down, a series of twelve, into another report that would be sent to the FDA. I would read these studies all day and then pithily summarize them. A study like the one in the story came across the desk. Cynomolgous monkeys.

It was this whole thing about one monkey that for no reason at all didn't respond to the drugs and couldn't be killed. They kept pumping up the concentration dosage, and it never showed any symptoms. After everyone else in its control group had died, this monkey was fine. The last line was, as it is in the story, "The animal was tranquilized via dart, removed from the enclosure, sacrificed, and necropsied." I almost started crying when I read it. You'd come to love that monkey for its Christ-like qualities, and suddenly it's dead.

I guess I was interested in the way that you could take something that never became literary—it maintained its voice and its scientific reserve—but still there was a story behind it. I turned up the volume just a little bit. As someone who read those reports all the time I could see how unusual it was, but for people that didn't I felt I had to turn up the volume in a few places.

DW: In the first or second line of one of your stories, I forget which, the narrator talks about "my coordinator." I wanted to go back and reread that story, but I couldn't even begin to guess which it might have been, or from what book.[1] I had no idea.

So many of your characters are in that relationship with a superior. And there's often a fault line, an easy slip into something more like bondage.

GS: Just look at our lives. You're always working for somebody. Even when you're not, you could fall between the cracks—and the system is not kind to the people who fall between the cracks.

A lot of it is just mimesis. I grew up in a working neighborhood. Everyone worked, and it cost people. And I always have to be careful—it's not as if going to a job is like going to the gulag. It's not. But it would be blind to say that working twelve hours at a factory, or working twelve hours at Google, isn't taking something away from you. When you come out of that, unless you're an extraordinary person, you're not as generous and present as you were at eight in the morning.

After grad school, I was trying to write, and I didn't like writing about work because it seemed boring. Well, what else is there to write about? Look at the literature. Hunting. I don't hunt. Exotic vacations where extramarital affairs occur. Didn't do that. The whole pantheon of literary subjects had nothing to do with the life I'd lived to that point, or the life that anybody I knew had lived. Then you have to say, "Okay, I have to write about work. I need to try not to make it dull."

And work isn't dull when you think about it. At one point, I was working for an engineering company. We were a small satellite office of a big company in Austin, and we were getting all these crazy emails concerning rumors about people that we'd never met, but that affected our livelihood. We would literally check our email to see if our lives were still viable.

It's mostly a matter of saying that my life has always been work, so how do I work that into the stories? The same idea as earlier: you have a blank page. What are you going to fill it with? Work.

DW: It reminds me of the guy in "Pastoralia" who's going to be in a shitload of trouble if they close Sheep May Safely Graze.

GS: A lot of people have an idea about corporations. I didn't ever want to work in an office, but I was at that place where I was either going to be Kerouac and run away from my family, which wasn't going to happen, or do something else. So I started working for this corporation, and it was weirdly beautiful. These were people exactly like me. They didn't have a dream when they were kids of someday sitting in a cubicle. But then you also saw that it was a cooperative venture: if we in the Rochester office could keep our heads above water, we could continue to have health insurance. It was interesting to get on the inside of that and realize that actually it's not *us* and *them*.

That became a way of thinking for me, which is to say, whenever you start thinking *us* and *them*, run around and get into *them*. Because people don't do things for no reason. Nobody wants to be diabolical. Everybody wants to be happy and good, basically. What gets interesting is when your definition of good and mine are at odds. That's part of the work thing. Let's get in there and see.

If you want to look for conflict in modern life, at some point you have to get down to the level of resources. If you and I were multi-bazillionaires with perfect health guaranteed for all eternity, there would be much less conflict in our lives. There would be some, I'm sure, but much less. For most of us, moral issues come up where there's a scarcity of resources.

DW: Which describes *The Brief and Frightening Reign of Phil*.

GS: Right. And what happens when you create the us and the them. *Since you're them, I'm going to turn you into something nonhuman so I can kill you without qualms.*

DW: Why didn't the characters in that book have human bodies?

GS: The book started out to be something entirely different. Lane Smith had challenged me to make them abstract shapes, but it just wasn't working. "The triangle said to the rectangle . . ." It seemed flat.

I was looking for a way to get a little more energy into the sentences. At one point, they were kind of like androids, but even that: *whoa, robots!* So just the idea of adding a plant part . . .

It was supposed to be a kids' story and kind of spun off track. At that point, I thought, *Maybe I should just skip it.* But there was something about it that I really liked. Really it was an ongoing experiment. What I loved was that dodge of constantly trying to stay out of the rut of the metaphor. *Is this about Bush? Um, not really. Kind of.* I tried to avoid the easy reduction.

When people review books, I think they assume you have a big plan. That book, I'd been working on it for six years. And I liked it. I didn't think it was perfect. In fact I knew the problems immediately.

DW: What was one problem?

GS: I started writing it way back when, and then 9/11 happened. My attention turned to Bush. Well, the story is not a good metaphor for that—it's set up wrong—but I couldn't help some of that leaking in. So I knew a lot of the reviews would say, "This is the most inept satire of Bush," and I'd go, "Yeah, I know." On a micro level, what was I satirizing? Actually, I was just trying to experiment and see if I could make the story play out to the end.

And then also there was a problem with the tonality. It starts off with a kids' book tonality, about genocide, and in some ways that's good because you don't have to get all heavy. You're really not allowed to because of the tone. But at certain points I found that I didn't have the language at my disposal to get the emotional depth I wanted. I didn't have the language to humanize those things as much as I would have liked, so I had to do it somewhat cartoonishly.

But that's what I love about art: everything is a problem. You have 360 degrees of possibility, and as soon as you write one sentence suddenly you're down to twenty degrees. You're eliminating options. You're writing yourself into something like those Chinese thumbscrews. Until at some point your trap becomes your way out—and you *can* get out, but not without conceding a lot of the ground.

When I was younger that was my biggest problem: I wanted to be every writer to every person. You learn the hard lesson that you have to choose, and choosing equals reduction.

I think it's why I write short stories. If I say, "I'm going to write a story that's all commercials," a voice in my head says, "That's going to be stupid. You're not going to get very deep on that one." But you say, "I know. But it's only going to be twenty pages. It's not going to take the rest of my life, so let's try it." It's like Houdini. If Houdini said, "I am going to get up from this chair," no big deal. But if he's chained into the chair and then he gets up, now that's entertaining.

If you make yourself a trap for the story—in one story, commercials—the odds are it's going to be a clever little story. And I knew that. So I wrote it and I wrote it, and it kept staying just clever. I liked the jokes, but . . . Finally, at the end, I hope I got a little extra out of it that moved it into the realm of the short story. Months before, I'd conceded that it wasn't going to be "The Dead." But for me that's the fun of it. Get yourself in a trap.

Phil was like that. Halfway through I realized, *Hey, this is complicated. It's not like anything I've done before. I don't know how to get out of this, and I'm not entirely sure that it's doing useful work.*

I'm not a deeply talented person. There are some little things I can do. If I get a story that doesn't put me to sleep, I'm going to finish it. I'm going to try to make something happen. If it doesn't happen 100 percent, I'll say, "Thanks, I'm going to be dead in forty years anyway. Let's move on."

DW: That's where the energy comes from, the tightrope walk. Maybe this isn't going to work. In the very first paragraph of *The Very Persistent Gappers of Frip*, a town is teetering that way. Will it survive?

GS: Right. If you don't have a risk, the reader feels it, and that's not very fun. It's like going on a date with somebody who's brought index cards. "7:06. 'Your hair looks very attractive.'" It's condescending.

Short stories are risky. They're like jokes—if it doesn't work, you know it. If someone tries to fake their way out of a story, a reader feels it.

Many times for me, the first half of a story is so much fun, and then you hit the point where you're like, *Oh God. Now I have to get out of this in a way that doesn't disregard what I just did. But what I just did makes it impossible to get out of this.* That's where the real fun starts. You're playing a kind of high wire, psychological game with yourself.

It often means going back, looking at the first part of the story, and outing yourself for your own falseness. There's a story in this new book called "CommComm" where there's a guy named Giff, a born-again Christian, an obnoxious, proselytizing, in your face kind of guy. I started that story because I'd been in contact with an old friend of mine who'd gone far right. He was telling me that Saint Augustine would be a hundred percent for the invasion of Iraq. I was so disappointed in what he had become, and I thought, *I'm going to take a few swipes at that way of thinking.* So I did. And it was really easy to make fun of that. But then you get halfway in and you're like, *If I was reading this I would think, liberal guy making fun of fundamentalist, and that's a little too easy.* So, okay, duly noted. That's where I find it kind of spiritually rewarding because you find out about your own bullshit.

A short story is not about nailing somebody. It won't hold. It's almost like relationships: It's fun to get involved, and then at some point you realize, *Oh, this is also about my shit. I can't put it all on you. I have to take responsibility.*

That's also why it's so slow. If it were so easy, it wouldn't be as harrowing. I wrote the first two pages of "Bohemians" eight years before I finished it. I kept looking at it and thinking, *Impossible.* But finally, over that eight-year period, one little trick let me finish it, and I finished it about a week after that.

DW: I must ask: What is your rating on the Ken Byron Manly Scale of Absolute Gender?

GS: I'm a 5 and falling. I'm getting more and more Fem every year.

DW: In many of your stories, characters suffer some kind of public humiliation. Care to share any personal recollections?

GS: I've had them, but in the stories it's more a symptom of being a not-subtle writer. To evoke sympathy, some writers would give you long pages of subtle, internal monologue. I just have a guy fall down.

But when you said that, here's what came to my mind. When I was a kid, I had a crush on this girl in our school. I'd see her during the week, and I always hated that I had to wait two days to see her again. On Sunday her family would go to Mass. My family had kind of stopped going, but I knew the Mass she went to, and I'd go just to see her. Something about seeing her with her family, there was something really novel. I'd only seen her in her school jumper. On Sundays, she had civilian clothes on, with her mom and dad, and I had the whole projected fantasy of *someday that will be my family.* Kind of creepily I would stand in the back of the church, basically living for the moment when she would walk out.

One day it had been snowing. If you got there late—and I always calculated to—you'd have to stand against the wall in back. So I'm leaning against the wall, and I have snow boots on. Partly to show that I was not really *that* Christian I leaned kind of jauntily. It was the quietest part of the Mass, and my feet gave out from under me. Instantly. I didn't even know I was falling. I was just down. Down on the ground with the memory that I had [and I] just went, "OOOMPH!" really loud.

"OOOMPH!" The whole church turns around and looks, and by this time I'm up on my feet but it's obvious I'm the one who's fallen.

That's what I thought of.

DW: What is the last really good book you read?

GS: I just reread all of Mary Gaitskill's work because we're talking tonight [at an event hosted by Portland Arts and Lectures]. Those are all amazing books.

I read the new Márquez, *Memories of My Melancholy Whores.* I hadn't read a book like that in a long time, that got me excited about writing.

Last year I reread a bunch of Jhumpa Lahiri that I was really thrilled with. But I don't read as much as I should. I think I have a little bit of a self-protecting instinct against reading too much because that's my job, teaching. I have to read too much.

DW: Give one example of something you've found that works in the classroom.

GS: The last grad class I taught at Syracuse, we committed to having no outside reading. We would read one story in class and talk about it for three hours. We also committed to keeping away from an academic approach. That was really interesting.

I would try not to read them beforehand. I had read them at some point but not recently. We would say, "Let's treat reading as truly experiential. Let's actually talk about what happened as we read it. If we can." Almost meditation-reading, where you're watching your own mind. And be comfortable being quiet.

It was amazing how deep you could get into stories that way, when you didn't have the option of bringing up four other stories. You'd read a six-page Salinger story in class, and you had to talk about just that one. And then when someone would make an observation, you'd have time to say, "Let's go back and see if that's true. Where exactly did you start to not like Character B?" And you could track it down, literally, to mid-phrase, which is really empowering. You realize that the emotional effects you were experiencing didn't happen out of the blue. You could literally trace them to lines in the text.

Also, you'd see where different young writers would be totally divided about the way a piece was working, and how that mapped their aesthetic values. As someone who wasn't really educated in English Literature, I have that insecurity about going into a class and having nothing to say. This worked against that. *Fine, I'm going to go in and we're going to read this son of a bitch. If we have nothing to say, we won't say anything. And if we start to say something full of shit we'll stop.*

That was a really productive class. You see that all the stuff you'd normally talk about, character and theme and all that, it only comes at you a line at a time. It's empowering to see that you don't have to have a big theory about theme or character; you just have to keep the reader going from line to line. Literally, when the mind shuts down, you've lost them, you're done. But if you can keep that alive, you're a storyteller, and all those other things will slot in.

Note

1. Editor's note: Weich is presumably referencing the story "Jon" here.

George Saunders's Wild Ride

Deborah Treisman / 2010

From newyorker.com, December 12, 2010. https://www.newyorker.com/books/page-turner
/george-saunderss-wild-ride. Reprinted by permission of Deborah Treisman,
the *New Yorker* © Conde Nast.

George Saunders's story "Escape from Spiderhead" appears this week in the *New Yorker*. Recently, he chatted with Deborah Treisman, the magazine's fiction editor, about good and evil, dosing while working, and the writer's main job: "to provide a wild ride for the reader."

Deborah Treisman: "Escape from Spiderhead" reminds me a little of an earlier story of yours—"Jon"—which dealt with teen-agers who were held captive in an institution as test subjects for advertising. That story was dark. This one is even darker. I'm sure you get asked this all the time, but where do these ideas come from?

George Saunders: Well, I should first say (thereby covering my ass for the entire interview) that I am not very good on questions of intentionality, i.e., questions of the "why did you do that?" variety. I think the writer's main job is to provide a wild ride for the reader. So most of what I'm doing on a given day is just trying to ensure that the wild ride happens, trusting and hopeful that the thematics will take care of themselves.

I've done a lot of (mostly defensive) thinking about this darkness thing, and have formulated a good amount of shtick along the way. So thanks for asking! One of the most truthful answers I've come up with is just to paraphrase Flannery O'Connor, who said that a writer can choose what he writes about, but can't choose what he makes *live*. Somehow—maybe due to simple paucity of means—I tend to foster drama via bleakness. If I want the reader to feel sympathy for a character, I cleave the character in half, on his birthday. And then it starts raining. And he's made of sugar.

Are people made of sugar? Is it raining? How often does a guy get cut in half on his birthday? Still, the story about the sugar-guy being cut in half on his birthday in the rain is not saying: *this happens.* It is saying, *If* this happened, what would that be like? Its subject becomes, say, *undeserved misery*—which *does* happen. We know that, we feel it. And maybe (the argument goes) it was necessary to make this exaggerated sugar-guy and cut him in half in order to remind ourselves, at sufficient volume, that undeserved misery exists—to sort of rarify and present that feeling so we might feel it anew.

Anyway, that's the theory.

But yes—this "why so dark?" question comes up a lot, both inside and outside of my head, and, when it does, I always have two opposing impulses. One is: "I know, I know, I'm so sorry, I'll try to do better, I really do enjoy living!" The other is: "Well, wait a minute, what do you mean by 'dark'? anyway? What makes this story 'dark'? I don't find it 'dark' at all. Jon chose love! Jeff chose to not kill! You want darkness? Watch TV! Like *C.S.I.*! Read *Little Red Riding Hood*! Chick makes one mistake, gets eaten by a wolf! And she's a kid! Or how about the Bible? Plagues of locusts, and then the nicest guy in the world gets crucified? Are you kidding me?"

Then I calm down and remember another shtick item: Chekhov's line, in "Gooseberries," where he says that every happy man should have an unhappy man in his closet, to remind him, with his constant tapping, that not everyone is happy, and that, someday, life will show him its claws. That is, stories can exist as a kind of "worst that could happen" entity, to remind us that the happy norm is not omnipresent; that good fortune is not proof of virtue; that statistical beneficence does not mean the miserable starving guy doesn't exist.

Sometimes, I think, we use the term "darkness" in a pejorative sense, to indicate that the fictive world has been (unfairly, or out of sloth, or cynicism, or bad craft) skewed in the direction of having more negative events than "real life" does. So I sometimes do a little gut check, to see if this is the case. In "Escape from Spiderhead," prisoners are used for the testing of experimental pharmaceuticals, even unto death. So I understand that this might come off as a little . . . negative. After all, we are not doing that now. (Well, just to animals. Like bunnies. And monkeys. Even to the big monkeys, so very much like us. But not to prisoners. Never to prisoners.) Would we ever do it? Oh, come on. No way. We are a happy, kindly people. Has there ever been a case, in recent human history, where a group of (up to that point kindly/happy) people treated another group cruelly, even unto death, just because they considered that group somewhat sub-human, and therefore beneath pity?

DT: Seems to me there are many layers of sociopolitical commentary here. Do you have a particular target in mind, or are there several? Animal-testing? Death row? Big pharma?

GS: I think what I do (more by inclination than design) is to put these surficial, quasi-political elements into my stories, just as a means of getting the story told; that is, their function may be more distractive than instructive. A reader might feel, at first, "Ah, I see, this story is making a social commentary—that's why it exists," and then, while she's distracted, the story does . . . something else. Hopefully something a little *more*, if you see what I mean.

Say a certain writer was able to generate pages and pages of people talking entertainingly about fish. That was just a thing he could do, poor bastard. Well, he might choose to set his story in the Monterey Aquarium, and make his two main characters, uh, fish scientists (I am blanking on the word for fish scientists, and keep coming up with "podiatrist"). Well, these two podiatrists would, of course, do a lot of joyful/entertaining talking about fish, and so the reader might think, "Ah, this story seems to want to be saying something joyful about fish—that's why it exists." But if the writer is doing his job the story will have an understory that steadily becomes more apparent—it might concern (say) the blossoming love between the two podiatrists, who, though they share a love for fish, are from different sides of the tracks . . . and hence the story (aided by the distractive device of apparently being "about fish") actually becomes "about love surviving difficult obstacles." (Boy, do I ever want to read that story!) One of said obstacles-to-love being, perhaps, that the male podiatrist's family hates the female podiatrist's family, and then there's a balcony scene, and in the end, after the podiatrists have committed double-suicide, by jumping into the shark tank, the families go, "Oh, we were so wrong, we have finally come to see the error of our ways: our kids were not podiatrists at all, but ichythyoligists! Is that even how you spell it? Come on, let's go find a dictionary—together!" And in the shark tank, the severed heads of the two lovers smile. But then a shark eats the boy's head, and the girl's head frowns and sinks to the bottom.

Anyway—if my intention were (just) to critique animal testing (or corporations, or our treatment of prisoners), I suspect there'd probably be a more direct, efficient, and emotional way to do that than "Escape from Spiderhead." But to use "Look, I'm taking a shot at animal testing here!"

as one of the *apparent propulsive elements* . . . I think that's more what I'm doing.

Likewise, in a story like "Jon," which was sometimes considered to be a satire on advertising—I mean, yes, it was that, but if it was only that, then I failed. There was an understory there (or at least I hoped there was) about having to rise to the occasion of love, about having to, salmon-like, swim against the current of one's prevailing mindset—anyway, that's what I felt was the heart of the story, but one of the means of getting there was a lot of invented products and commercials.

DT: Jeff, despite his "fateful night," is a sympathetic character. Do you think he makes the right decision at the end?

GS: I don't know that it was the right one. But I think it was the most interesting one. That's a funny thing about writing stories. We have that illusion that we are "deciding" what to make a character do, in order to "convey our message" or something like that. But, at least in my experience, you are often more like a river-rafting guide who's been paid a bonus to purposely steer your clients into the roughest possible water.

It's as if the writer has to keep asking, What choice is going to give off the maximum bumpage? And if you go that way—in the direction of the biggest bump—then the thematics of the story will change; but it's not really your decision to make. The energy of the story dictates it.

For this story, I had written many, many pages of a draft ("A novel," I was thinking, all last summer, "finally my novel!") in which Jeff escaped, and it became a story about him hiding down in the town. But it didn't really have much life in it—or so I found out, in August, much to my chagrin. I had all sorts of rationales for it—thematically and so forth. I knew what it "meant" and all of that. But somehow it was dull. So I had to backtrack to the point where the energy had dropped, and that turned out to be right at the place (in an earlier, June-era draft) where I'd had Jeff circumvent this decision re participating in the killing of Rachel.

As they say in cartoons, Wah, wah.

DT: Is there any form of redemption out there for Jeff?

GS: I think he gets some kind of redemption, just in that split-second of once again getting to (briefly) be someone who has never killed anybody. I mean, his life has still pretty much sucked. It was tragic, what he did, and that's not going to change or be equalized by anything he does now. But he sees, in those last few lines, that his identity as a killer, like every other kind of identity, is transient. And he also stayed strong and refused to kill Rachel, took the hit for her, etc., etc. So I guess that's good. But I also felt he did what he did there at the end partly out of sheer-ass weariness—he's tired of the fight. And he hasn't left his mother in such a great spot either.

I'm finding, as I get older, that I'm not much of a believer in redemption. I mean, I believe in redemption in real life—redemption does happen, and it's cool when it does—but I find myself getting leery of my desire for it in stories (especially my own). It feels more and more like some sort of apologist/capitalist construct: "See, all is well, and it always was! Us scrappy humans can redeem any dang situation!" What I don't like about this is that it implies that, when redemption doesn't happen, it's the unredeemed person's *fault*. Whereas, to me, it seems more and more like luck/fate/karma.

Having said that, there's a certain need-for-redemption built into the form, I guess, because the writer has so much destructive power. It's easy to put the bad/dark things in, and, in order to make what feels like a fair representation of the world, it behooves the writer to set things back up on their feet somewhat, I suppose.

More and more these days what I find myself doing in my stories is making a representation of goodness and a representation of evil and then having those two run at each other full-speed, like a couple of PeeWee football players, to see what happens. Who stays standing? Whose helmet goes flying off? It might not be the case that one character is purely good, but rather that good is lurking in that person, and the story is about whether the good gets to emerge. And likewise the evil: it sits inside a person, sort of latent, waiting for the right combination of circumstances. And so, to the so-called evil characters (like Abnesti in this story), the bad things they do seem almost reasonable—as, I suspect, evil does, to the people doing it, in those large, catastrophic, genocidal moments that periodically mar life here on earth—and even in the small, nasty acts that mar life here on earth every day.

DT: Do you ever wish for just a small dose of Verbaluce™ while writing?

GS: Well, define "small." I tend to use 50 ccs for fiction. For an interview like this, I'll use 25 ccs, which runs out in about an hour or so. Dosage is key. One doesn't want to underdose. Because an interview like this is important. Think of it: tens of thousands of readers reading me on there IPids. This is no time to take chanses. On a too low dose; their mite be a tendency: for my prows and sin tax and punch you ashun to get less presise. Which wud suk, sence I/am riting to the interview to the yew norker, one of are mast presijus, if not most, magizins, who stil even publich friction in are dekadint acche!

The George Saunders Interview

Patrick Dacey / 2011

From *BOMB Magazine*. https://bombmagazine.org/articles/the-george-saunders-interview
-part-1/. https://bombmagazine.org/articles/the-george-saunders-interview-part-2/.

Part 1

I met George Saunders in the fall of 2000 when I was a junior at Syracuse University. I had never read his stories (had never read much fiction at all outside of what was assigned in high school), and took his writing workshop to meet a humanities requirement and because I thought it would be easy. I ended up suffering over some long, melodramatic piece about a narrator's dead brother coming back to the beach where he had drowned and speaking from the beyond. There was no denying how terrible it was, but something happened for me in writing that piece, some kind of opening. It might have been knowing that George took an interest in my writing, though he's such a generous teacher and writer that I can't imagine he takes less time with any of his students. It was during this time that I read George's first book, *CivilWarLand in Bad Decline*. There are stories in that book—"Isabelle," "The 400-Pound CEO"—that have the capacity to make you laugh and weep in the time it takes to read them. George's writing does what it seems to me all great writing is supposed to do, which is to garner an emotional response. In *Pastoralia* and *In Persuasion Nation*, his second and third collections of stories, the voice of each character creates a narrative that lives in arm's reach of us. Secretly, we believe these worlds exist. It is not that George opens our eyes to something we may not have considered, but that he breaks through intellectual apathy and allows us to see, hear, and feel what is inside us.

After graduating from college and working a handful of dead-end jobs, I was offered a fellowship to the MFA program at Syracuse, the time to write, and three years to spend in the company of George. If anything, that time taught me the most important lesson for a writer, and one that George preaches often: be disciplined. Since graduating, I've been fortunate enough to maintain a friendship with George, follow his writing, and find places for my own stories to appear. Along with being an immensely talented writer, George is a kind, generous, and whole-hearted human being. That the two go hand in hand is probably no accident.

Patrick Dacey: It's been a few years since I was a student of yours at Syracuse, but I always enjoyed your classes because they felt more like conversations and I remember certain things you said that have been invaluable to me as a writer. A couple have stayed with me: "The moment when things get complicated, that's what we try to move towards." And: "A father and son in a bedroom doesn't mean that something sexual has to happen." Does it seem to you that writers sometimes choose to shy away from complications by going to the extreme?

George Saunders: Right—those two are kind of like bookends—although also, wow, what a terror, to be quoted so accurately at such great temporal distance. You may remember some of my other biggies, such as, "Any monkey in a story had better be a dead monkey," and "Aunts and uncles are best construed as the heliological equivalent of small-scale weather systems," or (the mother of all advice-quote-pairs): "The number of rooms in a fictional house should be inversely proportional to the years during which the couple living in that house enjoyed true happiness."

The first idea ("move towards the complicated") is, I think, best understood as a habit of mind generally worth cultivating. Basically: steer towards the rapids. Say we're writing "Little Red Riding Hood" and we've just typed: "One day, Red's mother handed her a picnic basket and told her to go see Granny, but not to talk to any strangers along the way." So—should we have her meet a stranger? Yes. Should that stranger be potentially dangerous, like, say, a wolf? Sounds promising. Should Red engage with the wolf? (What a drag, if, at that point, she takes Mom's advice and ignores the wolf: story over). Should the wolf she meets be evil, or a gentle, New Age wolf, who gives her some nice poems about daughter/granddaughter relations? Looking at a familiar story like that one, it's pretty clear: a story is a thing that is full of dozens of crossroads moments, and if we make a habit of first, noticing these, and, second, steering toward the choice that gives off incrementally more power (or light, or heat, or throws open other interesting doors, etc.), this will, over the long haul, make the story more unique, more like itself, more incendiary. (Although even as I type this, I find myself intrigued by the poem-giving wolf . . .)

That's where the second idea comes in: as we try to steer toward the rapids, we sometimes do so reflexively, thus overriding reality, or probability, or story-power, in a way that can seem like a tic. We often auto-choose the naughty, the verboten, the violent, the coolly uneventful, the "literary."

For example, a few years back, in our admissions pile at Syracuse, we were getting a gazillion stories where everyone over forty was a pedophile. Or, you know—if he/she wasn't a pedophile, it was through sheer act of will. And I started feeling that move as sort of habitual—it was what a young writer did when he/she didn't know what else to do: throw a pedophile in there. So that decision—which must have felt, to those writers, like "steering toward the rapids"—was actually the opposite: it had become the lazy, go-to solution—a way of avoiding complexity.

That second bit-o'-shtick you mention in your question ("A father and a son in a bedroom . . .") might refer to a larger principle, namely: we have to know what our reader is expecting and take that into account. If, for example, we make that father a Father—i.e., a priest—and have him call that kid into the dark, secluded back room of the church—well, at this particular cultural moment, certain expectations arise. And as writers, we have to know those, and deal with them somehow. If I say: a priest summoned an altar boy into the back room of the church—well, at some level we "expect" a molestation. We just do. Maybe in 1931 we didn't—but we do now. (And "expect" might be too strong a word. Let's say "molestation" comes into the realm of likely narrative possibilities.) So the writer has to know this and respond accordingly. The molestation could occur, of course, but we'd have to make it occur in a way that somehow takes into account the fact that molestation-by-priest has become a trope and a *Tonight Show* punch line.

We all know that nice feeling that happens when we are expecting Thing A from a writer and we go, "Oh no, not that, that would be just too obvious," and then she delivers, instead, Thing B, and Thing B evidences a bigger heart, or a wider experience, or just more attentiveness on her part, etc., etc. So: there in that back room, the priest might do or say something that suddenly reminds us that "priest" is a category that contains multitudes— from molesters (yes, sure, okay) to Merton-like spiritual beings of great kindness, like that priest at (I think it was) Auschwitz, who sacrificed himself so that some other people could live, and was then starved to death in a pit, and the others heard him singing hymns literally to the very end.

(Or, for that matter, the priest might do something that reminds us that "molester" is also a category that contains multitudes (!). That is, the molestation could go ahead and occur, at a level of detail/insight that astounds us and makes it all new again.)

I suppose what we're really trying to develop is the ability to see, at a given moment in a story (stuck there, sick of our own prose, blinded to it by the hours we've already spent), all the inherent possibilities, and then choose the one that is most . . . something. I would tend to say: The one that is most uncommon, i.e., the one that would take the most time/energy/ acuity of vision to come up with—the one that is farthest down the trail, so to speak. But I suppose that's what distinguishes one writer from another— how he/she might complete that sentence: Choose the one that is most (??).

And, of course, all of the above is mere concept—we "decide" how to write by doing it over and over, all the while trying to avoid nauseating ourselves—and then we look up afterwards and maybe try to figure out what we've done, and what we, therefore, must "believe" about writing.

PD: So building off this idea about the present and the reader's expectations affecting that choice, is it fair to say that in fiction some sense of realism has to be apparent for a story to work?

GS: I think so, yes. I'd make the case that the whole fictional thrill has to do with this idea of the reader and the writer closely tracking, if you will. Like one of those motorcycle sidecars: when the writer leans left, the reader does too. You don't want your reader three blocks away, unaware that you are leaning. You want her right there with you, so that even an added comma makes a difference. And I think building that motorcycle has to do with that very odd moment when the writer "imagines" his reader—i.e., imagines where the reader "is" at that precise point in the story. This is more of a feeling thing than an analytical thing, but all that is good about fiction depends on this extrapolation. Which is pretty insane, when you think of it. The writer, in order to proceed, is theoretically trying to predict where his complex skein of language and image has left his reader, who he has likely never met and who is actually thousands of readers. Yikes! Better we should do something easier, like join the circus.

PD: But is it that a writer must always consider the reader? I mean, I think it's clearly necessary in some respects, but I'm also thinking of the artist's impulse to create. A few years back, Neil Young gave an interview to

Charlie Rose, and he spoke about his songs as being gifts, and how he had to be open to receive those gifts, and to respect the source, be there for the source that provides him with whatever it is that gives him the ability to create. I guess I'm getting at a couple of things here. What do you think the impulse is for you to create and then give it away? And do you ever question that source or that story or line that strikes you at any given time?

GS: As far as "considering the reader"—I'm sure it's different for every writer. But for me, yes, I am always considering the reader. Although this is admittedly kind of odd: Which reader? On what day? In what mood? For me, that "reader" is actually just me, if I had never read the story before. That is, I'm trying to read/edit as if I have no existing knowledge of the story, no investment in it, no sense of what Herculean effort went into writing page 23, no pretensions as to why the dull patch on page 4 is important for the fireworks that will happen on page 714. I'm essentially just trying to impersonate a first-time reader, who picks up the story and has to decide, at every point, whether to keep going.

As far as the "impulse to create"—what comes to mind is something like this. Say you were standing in a group of people, and nearby some guys were throwing a Frisbee around, and suddenly one of them misthrew, and here it comes now, right over your head—that impulse to jump up and catch it is similar to what I feel when I'm writing. Why did you jump? Not to "honor the Frisbee" or "make a connection with the thrower" or "serve as the conduit/recipient of the Frisbee's symbolic journey, blah blah blah." You did it . . . well, who knows why, really? Partly the motivation is a "because it's there" kind of thing. You start a story and in rereading it, see a place where it could be made better. Well, why not?

As for the last question—if I'm understanding the question correctly, then yes: I think that's part of what we're always trying to learn: which storyline is going to prove to be a dud, which impulse is trustworthy, which is going to lead us to an eight-month editing nightmare . . . and at least so far, whatever I've learned is at such a weird, subtle, sub-verbal level that I can't really articulate it. I imagine it might be something like being a good athlete (and here I really have to imagine . . .). What does a really good tennis player know? There is, of course, some basic conceptual knowledge— the grip, general strategies for pacing oneself over the course of a match, or whatever . . . but what really distinguishes that player from the (lesser) player he/she was five years earlier is a series of neurological/muscle impulses and responses that he/she has "learned" in some sub-verbal place.

My feeling is that it's similar with art. You put in thousands of hours at the writing desk and the result is some refinement of your hundred-a-day micro-decisions. I am more convinced than ever that the talking and the doing are miles apart—probably mutually helpful in some complicated way, but still, miles apart.

PD: I believe that, too. I was late to writing, and, to be honest, reading. I had always wanted to be a professional football player, an offensive lineman. That was my goal up until I went to Syracuse as an undergraduate and realized I wasn't 6-foot-4 and didn't weigh 300-plus pounds. Then I took a class with Michael Burkard and became interested in writing, but I felt like I was so far behind, that I hadn't read anything yet and couldn't really explain what I was trying to write, but I was getting good feedback and beginning to write stories and I read your books and Denis Johnson's and Raymond Carver's and found out what books you and Johnson and Carver read, and so on. I have come to see not knowing too much as an advantage, not only in writing but in teaching.

I'm thinking about this student I had last summer when I was teaching an American Lit course. We were reading Melville's *Bartleby, the Scrivener* and I asked the class what they thought of the story and everyone was silent, but I could see this one student wanted to say something but didn't know how to articulate it, so I asked him just to say the first thought that came to his mind when he finished the story, and he said, "All I really know is that this Melville dude must've been smokin' some of that Kush weed." I'm pretty sure that's the exact quote. Now among crazy things a student has said, that's up there. But, at the same time, I found it kind of encouraging. He was later able to articulate what he meant and point out specific parts of the piece that were especially filled with "Kush weed"-induced moments. He had read the story and he was into it and into seeing how it worked and this, more than 150 years later, was his first emotional response and it was as though it gave the story that much more power, that it could be understood in this new way. Could you discuss how you came to writing, and, maybe more importantly, how you've been able to sustain your career and produce work that is original and your own? In another sense, how are you able to adapt to the new thing without relying on what was successful for you in the past?

GS: I like that: "the mentality of the athlete." That seems right to me. And I noticed you thinking that way even back when you were a student—you always had this very admirable sense of "whatever it takes" with regard to your own work. I always knew that if I said "Isaac Babel" you'd come back soon having read it all.

Anyway I came to writing sort of gradually. When I think back, I'm always kind of amazed that I didn't see earlier that it was what I wanted to do. Or maybe I saw it and it scared me. I remember having this sense, in my early twenties, that if I actually tried to write anything, it might suck, and then the dream would be dead. I vaguely remember seeing something, when I was very young (maybe three or four), about Hemingway's death on TV. My memory is: a photo of him in that safari jacket, and the announcer sort of intoning all the cool things he'd done ("Africa! Cuba! Friends with movie stars!"). So I got this idea of a writer as someone who went out and did all these adventurous things, jotted down a few notes afterward, then got all this acclaim, world-wide attention etc., etc.—with the emphasis on the "adventuring" and not so much on the "jotting down."

And yes—as your question intimates, one of the challenges of the writing life is to find new things to say and/or new ways to say them. And this is a paradox, because when you write your first book, you actually carve out a great deal of what you'll end up working with for the rest of your life. And you come to it (or I did, anyway) with this sense of stumbling on a virgin landscape: it's all new to you. You didn't know you could sound that way and, having discovered a new way of sounding, there's suddenly all this new material available to you, i.e., the new voice enabled, or even brought into being, all this stuff that previously you would have felt was sub-literary, or would just have been invisible to you as material. So that's genuinely exciting. But then there's the next sixty years to get through (!). A more mundane way of saying it: in your early work, if you're going deep, you discover your themes, your voice, your (ugh) "concerns." And if you did it right, you sort of plumbed your own psyche in this very intense way, and there's no turning back. You made a legit discovery about who you are, and about what things you can do well, and the things you can't, and maybe about your fundamental relation to the world, about what things you can make come alive, about (maybe most importantly of all) the way your mind works—its pre-inclinations, habits, prejudices, inexplicable fascinations.

Now, the hope would be that you'd have this virgin-landscape feeling for every book, but I'm not sure that's the way the brain is set up. We'd have to see the further books as deeper and more specific forays into that same landscape—so this model suggests, depressingly enough, a gradually shrinking field of play for the writer—a room which is getting smaller and smaller—sort of like that garbage dump scene in *Star Wars*. My experience of writing is that I had to work very hard to discover a tiny little wedge of talent, and almost immediately became aware that there were certain things I just couldn't do. So then the challenge became something like: get through the rest of my life while running back and forth on that little wedge of talent, without blatantly repeating myself. (While periodically trying, again, to do those things "I just couldn't do," to make sure I still couldn't do them, just in case). For me, that has meant working pretty slowly, doing a ton of revision, only producing one or two stories a year, walking this fine line between becoming so OCD that I blocked right up versus writing nice and loose but then producing stuff that wasn't sufficiently original and had to be thrown away. But, maybe paradoxically, I'm also finding that this tiny wedge o' talent, or gradually shrinking *Star Wars* garbage dump (or now I'll shift metaphors and call it a "ledge of talent"—a ledge which is, let's say, usually thinning/crumbling away, because much of what you feel inclined to do, you've already done) to be a deliriously interesting place to be. Much more interesting than, say, being granted an entirely new mind, and being allowed to write "another" first book.

PD: I never thought of your short stories as criticisms of American life or signs of what's to come, though—especially in *In Persuasion Nation*—the stories are topical; we can see them existing today, as some kind of reality. Do you approach each story with a subject in mind and then work through that story with that voice you're talking about, that way of seeing things?

GS: No, regrettably it's a lot more scattershot than that. Really I am just trying to find some little interesting (to me) thing to start out with: something small, even trivial. Preferably something that doesn't have a lot of thematic or political baggage—that is, a little crumb that is interesting but I'm not sure why, exactly. (As soon as I feel Theme looming, I know I'm in trouble.) Sometimes that crumb might be just a few lines in a certain voice, sometimes it's a bit of dialogue, or something more conceptual that feels like it would be fun to riff around—that story "CivilWarLand in Bad Decline" was like that. I think I have to use this approach exactly because I'm so prone to being political and didactic and reductive—this approach is a way of confounding that part of myself, throwing it off the scent a bit.

PD: Is this the same approach you take to your nonfiction writing?

GS: No—with that kind of writing (and what a relief) I feel like I'm confined and driven by what actually happened. That makes the "plot," so to speak. So it's a process of getting all of my notes typed up, then scanning through the notes, trying to extract or find certain vignettes that seem like they might write well—that might have a potential for good energy, shape, etc., etc. And then at some point I start stringing these together, keeping an eye on the word count. It's amazing how severe you have to be to represent a ten-day trip in 12,000 words.

The one thing the two genres have in common for me is that sense of trying to get the sentences to be minimal but at the same time be a little overfull—to encourage them to do a kind of poetic work. And I know you know all about this, Pat. That's one thing I love about your work: this sense of poetic compression—the way that omission and close, loving attention at the sentence level make something that is both of the world but somehow floating above it too—a kind of fabulist feeling that has a real sense of awe and open-heartedness about it.

PD: Everything moving forward quickly and purposefully. That seems to be the toughest part. Most of my undergraduate students think they need to tell the entire life story of their character (or their entire life story if it's a personal narrative piece). But it's unnecessary if you can do it with action and voice. I like to read to them the first paragraph of your story "Adams." The first five words of the story are about the only background information we get and that's less than half the words in the first sentence. The economy of language is so essential.

GS: Yes. I think the "purposeful" is really hard and important. My feeling is, we don't get any "points" for laying out something that the reader would otherwise assume or posit. Even writers we think of as being very big and lush and symphonic—like David Foster Wallace—are actually very structurally efficient. It's like a well-built house that can then support all sorts of fancy decorative frills, extra rooms, etc.

I like the idea that a story—well, that we don't really know what it is, exactly. And that this is actually the purpose of every story: to find one more active, breathing example of what a story can be.

Part 2

PD: I've been thinking lately about the impulse new writers have to imitate their heroes—they know they want to write, and they know what resonates with them as readers, so they fall into a kind of trap where they write toward a preconceived ideal, taking whatever ideas they have and fitting them into someone else's structure and style. My wife, Tara, taught a fiction class recently where two of her more promising students were Miranda July hopefuls who wrote stories full of nonsequiturs and quirky sweaters and neurotic inner monologues about mismatched shoelaces and Spam. What are your thoughts about the tendency among new writers to lean toward "what works" rather than pursuing a vision of their own? Is this maybe a necessary step for any artist, like the way a child learns to do things through observation and imitation before he becomes his own strange, self-motivated person? It also seems likely that by now there are more than a few George Saunders hopefuls out there who are trying to work versions of your characters or aspects of your style into their own stories. How does it affect you as a writer and reader when you come across this sort of thing, both among students and in published work?

GS: I definitely think this imitation phase is a good and necessary thing—or at least an unavoidable thing. I went through it in a big way, several times. I think what happens is that, as you get older, and start having more undeniably valid and costly life experiences, you start acutely feeling the distance between the prose you are imitating and your own life. It's painful, actually, that disjunct. It grates. And of course you never think you're imitating someone—you think you're "taking over the torch" or "doing the next thing for the lineage" or whatever. I went through this with Thomas Wolfe, then Hemingway, then Kerouac, then Carver, Toby Wolff, Isaac Babel. And after all that, once we had our kids, I started to feel a little sick at heart every time I donned the cloak o' admiration, i.e., every time I felt that little thought-bubble called "Who Shall I Imitate Today?" start to form around my head.

I've started to think that this is one of the hardest and most important things a young writer can do: look at his/her heart-influences and ask, very respectfully: OK, given that this great master existed in the world, what else is there left for me to do? That is, you love (for example) Tolstoy, you give Tolstoy his due. But then you have to say: All right, given that Tolstoy has already existed, is there anything in his worldview that I might, slightly, disagree with? Is there anything that I have known and seen and felt in my life that, perhaps (sorry, maestro!) is not fully accounted for in his work? If not—well, there are other things to do in this life. If so, go for it.

For example, I remember reading Hemingway and loving his work so much—but then at some point, realizing that my then-current life (or parts of it) would not be representable via his prose style. Living in Amarillo, Texas, working as a groundsman at an apartment complex, with strippers for pals around the complex, goofball drunks recently laid off from the nuclear plant accosting me at night when I played in our comical country band, a certain quality of West Texas lunatic-speak I was hearing, full of way off-base dreams and aspirations—I just couldn't hear that American in Hem-speak. And that kind of moment is gold for a young writer: the door starts to open, just a crack.

PD: There seems to be a good deal of negative press about MFA programs. That these programs are inorganic and that students are taught how to write a certain way. I'm really not sure what the argument is against having two to three years to focus on nothing but writing, being exposed to great writers and getting financed to travel, etc. The argument seems to be that writers "in the old days" would go out in the world, like, live in Paris or New York and drink and talk. Most of the criticism seems to be bullshit, but I'll admit I did feel a certain level of stress and self-consciousness I don't think was there before. And I was glad to get out for a while, try my hand at reporting, work on a novel in Mexico, mow some lawns on Cape Cod for a summer, before getting back into teaching. I remember you saying once that your writing became worse while you were getting your MFA at Syracuse.

GS: Well, worse and better. Short-term, my stories got worse. I was so intimidated and impressed by my teachers and peers that I sort of clammed up and got (shudder) "serious." That is, having been admitted on the basis of a kind of wildish story, I reverted to a kind of realism at which I'm not very good. So if you looked at the work I did while I was in the program, it was pretty flat. But I think all that time I was learning some deeper things about structure so that, when I finally got my voice back, I knew what to do with it. Before that, I could be sort of funny/wild but only for a page at a time.

My feeling is that it would be pretty hard to generalize about a phenomenon as vast and various as creative writing programs—it's kind of like generalizing about grocery stores. But I agree with you that, at their best, they aren't much different from the small writing communities of yore. (I like the idea of Hemingway in workshop with Fitzgerald and Stein and Joyce, and afterwards, having been trashed—("Maybe Nick Adams could have a little more inner monologue in here, Hem?" says Gertrude Stein)— Hemingway beats them all up.) The only thing I'm finding a little problematic lately is a shift in attitude I've seen over the last four-to-five years, in which an MFA is seen as essential to becoming a writer. Essential and sufficient: no way to be a writer if you don't have one, and pretty much a guarantee that you will be a writer if you do get one. Neither of these things is true, seems to me, and the sort of frenzy/desperation I see in young writers is troubling. It feels like there's been this subtle shift, wherein the insane act of writing fiction—which is pure vocation and lunacy—is becoming "a career." I mean, it can turn into a career, one hopes—but first it has to be a vocation, with all that implies: failure, isolation, dark nights of the soul, a tank-like resolve to do it no matter what the world says, private moments of realization, etc.

PD: Not only to becoming a writer, but a teacher as well. Yet many universities want to know what you've published and if you don't have those credits it can cause one to rush out work that isn't ready (I'm basing this on experience), which is a killer. So, it's difficult to talk about those last things you mentioned because they always exist, will always exist. I was going to pretend as if I had some sort of epiphany in the last few years about my own writing, but that wouldn't be true. It seems to be more of a spiritual matter, an attempt to connect myself with the other through some third thing that exists between the two, and if I'm aware of that existence, then I'm not concerned with what the end result provides me with.

GS: Back when I was just out of grad school, I think things were simpler. I remember feeling that there were two kinds of teaching a person could do: the teaching you did before you had a book (i.e., eighty-seven sections of freshman comp) or the kind of teaching you did after a book (grad teaching, light load, tenure-track). I'm not sure that was the case then, but that was my understanding of it. Given my various intellectual frailties and the fact that I'd never, at that point, taught, I had a feeling that the first option would be disastrous for me—a hunch that all of the grading and thinking about writing were not stage-appropriate for me and would fuck up my fiction. And I think I was right about that—I had a lot of learning to do after grad school, a lot of trying to get in touch with some wild part of my writing self that I'd lost, a lot of work figuring out how to use the things I'd learned in grad school. And that took a lot of quiet. That is, Joyce's "silence, exile, and cunning." A sense that, at least in that realm, I could do whatever I wanted and it would only cost me—not our family. So—again, given my psyche—this meant finding something that would support us adequately, and that would also allow some flexibility to write (i.e., some way to steal time from work.)

So I was lucky enough to have had an engineering background, and although by that point the degree was a little cold (like, seven-years cold) I found work as a technical writer. At that point my feeling was basically this all-the-eggs-in-one-basket feeling: I am going to keep working as a tech writer and doing fiction on the side until I finish a book, a book I really like, and at that time, if I feel like it and it seems advantageous (to my family life, to my writing life) I'll look for a teaching job. But only if I want to and only if it's a really good one. But I didn't feel all that urgent about getting into teaching. So my thought was to sort of hold my breath and eschew teaching until I could do it on terms that felt right for me. Which, given the feast-or-famine nature of teaching at that time, as described above, made sense.

Now it seems like the game has slightly changed. From what I can see, there are a lot of decent jobs teaching creative writing, at relatively sane loads, even for people with no book yet. Which is great, but also complicates things in the way you've described in your question. Because eventually the university is going to start looking for that book, and during the time the person was supposed to be writing it, he/she was teaching a load that, even if it was a pretty light one, would typically be more intense than that of the "post-book" hire.

But writing is funny. It's kind of like "farming by Escher." You can put down perfect seeds, in just the right way, in great weather, and get nothing (i.e., you can have all the time in the world, do a gazillion drafts, and . . . blah). Or you can be messing around one day and a seed falls out of your pocket and something really interesting and new grows.

The only thing I've really come to believe is that it's all about putting in the hours. The poet Jon Fink related this story to me awhile back and it's stuck with me. Robert Frost was apparently doing a college visit back in the 1950s and a student asked him some complicated, technical, conceptual question, of the "how must the poet proceed?" variety, and Frost answered: "Don't worry, work."

Now, at first this struck me as a little bit easy. (Hey thanks, Mr. Most Famous Poet in the World, I'd never considered not worrying before! That's super!) But it's starting to make sense to me. I'm a person who has always done a lot of thinking and worrying and planning and strategizing vis-à-vis my writing, but as I look back at the last twenty years, I can see that all the real big leaps, such as they were, took place in a sort of extra-conceptual place—they came at-speed, while writing, or over many days of writing—but in any case, through work, through the hours and hours of work, when the subconscious is being given free rein and hence can do the crazy things only it can do. That is, I never "decided" anything about writing that did me much good, that I can remember.

PD: Yes, there are those stories that just come to you in a shot, and then those ones that take two years or more to get right, and then, you look at them and maybe you never get them right. So, how then has teaching influenced your work and your life, beyond, you know, money?

GS: What I really like about teaching is that it reminds me that writing (and the effect it has on people) is real. We writers comprise a sort of embattled guild in the world, and it's a non-trivial guild. The things we are saying (the things that only we can say, i.e., the things that can't be said/ reached in films, songs, blogs, tweets, etc., etc.) are essential. But also: that a given person can be better or worse at saying those things, depending on how hard and how efficiently she works. Or, another way to say it: expressiveness, in humans, is mutable. We can get better at it. And when we get better at expressiveness, we get better at understanding, better at sympathy, better at bullshit-detection, better at experiencing pleasure, better at true engagement (with others, with the world, with ourselves). And in a time when (I hate this phrase but) "mass-media" seems intent on making us worse at understanding and sympathy, and is rapidly filling us with (cheerful, happy) (or faux-dark, doom-inflected) bullshit, and seems specially designed to make us less adept at experiencing (real, authentic) pleasure, and is bent on actively discouraging real engagement—well, at that time, our guild becomes essential.

PD: Well, it's only a matter of time before a novel produced solely in tweets is published (How inauthentic, unoriginal, and overly ironic! says the critic via Twitter). It seems strange to me that reading short stories isn't more popular nowadays, given our attention spans. I've often felt that, despite its popularity, the short story makes more sense, and that may be why the general public invests themselves in long thrillers, because the short story is too close to their natural way of relating information to others. We tell twenty or more short stories a day, to people we know and people we don't know, constantly revising those stories depending on who we're telling them to. And the best novels, to me, are the ones that don't rely on just one story, but are filled with multiple stories within whatever the driving force of that novel is.

GS: Right. Although, as someone who's been around since the late Pleistocene, when we used to write our short stories while riding around in horse-drawn carriages and all had untreatable syphilis, I can tell you that this idea that the short story is somehow under-loved has been around awhile itself. My sense is that the story is holding steady, same as it ever was: tended by a relatively small but passionate group of devotees around it, who keep it vital.

Now, having said that—and to your point—I talked to a really wonderful writer recently who writes both novels and stories, and I asked him what the difference was in terms of attention at time of publication. He said he will get about four-to-five times as much attention for the novel. Wah.

One thing about the short story is that it's kind of an exotic, hothouse version of the "real" story. It does a little more—there's more compression, of course, but also a higher expectation of shapeliness and some kind of aesthetic closure—a moment where the wires the writer has filled with current get a chance to really cross. So I think some "normal" readers don't know quite what to do when they get to the end of a literary short story that feels (to them) oddly shaped, or truncated—i.e., that doesn't follow the natural course of events out to the last days of the protagonist or whatever.

But there's another answer, which I'm pretty sure I don't believe, but which I'll simulate here anyway: contemporary short story writers have gotten too specialized/dark/mopey. They don't have enough "real life" in their stories—that is, they're not taking up the real concerns of real readers. They aren't storytellers, really (in that around-the-campfire sense) but margin-dwellers, writing stories in response (not to life itself), but to other hothouse stories, and all these stories do, really, is uphold a certain knee-jerk, lazy, default humanist ethic, etc., etc. Where's the joy? Isn't there lots to celebrate in life? This model (as you can tell) is dangerously close to reactionary ("Just write something I can read and I'll read it! Why so negative! You sure seem well-fed enough, mister!"), and I don't buy it for a number of reasons, the main one of which is that sometimes joy can express itself in strange ways, and also because stories have always been dark (i.e., Grimm's Fairy Tales, the Crucifixion).

But lately I have found myself wondering—aware of a certain tic in my own approach, a tic that seems to autoswerve towards a suite of things: drama, violence, darkness, speed. Is this an authentic and natural tendency of mine, and therefore to be honored? Or is it a sort of acquired and automatic thing, to be regarded with suspicion, and thrown off in favor of something else?

But I guess this tension is good, good to write from. God forbid we should wake up one day and know exactly what we're doing.

PD: In talking more about not talking about writing, do you have some inclination of why you've begun to move towards more drama, violence, darkness, and speed as of late? And is this "tic" what helps you to view your stories as a collection that work together in one book or does that not matter so much when putting together a collection? Meaning, did you have a certain tic that led you through the stories in *CivilWarLand in Bad Decline*, *Pastoralia*, and *In Persuasion Nation* that you see influencing the work that you'll include in your next book?

GS: I think this tic or habit has been with me from the beginning. I'll give you an example of what I mean. I've always loved this Chekhov story called "After the Theatre." It's this simple little five-to-six page thing. A girl comes home from a play, thinks about it, about certain boys she knows (it seems she's very pretty) and we hear her internal monologue as she's sort of rating one boy against the other, thinking about her future, etc., etc. At least that's how I remember it. But it's perfect: he really nails the adolescent sensibility. You can see the girl she is—pure, hopeful, kind—but can also feel the grownup she might become. You can see how the positive traits in her might get corrupted or eroded as she gets older and, best of all, you don't feel it as a judgment of her, really: just a beautiful little accurate portrait of what it feels like to be young.

OK, so I've been carrying that idea of "After the Theatre" around all these years, and one day I think: I wonder if I could do something analogous? That is, make an uninflected picture of a teenage girl. And I try it. It's funny enough, she's kind of sweet, but somehow it doesn't feel complete enough to qualify as a story. Suddenly, a guy shows up, and a few drafts later, turns out this guy is a potential kidnapper. And the story now has energy, and I suddenly know where to go with it, and off I go. But I'm interested in that moment right there, where my working definition of "story" requires me to introduce a kind of drama that (one could say) is a little, I dunno— melodramatic? Hyper?

In a sense this is all academic—or maybe just applies to the stories to come. When I got to that moment I had no doubts, and am happy enough with the story ("Victory Lap") that resulted. But I do love books where the plot/drama is either slight or where we understand them to be non-urgent, sort of like red herrings or MacGuffins, there just so that the comedy can proceed. I'm thinking here of, say, *Dead Souls* or *Confederacy of Dunces*.

I just (so far) can't do it.

As far as what powers the individual books along—I tend to just work for four to seven years and then at some point, I start to feel that group of stories closing out. I basically just trust that if I've been working hard all along, there must be something essential going on under the surface that will unite the stories, and hopefully in some deeper way than I could have planned or imposed. It's maybe something like if you were constantly tape-recording yourself for five years but at the end of every week you deleted all but the wittiest things you'd said. Then, at the end of the five years, you went through the edited things that remained, and edited those down. During that time, you were who you were—for better or worse.

PD: You mentioned earlier about things you keep attempting to do, to see that you can't do them, though feel compelled to keep trying. And I doubt you're alone. Are there specific instances of this that loom large?

GS: Well, it's funny—you sent me this question yesterday, and I've been wrestling with it ever since. It isn't the case that I have this 300-page sincere novel off to the side. Rather, I think it's more of a tendency I have to swerve away from certain material or ideas or notions, year after year, and then occasionally look back at the body of work that's built up, and think: Huh, you still haven't started on the Big Stuff yet. (I feel especially remiss when I think in terms of scale: Where is my epic? Why all of this obsessing on small canvases? This is probably the expected midlife crisis for someone who learned early that if my writing was going to have any power, I was going to have to radically concern myself with the lapidary.) Now, in some cases, this swerving is a good thing. I don't know how many times I've thought: "You know, what I'd like to do, is write a really big book about some really big city, and my themes would be, just, you know everything, and my main idea stylistically would be, uh, like: All is Allowed!" That has the feeling of something that, in order to avoid becoming a sinkhole, might benefit from a little more, uh . . . specificity.

But let me tell you a little anecdote, and with apologies, because I've been telling this one on the road a bit lately—but it's somehow central (in a way I haven't quite figured out yet) to this whole issue for me.

A few years ago I was cutting through Rockefeller Center, and I glanced up and found myself in front of that really nice chocolate shop down there—can't remember the name of it. But it was early December and they had the window all Xmas-tricked-out, and I got this involuntary thrill of the exact variety I used to get as a kid when I realized Xmas vacation was looming: kind of this presents-are-coming, freedom-is-approaching, life-is-so-beautiful leaping of the heart that felt both totally familiar and entirely fresh. It was corny, it was all Currier & Ives—but the feeling was as real as the pigeons over there on Fifth or that scrap of paper right there, you know? Just a little split-second thrill, really, with that kind of associated imagistic mind-nostalgia burst (*pinesmellgoldenpapercookiesnowman*) that, again, is as real as more familiar mind-states, like, say, anxiety, or dizziness. So as I was walking away I thought, as us writers are wont to do: "Hey, I wonder if I could use that in a story?" I felt that, yes, I probably could use it—that is, I could probably find a way to generate some text that would convey that sense, make it real, or some pleasure-giving exaggerated version of it—and that was exciting. But then I felt this blowback sense of discomfort, almost dread, that had to do with this feeling of: Well, okay but *then* what? Or, put more precisely: I was feeling a little insecure with the notion of letting that moment of positive energy just stand there, without some sort of ironic caveat. My first instinct, having written this little vignette (middle-aged man has a mini-burst of happiness), would be, you know, to make an icicle come down and impale him through the head. Or, maybe if I could locate him in some ironic place (a theme park, say [!]) I'd be able to "get away with it." Which was weird: Dickens would have let it stand. Ditto Tolstoy. If they had to complicate it (i.e., show that this feeling might have repercussions, or might be just part of who this man was, i.e., was not him in his totality) they would have had the confidence to wait a few hundred pages to do so.

So I've seen doing a lot of thinking about that: why do I always feel the need for what we might call the obligatory-edgy.

Now, this gets complicated. Because I first discovered the obligatory-edgy (and the happy effect it had on the energy of my prose) when my work was dying of complete boredom for want of it. So excising this thing (if it is, in fact, "a thing"), at least in theory, can feel like a step backwards. (And I've done this a few times over the years, in individual stories that then didn't fly, at which time I learned the whole lesson over again—I remember one in particular, set in an Episcopal church, that included all sorts of straightforward, precisely rendered, internal monologue bits that represented exactly the theological questions that were tormenting me at the time, and this story was a very nice, sincere, smiling bird, sans wings.)

So edginess can be a way of introducing energy, and/or an appropriate overtone of skepticism, a way of enlarging the frame, of accounting for the complications of real life. Are there fields of beautiful tulips in the world, through which two well-matched lovers stroll? You bet. But is the world an endless sequence of such fields? Ha. So, to underscore this, maybe we have a crop-duster fly over the tulip-field, and the pilot is listening to "Smells Like Teen Spirit."

In terms of the above (Rockefeller Center) example, that falling icicle has the effect of saying: yes, well, this dude is happy, but there are others out there who are not, and this kind of "I am happy, therefore life must be good and fair" mentality that he is enjoying is not without consequences for the rest of the world, etc., etc., and furthermore, his feeling of happiness is not permanent, since, for example, any minute now something bad might—oops. Icicle. That is, there's a reason to have that icicle come down through that guy's head, and that's to puncture his smugness. (Although that can devolve into, God help us, Moral Fiction—preachy, joyless, over-determined, unhinged from the very real pleasures of living.) But I think one of the problems with the obligatory-edgy is that it is a little impatient: it fails to account for the fact that this is an individual guy, not an emblem of something—there's time and space in his life for him to be a lot of things. So maybe, today, he's happy . . .

Also, the obligatory edgy component can also be just that: obligatory, i.e., a tic.

Sometimes when I read new fiction, I feel that the writers of it, myself included, have a somewhat dysfunctional relationship with our own culture. I don't mean we disapprove of it. I mean that we have absorbed so much habitual disapproval of it that we are no longer able to see it, and therefore are unable to disapprove of it properly. How can you disapprove (or approve) of something you no longer see? If your palette of possible modes of representation has been habitually narrowed and restricted (to the edgy, the snarky, the hip, etc., etc.), if that palette has been shorn of, say, the spiritual, the ineffable, the earnest, the mysterious—of awe, wonder, humility, the truly unanswerable questions—then there isn't much hope of any real newness there. Are the very real pleasures of being an American in 2011 underrepresented in our fiction? Are the very real terrors of living in other, less functional cultures, adequately taken into account when we critique our own? If America is sick, what is the exact nature of the illness? Beyond that, are we taking as much pleasure in the sensual as we should be: in, for example, the weird ways our towns and cities have accreted, the endless interesting American geographies (a line of U-Hauls twenty feet away from the pioneer graveyard, etc., etc.)? Is there joy enough in what we're doing, because God knows, life is short, and if we don't learn, by the end, to regard all of this mess with joy, it seems to me we haven't done our work properly.

Well, speaking of things "devolving," this is now devolving into the literary equivalent of some middle-aged uncle at a party, ranting about how disappointing all of Creation has become, just in the last few years, especially that a-hole down at the parking garage. And I really don't mean the above to be anything more than a representation of the kinds of swamp I find myself wallowing in, in order to keep my writing interesting, to me and hopefully to others—more of a gut-check than a manifesto.

And of course, in the end, all of the talk notwithstanding, you go in there and write the scene, and if the icicle version is more interesting than the sincere non-icicle version, you better go with it. Our hero strides away from the Rockefeller Center chocolate shop, visions of sugar-plums dancing in his head—and then you, the writer, look to see where that earlier-mentioned Frisbee is coming from, and do your best to catch it.

George Saunders Interview

Gary Percesepe / 2012

From *New World Writing*. http://newworldwriting.net/back/summer-2012/george-saunders
-interview/. Reprinted by permission of the author.

George Saunders is the author of the essay collection *The Braindead Megaphone*, the short story collections *CivilWarLand in Bad Decline*, *Pastoralia* and *In Persuasion Nation*, the children's book *The Very Persistent Gappers of Frip*, and the novella *The Brief and Frightening Reign of Phil*. A new collection, *Tenth of December*, will be published in January 2013. In 2006, he was the recipient of a $500,000 MacArthur Fellowship, and a Guggenheim Fellowship. He teaches Creative Writing at Syracuse University.

George Saunders is what used to be called "a writer's writer." James Salter is another of my favorite writers, about whom this is often said, but there is a trace of the romantic in Salter, a persistent lyrical wistfulness that at times tips into sentimentality (do a catalogue of "light" in Salter and Cheever and you'll soon see what I mean). It's hard to accuse Saunders of excessive lyricism; his work captures the spirit of an age tipping happily toward dystopia. Saunders writes fiction for postmoderns who don't want to be caught hoping but catch themselves trying; charting his cultural targets is a syllabus of stupidity. His writing is so tight it cuts the flesh, his humor so demented it deserves its own show, his ear for techno-talk and psychobabble so keen it turns at times on the placement of a sly pronoun or participle.

Saunders renders and skews an absurdist national circus where sentences like this are possible:

"Listen to me carefully, Brad," says Doris. "Go up on the roof, install the roof platform, duct-tape the AIDS baby to the roof platform, then come directly down, borrow your butter, and go home."

And this: "A giant can of Raid gave me a snuggie," said Voltaire.

That he succeeds in making you care about these sentences and the addled denizens of the "persuasion nation" who utter them, is the miracle of fiction.

Jean Baudrillard employed the concept of the *simulacrum* (the copy without an original) to address the concept of mass reproduction and reproducibility that characterizes electronic media culture, philosophizing about history in retreat, a great trauma brought on by the decline of strong referentials, a culture traversed by currents but emptied of references—but could he have imagined the narrator of "CommComm" (perhaps Saunders's greatest short story) fielding a call from Jillian in Disasters about the Air Force poisoning a shitload of beavers, or Mr. Rimney's immediate response: "We may want to PIDS this?" Or the narrator's task: *admit, concede, explain,* and *pledge*. I'll never read this story again without thinking of Mitt Romney's Irish Setter, Seamus, strapped to the roof of the car for the trip to Toronto.

Saunders's work has been compared to Vonnegut, Orwell, Huxley, Pynchon, Beckett, Bradbury, Atwood, Swift, Twain, with a dash of Dr. Seuss. We caught up to him in Syracuse just before he set out overseas. He graciously consented to this interview.

Gary Percesepe: Mary Gaitskill once told me that for satire to work, the satirist has to have some sort of secret love or empathy for the thing she's satirizing. Do you see yourself as a satirist? Are you a moralist? How do you understand these terms?

George Saunders: I think she's absolutely right. Otherwise it's just the writer using his unfair advantage as the creator to go ahead and create a world in which the target he has in mind can be easily kicked, out of spite. Satire as I understand it is all about simultaneous love/hate. Or attraction/revulsion. It's about, I think, the miracle of love (or the miracle of the potential for love) existing in the face of aversion. We start out to blame, but praise instead, like what's his name in the Bible. Something like: if we are satirizing or mocking or calling out the defects of something via the method of paying very close attention to it, then that's an act of faith: we are conceding the possibility that we might be able to convert our (first-level) aversion into something else—or even if we can't do it, it still might, theoretically, be possible.

I've never really thought of myself as a satirist. My goals are pretty much the goals of the serious literary fiction writer. But I found out early on that for me to do that work, I had to use humor. I think this is because the world feels comic to me—not funny, necessarily, but comic, i.e., weirdly designed, given our basic human desires for love, dignity, continuity, order.

GP: Your work is filled with irony and humor, which I have always understood as distance techniques, keeping something at bay, operating at a "remove." Donald Barthelme was sometimes criticized for this by those who thought his characters suffered for it, as they were so removed we couldn't possibly care about them. Ann Beattie, another ironist, was tagged with this. In my introduction, I mentioned "Brad Carrigan, American," and "CommComm" because these stories, while uproariously funny, never feel manipulative, and the characters, while sketched incompletely, nevertheless elicit compassion. But in the arc of your work and the construction of your personal aesthetic, has this been a problem for you?

GS: Actually, for me, it was the opposite: as mentioned above, I was never able to get any real feeling into my work until I gave myself permission to—well, I wouldn't have said "to use irony and humor," exactly, at the time. What happened was, I finally admitted into my writing certain things that were always in me personally, and were in me in abundance, especially when I was feeling the world intensely: humor, yes, but also velocity, a more vernacular approach, compression, flippancy, etc., etc.

These were all natural parts of me, especially when I was feeling moved or anxious or excited or engaged—but I was badly read as a young person and so always equated "literary" with "serious," i.e., tight-assed. So [I] omitted these things from my work, at that time.

There's a kind of humor that is distancing, yes—but there's also a kind of seriousness that's distancing. If we imagine a guy who is never really present to what's actually happening because he's always cracking a joke—well, not great. But likewise: his alter ego, the guy who is never really present to what's actually happening because he is so insistent on a serious or tragic view of things, or is so fixated on being in control of his circumstances, or viewing himself as a serious person, or using high diction, or not admitting, in his fiction, that he sometimes goes to WalMart, and actually likes it, sort of, while feeling unclean: also not great.

What these guys have in common is *inattention to the actual*. They have their method and they're sticking to it. That is, distancing stems from a failure to engage, or some sort of root dishonesty: rigid humor and rigid seriousness are two sides of the same coin. I think what a reader wants is genuine engagement from a writer: that is, he wants the writer to tell the truth as she sees it, and for the form of the telling to somehow be authentic to that which is being told. The reader wants the writer to be brave enough to step away from pre-digested forms or modes, as necessary, in pursuit of beauty.

GP: What is beauty?

GS: Beauty is truth, packaged efficiently. Pithy, right? (I can almost hear you, Gary, standing there in your toga, saying: "Ah, yes, but what is truth?") Well, okay: I think truth, for artistic purposes, is that set of things that we feel deeply, or have felt deeply, but can't quite articulate, and can't quite "prove," and, the direct statement of which feels deficient. "The Overcoat" is beautiful in part, because it says, pretty bluntly: cruelty is real and sucks. But that's only part of it. Anyone can say that. It's beautiful because of the way it says it—the line-by-line progress of the story, the resistance to a too-easy illustration of the precept, the delight it takes along the way. And also, maybe, because Gogol didn't "know" that he was saying that cruelty is real and sucks—it certainly wasn't his "intention" at the outset, I don't think. That insight—and the hundreds of insights that could come from reading that story—was more like a blossom, a blossom that came out of Gogol's imagining of that world, in real time, for fun. And that is where, I think, rationality has to back politely out of the room and let Gogol do his thing.

So art—I think one reason we value art so highly is because it really is, and has to remain mysterious—in its intentions and procedures, everything. We can't talk the life out of it. Well, I mean we *can*, and often do. But we can't *get at* the life of it via talking.

We humans tend to reduce. We live through a great day, full of literally millions of perceptual instants (a beach, a love affair, a really weird old couple who mysteriously keep saying incredibly insightful things while picking off of one another bugs that aren't there; a stream, a snake under a faded sail, etc., etc.), and at the end that day, we go: "Wow, that was awesome." Art is the inversion of that process: paying hyper-attention to the things that make reality what it is, resisting reduction, trusting that the truest (and most beautiful) thing that can be said has something to do with the accretion of those small instants.

Like that famous definition of pornography: we know beauty when we see it. And this is even true as we're making it, I think, and the pisser is, we have to trust that. There will never be a definition of beauty that helps anybody make some. (And certainly not this one.)

GP: Oh, what the hell, as long as we've donned togas we may as well complete the Platonic trinity: you've spoken of the beautiful and the true, but what of "the good?" Your work clearly engages with all three, in a way that's philosophically interesting to me. And I agree that these terms, especially now, need to be approached indirectly, from the "slant side," as Emily Dickinson put it. But I notice you've not published a novel, preferring shorter forms. Is this because you're not interested, or suspicious of "the big social novel," e.g., Jonathan Franzen's *Freedom*, *The Corrections*, Updike of the Rabbits, Roth's *American Pastoral*, DeLillo's *Underworld* (to name just a few), where (mostly male) authors deliver themselves of chesty opinions, or you don't prefer that big a canvas, or you just haven't gotten around to writing a novel, your agent is insufficiently brutish, or some other reason?

GS: No, I'm not at all leery of the "big social novel." I love those novels you named (plus a bunch of other big novels) and love the idea of the big novel in general. But I just haven't found a way in yet. Flannery O'Connor said (paraphrasing), "A man can choose what he writes, but he can't choose what he makes live." And I guess to date I haven't found a way of thinking about a big novel (or for that matter even a small one) that gets me fired up. I'm working on it though.

GP: Speaking of philosophy, did I read somewhere that you were once interested in Ayn Rand's "philosophy" of "Objectivism?"

GS: Yes, I loved that book, *Atlas Shrugged*. It basically was the reason I went to college. These two high school teachers I adored gave the book to me and I fell hard for it. I think it was for two reasons. First, it really helped me out of an identity crisis—I loved the authority of it, the us vs. them aspect, the way it turned the world upside down and made selfishness a virtue and simplified life into a sort of "power is all" ethos. I liked the way all of the Good characters were also Good-Looking: it made ethics easier to parse. I liked all of that then, I think, because—well, I was a teenaged dude, who was just starting to realize he wasn't as smart as he'd always thought he was, and that he maybe should have been working a little harder at school, and was, actually, outgunned, even at the local intellectual level. The second reason was just that it was the first novel I'd read in a long time and certainly the longest and most "intellectual" one I'd ever read. So that immersion experience was powerful. All of the usual novelistic charms kicked in: I felt I was there, I wanted to be there, the world presented in 3-D, etc., etc.

So then I went to engineering school and met a lot of other people who loved that book, also for weird reasons (mostly something like: "Ugh, those environmentalists are just like (NAME ANY REPREHENSIBLE SNIVELING CHARACTER FROM RAND BOOK)." For me, the last straw was going to work in Asia after college and seeing firsthand that there were good people who were working much harder than anyone I'd ever met and yet still living in abject poverty, and their teeth were rotten and their kids were dying, and it had nothing, apparently, to do with any sort of moral failing on their parts or any desire to rob the rich of their fairly gotten gains or anything like that. It just seemed like *luck*—that they were born there and I was born where I was born. And at that time all of my childhood Catholic teachings came back, and I saw that these people, these Asian people (who were unfailingly nice to me, while struggling against a system they'd never made, while I was walking around in my pocket with twenty times what they would earn over the next ten years) were the meek that the Bible said were blessed—and I left Ayn behind.

GP: How did you develop your ear as a writer, and your distinctive voice? What were your reading and viewing habits growing up?

GS: I read a lot of books about baseball and World War II fighter pilots and so on, and watched a lot of TV. I especially loved comics like Jonathan Winters, Robin Williams, Steve Martin, George Carlin, Monty Python—intelligent, language-based, joyful.

Also, my humor has a lot to do with having grown up in Chicago—there's a certain South Side style of discourse, which is satirical and abrupt and insulting but also overflowing with tenderness and feeling.

GP: "CivilWarLand in Bad Decline," the title story of your first collection, puts me in mind of Baudrillard's *Simulacra and Simulation*, where he writes, of another amusement park: "Disneyland is presented as imaginary in order to make us believe that the rest is real, whereas all of Los Angeles and the America that surrounds it are no longer real, but belong to the hyperreal order and to the order of simulation. It is no longer a question of a false representation of reality (ideology) but of concealing the fact that the real is no longer real . . . [T]he imaginary of Disneyland is neither true or false, it is a deterrence machine set up in order to rejuvenate the fiction of the real in the opposite camp."

GS: Well, I don't know. This quote feels a little over-conceptual to me. Did Disney, when he was designing Disneyland, do so "in order to make us believe that the rest is real, etc., etc.?" I don't think so. I think he was having fun and trying to make some money and do something that was, by his lights, great. Now, his definition of "great" was a very American definition: clean, supersized, hygienic, divested of the naughty bits, safe for all, mad idealized, let's say. But my guess is, he was just thinking: God, this will be so *cool*. Likewise: "Los Angeles and the America that surrounds it are no longer real." Ha. Try walking across them.

What interests me is this: when Disney, a great American genius, decided to make a simulacrum of America, what did he do? He *edited* it. In what direction? In the direction of nostalgia. In the direction of perfection. In his French Quarter, there are no washed-up junkie jazz musicians panhandling. Why not? That's interesting to me—that his fantasy erred on the side of the clean/perfect/tidy. I've sometimes had the thought that, for someone like Disney, who grew up (I believe) rural and poorish—and maybe for his whole generation, just removed from the farm, and hardscrabble paucity, with WWI still in memory—a world free of sweat and labor and dirt and grime must have seemed like heaven.

I mean—this is what Baudrillard is getting at, I think: our American desire to eliminate the nasty or "actual" (which is a form of retreating from poverty(?)) has become a national obsession, and has had the effect of negating the personal, or the intimate. Maybe. But I don't know. Maybe what's required here is a wider version of what's "real." LA not "real"? I have to say I don't buy the hankering after so-called authenticity evident in the Baudrillard quote. What is, is real. When were things "realer" than they are now, and how could that be? Whatever LA is, it's real. I mean, even if something is hyper-stylized, cosmetically enhanced, all glass, fake, fake, fake: there it is, evidence of some human tendency or aspiration or desire. It's real.

I think there's something deep and interesting about this theming impulse—which is not just American and not just contemporary (think, for example, of the elaborate spectacles in the Coliseum—mock naval battles and Gardens of Edens with real lions, etc., etc.). It seems to me this theming is sort of a celebration—a celebration of the original on which the themed thing is based. The American twist, I think, as mentioned above, is that our theme parks don't really try to be "real." They try to be cleaner, less complicated versions of the things they represent. Why? I think this may have something to do with the American tendency towards (what we call) "optimism"—the idea that all is well, and that any indication that things might not be well equals negativity/cynicism—a tendency which sometimes presents as radical rewritings of history ("and civilization was thus spread across the Great Plains, replacing the savagery that had previously reigned") and also radical rewritings of now ("a concerted effort against terrorism is going to unfortunately from time to time involve losses and damages, in terms of non-enlisted entities and or liberties, that will be, in the end, seen as regrettable but necessary") and sometimes presents as, you know, the "Great Mining Train Adventure!!" or what-not.

GP: Speaking of LA, not long ago I visited the Getty Villa in Malibu, where various statutory "muses" from antiquity are on display. And it set me to wondering, again, about modern artists and muses. Do you have (a) muse(es)?

GS: Hmm. Well, in a very literal way, yes: my wife. I've always, since the first moment I met her, really wanted to impress her. And she has very high standards and great taste, especially in writing, and especially in the way that she will not tolerate bullshit, and very much values a piece of writing that is really trying to say something important—she has little patience with the merely literary. So when I'm writing she is always in my mind. I am always hoping that what I write will move her.

In a larger sense, I think people write better when they're happy. (Allowing for a broad definition of "happy.") Maybe "feeling exultant" would be a better way of saying it. So for someone to have some idea, or person, in mind that makes them feel exultant: helpful. Or that feeling we get when someone is making us feel exultant—that feeling of anticipation of wonderful things and places in our future?—that's a good feeling to work from, I think. I sometimes get a feeling, when I'm working, that what I'm working on will somehow expand my life, expand my circle of influence and influences, break me out of myself—all good, I think.

GP: Do you watch a lot of TV? *Mad Men*? Reading *In Persuasion Nation*, I wondered what your thoughts were about the Don Draper character, who is given to such pronouncements as, "Advertising is based on one thing, happiness. And you know what happiness is? Happiness is the smell of a new car. It's freedom from fear. It's a billboard on the side of the road that screams reassurance that whatever you are doing is okay. You are okay." And, "What you call love was invented by guys like me, to sell nylons. You're born alone and you die alone and this world just drops a bunch of rules on top of you to make you forget those facts. But I never forget. I'm living like there's no tomorrow, because there isn't one."

Draper operates on the assumption that people *want* to be led, they *want* to be persuaded. Someone might as well do it, and be paid handsomely. Which is why he says, "Just so you know, the people who talk that way think that monkeys can do this. They take all this monkey crap and just stick it in a briefcase completely unaware that their success depends on something more than their shoeshine. *You* are the product. You—*feeling* something. That's what sells. Not them. Not sex. They can't do what we do, and they hate us for it."

GS: To me, advertising is just a slight corruption or utilization of our human desire for beauty (or sex/glamour/adventure, whatever). People want to be charmed and want to be involved in beautiful things. I'm not, maybe, as against advertising as some of my work might suggest. I just see it as this thing that humans do—a form of creation. It's false at its heart and will stop at nothing, true. But it's also sort of like one set of birds calling out to another: Come see my nest! (If, that is, the other birds had to pay to see the nest. Hmm.)

The thing is—I know advertising, from the hours of TV I've watched. It's something I can "do." Unlike, say, nature description. So that's one reason there's so much of it in my work: I can do it. I can make a surface out of the stuff of advertising.

As far as Don Draper—he's a great character. But if we want to think about actual advertising people, I don't know . . . I always like to move my gaze to the way things might work in the real world. Who does advertising? I think they're generally talented, creative people who decided, at some point, that it's better to do something you're good at than to be a mediocrity. And I get that. (You can make a case that fiction is a force for good in the world, but if somebody could prove otherwise, would I quit? Hope so. Doubt it.) And then they say: Well, let's do this job as honestly and well as we can. And they put all of their urge-to-create and their sense of beauty and their wit into their work, and hence ads get more and more astonishing and convincing all the time, and encroach upon (or encompass) areas that are harder and harder for us viewers to wiggle out of or dismiss. So we get ads that sell products AND funnel money to AIDS research. Or ads that use amazing cinematic techniques and so you find yourself crying during a frigging Hefty Bag ad.

At this stage of life, I just find it all kind of wonderful: a crazy-ass display that I'm happy to alternately despise/satirize/expose and then enjoy/celebrate/ wallow in.

GP: Please tell me that Rimney in "CommComm" is not Romney. Or Rumsfeld.

GS: He's not. Just liked the sound of the name.

GP: MFA programs have been known to teach students not to employ brand names in fiction. You obviously don't agree with that advice. What other "writerly advice" don't you agree with, and, more positively, how would you describe your philosophy of teaching, particularly when "work-shopping" stories? And how do you respond when someone asks you, in a skeptical voice, "Can writing be taught?"

GS: I don't agree with that advice, no. Whenever [someone] says "never do that," someone should try it right away. The game is: know rules, flout same.

There's this wonderful book I just read in galleys (*Mr. Penumbra's 24-Hour Bookstore*) that directly flies in the face of this "no product name" advice—Google is in there, the actual campus, and all kinds of other companies and products, some real, some invented. I had a great time reading it, flew through it in one sitting, in fact. The book has a wonderful undeniability: the reader gets that deeply satisfying feeling of entering a wholly created world, and looking on in wonder as that world gets created by the author's fearlessness and disregard for convention. It's a beautiful fable that is given legs by the author's bravado use of the real to sell us on a shadow world of the unreal/speculative. The writer (Robin Sloan) comes across as so big-hearted, so in love with the world—the ancient world, the contemporary world, the hi-tech world, the world of yellowing scrolls, in love with love, in love with friendship, you name it—and the reader is swept along by his positive enthusiasm, by his authorial courage, and feels the inclusion of this real stuff to be essential to the velocity and the emotional content of the book, in other words. It's a lot of fun, a real tour de force, and what's particularly amazing about it is the absence of cynicism. Sloan likes technology, he thinks Google is amazing, and then he shows how and why Google is amazing; he thinks our technical abilities can serve as conduits for beauty, and shows this—but also shows the flip-side, i.e., how these superpowers, like all superpowers, have the potential for getting too big for their britches and going awry.

Now—could he have done it without using Google? Probably. But there was something ballsy and insiderish and convincing about using the real thing instead of a stand-in that definitely made for a more powerful reading experience.

So in other words, rules/shmules.

One of the things I was enjoying about the book was the way Sloan set this almost Harry Potteresque adventure against a very real and contemporary backdrop (techie San Francisco) without batting an eye. I was enjoying his boldness and his unself-conscious immersion in his story, in other words.

Can writing be taught? I don't know, but the thing is, at the MFA level, in a place like Syracuse, you don't have to teach it. This year we got 520 applications for six spots, so the people we accepted are way past the point of needing to "learn to write." We can mentor people, and give them time and money, and the occasional encouraging or focusing word—and that's all it takes.

The thing about teaching/mentoring writing is, you just have to refuse to coast. Never lean back on your accrued dogma. See this new group (so much younger than you!) as valid, explosive, wonderful—and honor them accordingly.

GP: Meg Wolitzer wrote a piece for the *New York Times* recently, titled "The Second Shelf: On the Rules of Literary Fiction for Men and Women," where she laments the fact that many first rate books by and about women go directly to "the women's shelf" and never make it to the top shelf where certain books, most of them written by men, are prominently displayed and admired. Meg cites statistics compiled by VIDA, a women's literary organization, showing that women get shockingly short shrift as reviewers and reviewees in most prestigious publications (e.g., of all the authors reviewed in the publications VIDA tracked, nearly three-fourths were men). She concludes that women writers are still fighting to have their work taken seriously and accorded as much coverage as men's. The unfairness of this "system" is striking, especially when one considers that the vast majority of people reading literary fiction—and of writers applying to MFA programs and attending writing conferences—are women. What are your thoughts on this, generally? And specifically, in regard to your own work, I am wondering about how you approach writing characters who are women, and the role(s) of women in your work?

GS: I hadn't read that article but I'm glad I did, just now.

Well, the former scientist in me gets all jangly. Like: let's do a study! Why are three-quarters of the reviewers men? Is this a defect in the process of approaching potential reviewers, i.e., are mostly men approached? Are there fewer women interested in writing reviews? If so, why is this? And so on. Suffice it to say there is clearly a problem and I, like everyone else, apparently, can't quite put my finger on the cause. But this kind of shot-across-the-bow article is a great thing to do, a vital kind of activism (or a great thing to keep doing: sadly, I've been reading pieces in this spirit for as long as I've been writing, i.e., since the mid-1980s).

As far as women in my work—honestly, I find that production happens in a zone where I am not thinking quite rationally. If I go into a piece thinking: Hey, let's make sure and be fair to the women (or the men, or the kids, or the Bolivians, whatever), that skews the whole thing. That is, my goal is never accurate representation anyway. I try to go in thinking: Be fair to everyone, *in the final analysis*. Or: Make the moral compass here such that it would be acceptable to a just and loving God, who is also pretty patient with naughtiness. So there are crummy women in my stories and crummy men, caricatures abounding, assholes of both genders, cliché male and female archetypes, etc., etc. I really don't care. I don't like any constraint, self- or otherwise, when I'm working, and so I just trust that, if I write and rewrite like crazy, any surficial bias or cheap humor will either vanish or, in the end, be doing good work. I think you have to keep your eye on the work the story does as a whole—the *fairness work* that results at the end, if I could say it that way.

I've often thought that all of the horrible systemic injustices mankind has invented—sexism, racism of all sorts, homophobia, regional genocides, you name it—are best understood and diagnosed and fought as manifestations of a greater spiritual glitch—a design flaw, maybe. Take three people, let there be even the slightest difference between them, and soon two of them are going to be kicking around the third. Why is this? I'd say—and to really get at this would require another thousand pages of typing, and it's a beautiful summer day up here in the Catskills, and we have a new puppy—but I'd say it's because each of those three individuals is too convinced he/she is real and central to the universe. As soon as we think that, we start finding differences between us and others and preferring whatever it is we have that they don't. And we start grouping and generalizing and conceptualizing in order to maintain our advantage—to uphold that initial delusion of self-eminence.

GP: You've been compared to so many writers: Vonnegut, Orwell, Huxley, Pynchon, Beckett, Swift, Twain, Bradbury, Atwood, David Foster Wallace. Which comparison seems most apt, which least persuasive?

GS: Ah, I don't know. I'd take any of the above. I feel a little like the Steve Martin character in *The Jerk*, where he says, with respect to the possibility of watching the Bernadette Peters character make love to her boyfriend, "I just want to be in there somewhere."

GP: Was Donald Barthelme an influence for you?

GS: He was, although early on I wasn't reading him correctly. I was admitted to Houston when he was there but didn't go. I think, at that time, I felt about his work a little like you described it above—I was misreading him, being young and stupid and sentimental, and wasn't able to feel how full of emotion and longing all that crazed language is. I feel it now, though.

But you know, if I was going to be honest about literary influences, they were and are mostly realists. I'm just genuinely down with the realist agenda: making emotional power via the invocation of the real. The problem is, when I try to do it, it doesn't work. So to generate emotional power I have to use a different bag of tricks. Or another way of saying it: I have to abandon the so-called consensus view of reality in order to get at the emotional reality underneath it, maybe? I believe that fiction is about real human experience, and about emotion, but have found that I can only get at any sort of power if I let go of the idea that the fictive surface should resemble "the real." To get at the deep stuff I have to make a strange surface.

Which, I suppose, makes sense: life, as it is lived and as we feel it, is strange, deeply strange, and the only reason we don't feel it that way is because we habitually normalize it. That's necessary, that's sane—but it's also only partially "representative" of what actually is.

GP: Who is your ideal reader, or is there such a thing?

GS: Someone who has just gotten some really good news and is in the middle of an orgasm.

GP: What frightens you most in America today, and what brings you the greatest pleasure?

GS: What frightens me is that we are becoming a very materialist, literal group of people: always taking the straight, logical line between points. We feel that mystery, difficulty, the inarticulable are for babies, etc., etc.

What brings me the greatest pleasure is the way that, corny as it sounds, people tend to be pretty kind to one another, or at least try to be. Obviously, they aren't, always. But I've enjoyed finding out that, if you proceed as if most people you meet are generally like you, in their desire to be and do good, you won't be disappointed all that often. Well, unless you're in a war zone, I guess. Or it's a depression or the apocalypse or something. Or it's Germany in 1933. Or you're gay and it's 1971 and you're in Kansas.

GP: What is the most important thing for a writer?

GS: Hmm. I guess it would depend which one we're discussing. I mean, in general, I think a tank-like refusal to quit is pretty useful. Or a perennial hope that current difficulties will lead to beauty down the line. Engagement? A willingness to step into any reality and go: Ah, so this is how it is, right here and right now: excellent.

GP: Marx, Nietzsche, and Freud, whom Paul Ricoeur called the modern "masters of suspicion," taught us to look away from religious belief as evidential (that is, whether or not these beliefs could be "proved"), and to focus instead on "what work does religious belief do in the world," or more pointedly, "how do religious beliefs function as masks to disguise and advance self-interest." What is the function of religious belief in your stories, your version of a spirituality adequate to the times, and how did this govern your employment of terms like "Christ-portion" and "light-craving" in "CommComm?"

GS: Well, sounds like Marx, Nietzsche, and Freud had it all figured out. And yet, where are they now? Ha ha ha. No: I think a spiritual approach to life just means that you are smart enough to negate the idea that everything you know at this moment just happens to be everything there is to know in the universe. Wouldn't that be weird? If our generation just happened to be the one alive when our intuitive, sensory-based understanding of how things work was EXACTLY right?

A human being is exactly: a fish out of water. There is limited time, the situation is unsustainable, just lying there is not an option. So if the fish goes: Ha, you religious weirdos, what are you getting so frantic about?—he seems . . . dopey. Self-satisfied. Doomed.

There's this incredible place in one of Freud's books where he's talking about Eastern mysticism and says something like, you know: Now, it is said that certain practitioners can alter the state of their minds, and thus alter their perception of reality—but we do not need to concern ourselves with this at this time.

Doh.

My feeling is, Freud missed the most interesting exit ramp there.

What we know: we're going to die and are not ready to die, because we like it here too much and are too fond of ourselves and our loved ones. If we look to the known and common-sensical world, there's not much help being offered. It mostly says: get yours. Be a success. Or, as Dr. Seuss said it: "Fame! You'll be famous as famous can be. With the whole wide world watching you win on TV!" But anyone who's lived and/or succeeded and/or failed at all can see that this is a dead end. As much as we win, we are going to be in for a big shock on our last day, if not before it, via bad luck or ill fortune etc., etc.

So what are we waiting for? I'd define "the religious" as: "that field of inquiry that ardently seeks to know that beyond which we lazily know."

So I like: "focus . . . on 'what work does religious belief do in the world,'" but find "how do religious beliefs function as masks to disguise and advance self-interest," a little dismissive.

I'd say: religious beliefs, at their best, are a series of complex metaphors that are so accurate they cease to be metaphors. If having religious beliefs, and pursuing religious practices, and thinking in religious metaphors, has the effect of transforming the individual and moving him towards more presence and more kindness and more openness—than the distinction between the real and the metaphorical has dissolved.

GP: I read where you once said, "The number of rooms in a fictional house should be inversely proportional to the years during which the couple living in that house enjoyed true happiness." Please unpack this comment, with constant reference to Tolstoy. And thanks for spending time with us today at BLIP.

GS: Yes, that was a joke. A joke meant to undercut the idea that writing dictums are any damn good. Writing dictums are the equivalent of replacing the tightwire with a wide plank: a lazy man's approach. Safer, but less thrilling.

My pleasure, and thanks for asking me. Great questions . . .

Real as Hell

A Conversation with George Saunders

Maria Bustillos / 2013

From theawl.com, February 19, 2013. https://www.theawl.com/2013/02/real-as-hell-a
-conversation-with-george-saunders/. Reprinted by permission of the author.

While interviewing author George Saunders last week on the release of the
audiobook of his new story collection, *Tenth of December*, my Skype connection cut out maybe four times. Such a miserable and embarrassing development on so many levels—maybe the worst being that Saunders is one
of the best talkers I've ever met, and in the middle of this incredible riff his
voice would just float and burble off, culminating in that awful, plopping
Skype disconnection sound. Indescribable, like getting a long letter from
Oscar Wilde and someone sets fire to it as you're reading, or you've just
been poured a delectable glass of Château d'Yquem and suddenly there is a
massive earthquake and it's splashing all over the place.

Manfully resisting the urge to hurl my laptop across the room and stomp
on it screaming until it was a pile of shards, I reestablished our phone connection, gave up on making a Skype recording, and resorted to taking notes
for the last part of our talk. Which turned out to be a blessing in (a very,
very good) disguise, because Saunders most graciously agreed to proof the
results of my notetaking over email. What revelations came then!

I try to be very careful about transcribing interviews into text as I go, thinking over stuff like, well, was that a dash? Or was it maybe a semicolon? So
when I sent along the transcript of our talk, part of it was as faithful a recording of the author's speech as I could make, and the rest the sketched-in notes.
Which came back shortly thereafter—marked up, edited, augmented, with
comments. And thus it was that I learned a great deal about George Saunders's working methods not only from the conversation that follows, but

from its eventual documentation. There was careful, very careful rephrasing of line after line. He had his own ideas about certain exclamation points, ellipses, commas. In fact, this amiable perfectionist thought one of my questions could use a little tweaking. The author is famous for reworking his pieces over and over, sometimes taking years to finish a story. And even in this interview, one of dozens he's had to conduct in recent weeks, the layering-up of his attention resulted in a document of far, far greater richness and clarity than the original.

And another thing: he's a two-spaces-after-the-period man.

Maria Bustillos: This audiobook is just GREAT.

George Saunders: Oh, thank you so much.

MB: You went around saying in interviews, though, that you can only do like four voices? What a fibber! You're like a cast of thousands, in this thing.

I was already a terrific fan of your title story, "Tenth of December." But for me, "Victory Lap" was hugely improved by being read aloud, while I think I maybe preferred reading "Tenth of December" to myself? Just a little bit, but I thought, why should that be? Maybe it's more internal of a story? Do you feel, yourself, that some of your pieces read out loud are better, and others read to oneself?

GS: It might also be—this is maybe sort of mundane, but I've read "Victory Lap" a lot, over the last year or two; when I go out and do a big reading, I'll read that one. So I've kind of got it down a little bit, the rhythms and stuff. I think, "Tenth of December," I read it once for the *New Yorker*, and the audiobook would only have been the second time I ever read it.

So I have a feeling I—for example, I have no idea how to do that little boy in "Tenth of December"; I've never quite stumbled on the right way to do him. So it might just be, if I did it a bit more, I would—

MB: Oh, that's so interesting! Because you really are able to voice—for example, Alison [a fifteen-year-old girl], it's amazing to me how evocative your reading is.

GS: It's a little spooky for me. It's almost like, when I was writing those stories, I could sort of "hear" a voice in my head, and then channel it down. But the voice I can hear is much more subtle than the one I can actually perform. So as I read it out loud over and over, it's as if I'm working my way back to being able to do that Platonic version. But because I'm not an actor, I never quite get it exactly; she reads a little more broadly to me when I read it out loud. And you get more laughs that way, but I think maybe she becomes a bit more cartoonish in the out-loud reading—she's a little more of a space cadet. Whereas when I was writing it, I felt she was pretty bright, and I don't really disagree with the things she says.

MB: Oh, no! Nor do I. ("Egads!"—I love how she talks.)

GS: Reading is a totally different skill set. Performing your stories is kind of a plus, it's helpful, because the gigs are, you know, reading. But what if Henry James had had to go to Barnes & Noble, you know, that would be . . . a little hard to take, maybe—but it's still great writing.

MB: I was completely zero surprised to hear that you have daughters; there's that moment, so specific, where they're on this really magnificent sort of knife-edge between childhood, and being really snarkily dismissive with their sort of sexual power at the same time.

GS: Yeah, it's interesting.

MB: Isn't it? But like, Alison and Kyle had been friends earlier, I thought, because they BOTH would say "Egads!"

GS: Right, right. That's exactly right. But I always felt that that "Egads!" kind of snuck out of her; if she was out in public she wouldn't have been saying that. Not at this stage of her life. She's de-nerdifying herself. It's funny . . . you know, I don't really, um . . . on that story, the honest truth is she's more *me* at fifteen than she is my daughters. My daughters, for me, are sort of sacred, roped-off, I would never really want to write about them. Because my writing—tends to be kind of cartoonish, I would never make an attempt to depict someone I loved. So with her, I was really thinking about me at that age. And that was *so* much me, like that kind of slightly arrogant optimist, like—"Oh! People have always had trouble in this world—those poor idiots! Why don't they just do it *right*?" That kind of feeling.

MB: My husband's famous phrase to describe the worldview of a kid. "How could anyone possibly object to *me*?"

GS: [*laughter*] "I'm here! Don't you *see*?" I think that's deep. We think of kids as being kind of dumb, you know; they're inarticulate and they don't know how to start a car, and so on. But when I think back to being five or six, I can remember a fully formed human consciousness that was very sophisticated, and very judgmental and very egotistical.

MB: Oh man, I'm right with you.

GS:—and very discerning. But I suppose, you know . . . at that age, you can't speak it, but I remember being very . . . complex. Like when Kennedy was killed, it was 1963, so I would have been about four. And I have a really distinct memory of standing in the driveway, and this friend of my mom's came *flying* by, distraught, and I remember being very offended that she didn't say hello. I was like, "Who do you think you are?! You just went right past me, madam!" And I went upstairs and they had turned the TV on and were crying, and I just remember my reaction was: "Who's *this* dude, 'Kennedy,' who's usurping all my attention?! Like, *Mom*? Hello?!"

MB: And then you're capable of being overtaken by really, really serious emotions, but you have no defenses against them.

GS: That's right, they just come on you like a storm, and you don't know what to do with all of that. So I'm interested in that. In those internal monologue things, I'm trying to take away the overlay, the habitual way we think about thinking, and just say, wow, if you could really drop into a human mind at any moment—look what's actually going on in there, it's crazy shit!—it's multi-level, layered, and confusing and contradictory, and poetic and all that kind of thing.

MB: I love the tension in your stuff between innocence and experience. So much seems to kind of hinge on that, between recovering the innocence of adults, and children losing it? Kyle—this is one of the great crescendos in literature, for me. When he's running, it's so good—I'm sorry, I'm just such a superfan, so this interview is going to sound really idiotic.

GS: I'm loving it so far. Keep going. I'll just every so often go "uh huh" as you praise me.

MB: Okay but I have real questions too! I do. Talk to me about Catholicism.

GS: Okay. Are you Catholic?

MB: Cradle Catholic, yeah. Utterly lapsed, but there you go.

GS: Right. Well, for a lot of years I played it for laughs, you know, like the "inner nun" and all of that. But recently I was thinking about the Stations of the Cross, a lot. Did you do those, as a kid?

MB: Yes.

GS: I was thinking about how profound that is, as a fictive exercise. As I remember it, you sit there, and there's a little bit of a reading from the Gospels, talking about the scene, and in our church they were these kind of highly seventies-stylized pictures of the different stations. And I kind of remember being encouraged by the nuns to visualize and to think: "Okay, what's Jesus thinking? What's Mary thinking?" And even: "What are the Romans thinking?" So, that was deep. To be sitting there trying to imagine what the murderous Centurion was thinking as Jesus stumbled past . . .

I think as I become older, I'm becoming more and more grateful for that rigid Catholic background, on a lot of levels. The language training was terrific—the English stuff was great. We diagrammed sentences and that whole thing. But also in Chicago when I was growing up in the seventies, there was a lot of that kind of Dorothy Day activist component going on, and at the time I thought it was the coolest religion, because, compared to my perception of the Protestant church, it was so in the world, on its feet and sort of activist. It was all about Jesus as an advocate for change. I loved it; and I had a couple of really deep experiences in church that were—one in particular where I just had this—I can't really even articulate it, but it was just this profound feeling of connection with the lineage of the Apostles, and so on, just real as hell, and also the feeling . . . this fear that that heightened feeling would fade. Which, of course, it did. That night we went to dinner at a friend's house, and I could feel that feeling waning, and it felt bad, because I was just in this incredible zone where I thought: Wow, now I know how to live the rest of my life; and it was like, living for others, and living in a state of love, and I just felt it like a total buzz; and then it started to drift away, and I lost that feeling. And that really was a sad thing. I remember my friend and I were playing this board game called *All-Star Baseball* or something like that, and part of me knew I had to be a regular kid, and play the game, but with each turn I could feel that exalted feeling diminishing more and more . . .

I don't know if I'm answering your question.

MB: Well, yeah, obviously, I want to hear all this! And I had this other thought about it . . . when I first read your work, it was strange, I don't know why I thought this, but I thought: this guy grew up Catholic. Right away. And I thought, well, why do you think that?

Also: I went to public school, where we also learned to play religion for laughs all the way. We used to rib each other mercilessly. Kids from all these different backgrounds, there was no other way to deal with it.

GS: Did you call them "publics"? In the Catholic schools we used to say, very sorrowfully, or disdainfully: "Oh she's a *public.*"

MB: No, we didn't have that! I never went to Catholic school. But I went to Sunday school and was about to be confirmed, when I finally quit. I'd asked whatever nun, what the heck, I mean, what if you're from China? And you've never heard of this ever, and you've lived a perfectly blameless life? And she goes, "There's a special place for them."

GS: Yeah: Hell! A *really* special place.

But I loved growing up Catholic. There was something so powerful about the way they respected metaphor, and all of the symbols, and the incense and so on. They expected you to understand that there are truths that are not overt, but implied, and that the best way to imply that kind of truth is through metaphor and ritual. I think that once you get immersed in that kind of beauty, and really feel it, even once, you will always be looking for

that. Which is maybe where art comes in later. There was some kind of correspondence between the early, sort of sublingual kind of magic in Catholicism, and the desire to kind of get back into that space.

MB: I felt this too.

Another thing: guilt! You have a lot of guilt in your work, and it seems to
me to be of a very Catholic flavor. What is that?

GS: Well, I think my guilt kind of predates my Catholicism. It's like birth-
guilt or something. I think the Catholics picked up that preexisting guilt in
me and sort of super-charged it—but it was already there. I have really early
memories of feeling inadequate: arrogant, and inadequate at the same time;
I think that's neurological maybe, I don't think there's any . . . I don't know.
But I've always felt not quite up to the task. The task of living, you know. So
I always felt a lot of real fondness for life, and a kind of enthusiasm for people, somehow linked with the feeling that I wasn't quite good enough to be
at the party. So you add those things together, it equals a desire to achieve
something. I felt like: if only I can DO something, I'll be worthy of all of these
people and all of this beauty. Not exactly, uh, a high-functioning mental attitude. But there it is. So I know better, but that's how it felt to me, always.

MB: Do you think there's such a thing as "Catholic guilt"?

GS: Yeah, it's taught, certainly. At our school, when you did something
wrong, there was a vague sense of, "Oh yeah, you *would* do that." Plus,
Christ died for your sins. But *guilt* . . . my sense is that it has a lot to do with
that other set of delusions that we are born with. The delusion of your own
permanence, the delusion of your own centrality. So if a person says, I'm
here, I'm born, I'm three or four, I am the center of the universe; everybody
is here for my amusement . . . Well, that is an intensely egotistical position,
and there's a backlash for it. The guilt might be sort of the backside of that.
If you're responsible for all reality—well? That's a lot to take on.

Also, guilt is funny, comical. Guilt is ego, actually, when you think of it.
If I'm at a party with you and I'm trying to be clever, and I say something
hurtful and afterward I feel guilty about it, in a way that presupposes that
I should be so in control that I would never make a mistake—that's ego.
The thought that I—I, so perfect and above reproach—would never make a
human blunder. Which is—you know, that's very egotistical, to understand
yourself as He Who Never Blunders.

MB: Maybe guilt is also: I could have done better. I am, or I want to be,
better than this.

GS: So I suppose a preferable moral position would be (1) make the mistake, (2) go: Oh, I see, interesting, this person that is "me" just made a mistake,

(3) very calmly assess, to see why that happened, and (4) adjust as necessary. That would be sort of the ego-free version. Me, I tend to get stuck at (1), and then a modified (2), which is: You big idiot, how could you do that, you suck.

MB: Ah. Yes, eek, I'm familiar. Though in the Saunders universe, the world of your books, everybody is constantly aware of his capacity to blunder.

GS: Yes. As is the case in my head.

MB: That's what I love about it so much; there's such a lack of that in fiction, where people generally are chugging smoothly along on the preordained paths of their intentions, fulfilling a "role."

GS: Hmm. Right. I don't know how other people's minds feel to them, but to me . . . I'm really aware of all of those funny little micromoves we do in our heads—the little swellings of pomposity, the crazy unlikely mini-fantasies ("And then President Obama calls me, and asks me to write a speech . . .") And my working assumption is that, if I put those things into a story, the reader will rise to the—will go, "Aiyee, I do that too." And then . . . we're more connected. So when I put those things in, it's sort of a rhetorical moving in the direction of assuming that everybody's shit is basically the same. Our minds basically—basically—do similar things, in a given situation. So that is the basis for that effect in fiction, where someone from another time, long dead, rings your bell from afar.

If the two of us go to a real fancy party, I am probably correct in assuming that the two of us feel basically the same about it (of course, with some variations). So a lot of comedy comes from that. Somehow this also brings to mind the joke about if there are two people in an elevator and somebody farts, everybody knows who did it. What's funny about that is that little instant where farter and non-farter are on the same page, so to speak. So I love the fictive equivalent of that—that willingness to look at the minutiae, that maybe your prideful self would have you look past. To be aware of all of the little mind-blips and hesitations and so on—that is really the root of the comic, for me. To let out into the open those things that we normally edit out in the re-telling—even if we are only re-telling it to ourselves.

When I was younger, all my heroes were very Hemingwayesque, and aloof and powerful and in control. They knew what they thought, and did what that thinking told them to do, and so on. And then at one point you get a sense of the disconnect between the way you're actually functioning in the world, and the way your characters are moving around, with trench coats, and attaché cases and perfect haircuts . . .

MB: Which is fun, though!

GS: Trench coats and so on are totally fun, yes. As were—you know—stories about fishing trips or stories where no one actually worked and so on. But in my case they started to feel so false—such a betrayal of what life really felt like, both out in the world and inside my mind. So at some point I think the youngish writer has to make a choice: either continue to inhabit the world of his masters, where he is always going to feel like an imposter, or go down (and it really felt like down to me) to his own fictive world, come what may. In class I do this drawing of this big mountain, that I call Hemingway Mountain. And talk about how, early in my writing life, I just wanted to be up there near the top. And then I realized: Shit, even if I made it to the top, I'd still be a Hemingway Imitator. So then you trudge back down—and look, there's Kerouac Mountain! Hooray. And then it's rinse, lather, and repeat—until the day comes when you've completely burned yourself out on that, and you see this little dung heap with your name on it, and go: Oh, all right, I'll take that—better to be minor and myself. So that is painful. Especially at first. But it's also spiritual, in a sense—it's *honest*, you know. It's a good thing to say: Let's look at the world as it is, as opposed to the way I'd like it to be. Let's see how the world seems to me—as opposed to the way it seems to me, filtered through the voice of Hemingway (or Faulkner or Toni Morrison or Bukowski—whoever).

MB: Yeah, wow.

[Long pause (also, on the part of the interviewer, a little vertigo).]

Hmm.

Can we talk about Syracuse? [That is, the graduate writing program where Saunders is a teacher.]

GS: Sure.

MB: So you were saying there are 600 applications, to choose six people, in your program.

GS: 566 this year. Actually I am supposed to be doing that this afternoon.

MB: So tell me, what makes someone one of those six, for you?

GS: It's really a weird process. I don't think we've ever been able to articulate it, but it's maybe like that old definition of porn: you kind of know it when you see it. The weird thing is, we'll have usually four of us, reading. And when we get together at the end, we always agree on the top ten. For sure. Maybe when we go to six, then there's a little quibble. But I think making it into that top six has something to do with an eagerness, and a willingness, to communicate directly with the reader. The person really comes through, and there's an openness and an understanding that what she is about, is communicating something urgent to another intelligent person. On the other side—the people who don't make it in . . . maybe we can feel that they aren't so interested in communicating, but more in *impressing*. It's hard to generalize—there are so many applications and generally so, so good. Last year we agreed that we could have gone as deep as #75 or so and still been VERY happy to work with those people.

You read thirty or forty applications, and go, "Maybe, maybe, I dunno" . . . and then someone comes along and you go, Ooh HERE'S a human being. An urgent, human voice. And that's very exciting. Other problems, like with structure, you can work with those. But there's not a lot of debating among us, generally; the cream really does rise to the top. On the one hand it's a lot of work—you dread it—but on the other it rewires you, makes you see again as a reader.

It wouldn't be ethical, but it would be so great if our current students could read that pile; there are so many commonplace moves in fiction. If you could learn about those in advance, you could sort of veer away from them. You know, the things that we all habitually do as writers. And that, reading at that volume, your eye tends to race past.

MB: When interviewers have discussed your own originality, you've sometimes commented on that as maybe having to do with a lack of training as a writer. And yet later, you got all the training, and now you teach. And all that's happened is you've gotten better and better: so?

GS: It wasn't so much that I wasn't trained, but that I was coming into writing from a weird angle. I had the engineering background and wasn't very well read in postmodernism and came at fiction from a very traditionally realist, Steinbeck-Hemingway-Thomas Wolfe place. So it was like if you learned to hit a baseball without ever seeing a professional swing. There was a sort of functionality in what I was doing but it always—still does—look a little odd. This unusual quality, that I feel like I picked up from coming at writing from a weird place—it helped, but also maybe hurt? Because, for instance, when I came to Syracuse I hadn't had the experience of reading dozens of novels, and that might be why I haven't written one. I think if you read a lot and well as a young person, that loads you up with a sort of deep knowledge that is very helpful, and makes you confident—I feel like that's maybe what I'm missing—that feeling that would come from having engaged deeply with newer novels, when I was a young guy, coached by people who really knew that work. But during those years, I was in engineering school. For better or worse.

But now I wish . . . I think it would be fun [to write a novel]. I love that thing you can do in a novel where you are riffing on something just because it's fun, absent the constant pressure of escalation that is a necessary part of writing short stories. Just those wonderful digressive riffs in a novel that earn their way by being great writing, even if they are peripheral to the "real" story or a little digressive. A story doesn't leave much room for things like that.

MB: Yes. I endorse this idea of you writing a novel, and I am certainly not the only one. That brings me to the matter of your audience, because I guess suddenly you are so famous, now? Which came as a complete surprise to me, because I thought you were a superstar already.

GS: Ah, it's hard to know about any of that. This one's actually selling, which is new, and very nice; the others had good reviews and so on, or mostly good reviews, but they didn't really sell. So that has been interesting. But . . . a year ago, I was perfectly thrilled with where I was: it was sort of perfect. I had everything you could have as a writer, but at a cult level; good responses at universities, things like that. Lots of peace and quiet. I think if we had talked then, though, one of my concerns would have been: OK, am I finding my full audience? And if not, is that somehow my fault? Am I somehow writing in such a way that good, serious readers are put off? Is there some sort of stylistic tic I am guilty of that is not essential to going deeper, and is having the effect of ghettoizing my work? So now . . . well, now I don't know. I just heard that the book is coming in at #2 on the next *New York Times* list, so that is amazing. At fifty-four, I'm very happy, it's like, okay. Wow. And it has made a really interesting, sort of anthropological, opportunity to look into parts of the culture I didn't know about (TV, for example, and the things that happen when a book sells, just in terms of demands on one's time and effect on the mind/ego, etc., etc.). And also it has been great to meet so many readers all over the place. It's made me feel really good about the state of American literature, to see and meet so many articulate people, for whom writing and reading are so important.

MB: This is very interesting to me. It's a rare thing, when there is a keen pleasure to be had on the surface, but the work continues to repay the investment of attention (cf. Austen, Shakespeare, Springsteen, Wodehouse, Louis C. K.) What do you think about "difficult" versus "easy" in fiction?

GS: Well, I think you'd want to be as difficult as you need to be, you know? I've often thought that when we find ourselves situated on a binary (i.e., experimental versus realist, or difficult versus accessible) the most interesting answer is along a different axis. That is, I can't imagine anyone interesting saying, you know, "I will ONLY write in a difficult mode!" Or: "I refuse to be anything but ACCESSIBLE!" The point would be to have your eye on a different goal—so, if we said, "My goal is to evoke deep feeling in an honest way," for example—well, would that prose be "difficult" or "accessible?" And the answer would be: both. Yes. Or neither.

MB: Do you still read and/or enjoy genre stuff? Did you grow up on that, or were you mostly a reader of serious fiction?

GS: I was never a big sci-fi person although I did see a lot of sci-fi and horror movies. I also read a lot of sports books and a lot of genre books about WWII—stories about famous pilots and so on. Then I had a period in high school and college where I was reading a lot of sort of schmaltzy light philosophy-type stuff—*Zen and the Art of Motorcycle Maintenance* and Kahlil Gibran. And an Ayn Rand phase. We used to get those *Reader's Digest* Condensed Books and I'd plow through those . . .

MB: So what *does* it do to your ego? Or rather, what does it to do *your* ego.

GS: Well, it's roughly like a sugar buzz. You get some praise, you are all modest about it, at least on the surface, and then almost immediately start craving more good news. Or—it's like eating beans. If a person eats beans, he's going to get farty and bloated. That's just . . . the body. So the trick is maybe to just hold back a little bit and observe the process. Huh—here the metaphor gets weird. But anyway—so far, so good, and I think these many years of writing have been good training—I really am just getting hungry to get back to work and try to, like, live into all of this attention, and do right by it, in the next thing.

MB: So you have this huge, diverse audience, now. Let's talk about all the terrible Amazon reviews you have!

GS: Haha, yeah. My friends are very politely saying, Well, it seems like your book is very *polarizing.*

I don't have the nerve to actually read them. But my guess is that a certain number of the people who came to the book from the *Times* piece, or from seeing me on TV . . . I mean, I come off like a nice guy—I mean, I am a nice guy . . . and maybe, when I talk about it, the book seems a little more, uh, Chekhovian or happy or something, and also more accessible, so . . . the book might not be quite what they expected?

MB: Oh yeah, I think there might be a lot of people who aren't realizing that it's actually a very *scary* ride, not just a fun one.

GS: Yes. It's dark. I've also heard some talk about it being difficult—which, to me, it's not that difficult, particularly, especially to those of us who read a lot of contemporary fiction. But it's possible that, with the *Times* piece and the TV and so on, people who don't normally read contemporary literary fiction are finding it, and that it might be surprising to them. But within that group of people who've found it, I'm hoping, there are also people who don't normally read contemporary fiction, and—like it. And I'm getting emails and stuff that indicate this is the case, which is nice.

As for the darkness . . . I think about that a lot. The real and primary truth is contained in that Flannery O'Connor quote about how, you know—a man can choose what he writes, but he can't choose what he makes live. When I follow my own energy, I tend to set stories at the end conditions—those days when things go wrong. That's not entirely new—I mean, that's storytelling. That's the Crucifixion, that's the Garden of Eden, and so on. So I think a sophisticated reader understands that, if you put a baby near a cliff, you're not saying that all babies live near cliffs. You're just saying: what if there was a baby near a cliff? And/or you're saying: isn't it the case that, sometimes, babies get near cliffs? And/or: doesn't life sometimes feel like you're a baby and you're near a cliff?

There's a school of thought that understands stories as being the reflection, of life, in a very clean and non-distorting mirror AND thinks the writer should make sure to point the mirror at "average" or "typical" situations, AND makes sure that the events of the story produce some kind of "uplift" or "hope." I don't really . . . well, I don't really have a gift for that kind of story. I think whatever hope or uplift a story has can, in a completely valid way, come from the way in which the story is told—the verbal energy, the humor, and/or the ways that, in a terrible situation, a person may rise—or merely even try to rise—to the occasion.

So, to me, fiction at its best is not supposed to just be this flat, perfectly reflective mirror, that presents a linear position of "life as it is." We should expect and enjoy some distortion in the baseline representation. I think we do this all the time. I mean, let's say you're watching Charlie Brown . . . nobody turns it off because they're thinking, "Hey, no one could actually stand up, with a head that big."

[*laughter*]

That's not exactly fair, you know? That viewer's not being a good sport.

Reading fiction requires a little bit of that willingness to be a good sport. To say, you know: I will grant you, writer, your initial offset, whatever it is—darkness, talking forks and spoons, you name it—but I'm going to judge your artistic efficacy on what you do with my faith. It would be a bad or ungenerous reader who'd say: "Wait a minute, Kafka, we all know that people don't transform into bugs. I quit. Your story sucks." What really makes or breaks a writer is what he does with the initial setup. "If I grant you that Gregor turns into a bug, what will you do with that, what will you show me about human nature that I couldn't otherwise have seen?"

But anyway, I love that there's dissension and so on. It's great, too that people are reading it, maybe being challenged by it.

MB: Right? Even if it's so weird to you that maybe you don't like it at first! *The Rite of Spring*, or whatever.

GS: Yes. And if you don't like it, take it back! You can return it. [*laughing*] Get your money back!

But I can see that a lot of this is just . . . when you get to a certain level it's just like, you have to put on the big boy pants. You have to have kind of a thick skin sometimes. I don't, really not naturally—I'm kind of a defensive person. But you have to accept that, if a lot of people are reading your work, there are going to be a lot of different reactions, and the fun part is, to be out there, in peoples' reading lives. I mean, if we'd talked before the book came out, I might have said, fiction has such a small audience. It's largely read by other writers; we're ghettoized, we're in this MFA bubble. (All of which really meant: MY fiction has such a small audience, I'm ghettoized, etc., etc. Ha.) I think my concerns, back in, say, November, would have been to figure out a way to get my work out to those X number of readers who would get it if they only found it. And I think we found them. As well, apparently, as some people who found it and maybe wish they hadn't. Based on the Amazon reviews. But more the former than the latter, it feels like.

But really, this is great. It's fun. To be read, and to create a little friction—good things, really. I think it's important to remember that art is a game. A big, high-stakes game that takes so much of its energy from being like life, or about life, or from life—but still, a game.

MB: When you are threatening innocents, like, say an animal, in your stories, it's a mark of your skill that I will even make that trip with you, on account of my being totally unable to take the idea of a beast in danger (this is forever for me, in your work, since the raccoons years ago.) Like when I see one in a movie—you can always tell a doomed beast in the movie—I'm basically diving under my seat and avoiding the whole thing; an old boyfriend once invented an advocacy organization just for me, the Society for the Prevention of Cruelty to Fictional Animals.

In any case, when you in particular endanger someone, it will throw even a reader who is very familiar with your work into a complete panic, because this thing could go either way. You're not necessarily going to rescue anybody. You never know how it's going to go.

GS: *I* never know how it's going to go. It's true, I never know how it's going to go. That would have to be the case, I think—I mean, if you are really writing openly, and the energy of the story said a bad thing had to happen— then there you go.

One reason, though, that I tend to put animals and kids in danger and so on, is just a lack of subtlety. I don't have a real finely developed sense of finesse and so, when seeking drama, I just tend to grab the nearest and most innocent thing and . . . menace it. Or like, in that story "The Barber's Unhappiness," when I was trying to increase my feelings (and the reader's feelings) for the main character, who I'd been parodying pretty fiercely, I just suddenly found myself stating that he'd been born with no toes. Bango! Sympathy.

In writing, I think we are often just trying to get into relationship with our own weaknesses and deficiencies and, by fessing up to them, trying to convert them into assets.

MB: That is the real uplift. The rest is just Hallmark bullshit. You fess up, I fess up, we share all these incalculable weaknesses, shocks, terrors, failures (delights, jokes, also) that we've *survived*. And look quietly back together. Now what?

GS: Exactly right. The uplift is: a thing done honestly or well. We like seeing someone else in a state of transport—even if the "frame" of that state of transport is "dark." I think of music, for example—think of the saddest song ever, but if it's done beautifully, you feel "uplifted" by the singer's passion or presence.

MB: What I feel most is the not-alone thing; I'm so comforted, because there are at least two of us, now. (A couple of babies at the edge of the cliff, you might say. Hand in hand, listening to the pebbles rolling off the edge.)

I read some, not a huge amount, of modern fiction. But you seem to me to be unique, or nearly so, in the degree of focus your work has on the reader's attention, moment by moment, anticipating what I'd be thinking or feeling. How much of this is deliberate?

GS: You're describing 100 percent of my process. That's the goal. To know where my reader is at any moment and do the next thing with that in mind. Though I can never be sure, exactly, of course, that I know what the reader is really thinking at any given moment . . . but you try to simulate that state . . .

MB: Oh yes you do. Allow me to tell you—certainly yes, you do, rest assured.

GS: What I do is try to simulate the experience of being a first-time reader. I imagine there's a sort of meter in my forehead, with P for Positive on one side, and N for Negative on the other—and the process of revising is just reading what I've done, while trying to posit where that needle would be for a first-time reader, and adjust accordingly. So when I rework something, I'm trying to get back to that experience, of reading for the first time . . .

MB: It seems like there's a danger that reworking would almost necessarily take you farther away, instead of closer, if your focus gets too far in . . .

GS: That's exactly right. It does. Your own words become a bit dead to you. What I do is, I try to figure out tricks to help me readjust my eye, sort of reset my capacity to see it as if for the first time.

MB: Like what kind of tricks?

GS: There's maximizing the time between reads, for example. Or now I can sort of reset . . . I have the capacity, more or less, to reset at will. To—it's hard to talk about—but there's a little mental adjustment that, if I can do it, clears the slate, so to speak. It's just a little mental adjustment that I have a hard time describing.

But the main thing is—to be patient. Go through the piece many, many times, making small adjustments each time. There's a sort of saving grace in this iterative approach—the truth will gradually, mysteriously, assert itself. If you iterate enough, the piece will increase in clarity, intelligence, humor, and kindness: your vision will become more sympathetic and true. I can't really explain or defend it—but I know it's true for me. It's as if going through a piece many times gradually chips away at my habitual falseness. It's maybe like—if someone asked you a hard personal question and you had to answer it in 5,000 words, on film. And then you got to come back, day after day, and slightly alter your response. Over time—if your intention was to tell the truth—your account would get more and more honest. And in fiction, honesty means—well, complexity and ambiguity and—and this is the weirdest part—it means that you gradually give your character more credit. Even if he's a bad guy, you start looking at him deeper and understanding his motives more generously.

MB: It's like, as you edit, your moral capacity to understand what you're trying to achieve can become larger, and more clear?

GS: Yes, exactly, that's exactly right. Like in the title story, "The Tenth of December," there's a guy maybe minutes from death and he's thinking about his son, and at first, I had him thinking something about his son's wide hips—something harshly physical, something meant to be a little funny—but it was sort of mean. Later, I thought: In that moment, would he be so critical of his son? And when I changed it, it felt truer—more like him.

MB: Oh God, though, but it's just so *great*, how he is able to see his son with this gimlet-eyed clarity, the truth of him . . .

GS: But in the final version I softened this—he sees a certain moral weakness his son has, and sees it very gently—but the earlier little barb about his son's looks is gone now.

MB: Yeah.

GS:—and it felt so much better.

[*A silence, here*]

So the reader might be thinking, "this is dark!" or "this is scary!" and you notice that, or know that—and then, in response, you leaven it with something else. You're basically saying, "Yes, I agree, this is pretty dark. Let's see if there's anything else here, so that you and I, dear reader—who, of course, live lives that are not dark—can feel some connection with these unfortunate characters." These feel like language adjustments, but it's what you said: they're essentially moral adjustments.

George Saunders

The Kind Side

Nick Curley / 2014

From *Barnes and Noble Review*, May 7, 2014. https://www.barnesandnoble.com/review /george-saunders-the-kind-side. Reprinted by permission of Barnes & Noble, Inc.

In the title story of George Saunders's latest short story collection *Tenth of December*, a dying man reflects: "He was fifty-three. Now he'd never deliver his major national speech on compassion." Last year, at age fifty-four, George Saunders delivered his. In a 2013 commencement address at Syracuse University, the National Book Award nominee spoke about themes that animate many of his most celebrated stories: empathy, communion, self-examination, and generosity. "That luminous part of you," proclaimed Saunders, "that exists beyond personality—your soul, if you will—is as bright and shining as any that has ever been. Bright as Shakespeare's, bright as Gandhi's, bright as Mother Teresa's. Clear away everything that keeps you separate from this secret luminous place. Believe it exists, come to know it better, nurture it, share its fruits tirelessly."

The speech circulated rapidly online, producing a surge of admiration during a banner year for Saunders, who had already cultivated a devoted readership (David Foster Wallace once called him "the most exciting writer in America"). With *December* he found an even wider audience, acutely receptive in our bewildering time to hilarious and poignant scenarios in which the marginalized become heroic, and divides between neighbors are erased. A revised and expanded edition of the Syracuse speech has now been published as *Congratulations, by the way: Some Thoughts on Kindness*, providing on the page what those who've met Saunders have already encountered: mush-free warmth and wisdom born of exuberant curiosity.

A gracious and game Saunders spoke with me about the book and what led to it over coffee on a breezy April morning. He would appear as a guest on *The Colbert Report* later that day. "Usually I'd be in my room hiding under the covers right now," said Saunders of his imminent TV outing. "But jeez, you know: I think this chilled me out."

Nick Curley: To set the table, I want to ask how you became a teacher, and how the job has prioritized and influenced your belief in kindness.

George Saunders: Sure. It's morning, so I've got to get the wheels going a little bit. I'd done a little adjunct teaching, but then, after *CivilWarLand* [*in Bad Decline*] came out . . . Tobias Wolff had been my professor at Syracuse. He called and said, "Would you like to come teach for a year?" At that point, I was happy to do that, but I wasn't sure if I would like it. I wanted to see how it affected my writing, to be honest with you, because I'd been working this corporate job, and it was all right.

What you find with teaching is that you are plunged into a relationship with people that you don't know at first. When you walk into the classroom, what are you going to do with all your anxiety and your projections about them? But then I got some advice from an older teacher. I had a particular class that was a little hostile. This professor said, "When you go in there, just before you go in, imagine them, as a group, as they will be when they are forty. Now they're young, but that's not them. They're just nervous. But when they're forty, they're going to look back on your class, and what will they remember?" That was really helpful. Then it was like, "OK, whatever awkwardness or indifference or sleeping is going on in here, they're young, and I'm teaching to their best selves."

That became the ethos for the whole deal. Your job as a teacher is to abide and receive whatever they have, then somehow try to convert it into something positive. Especially at a grad[uate degree] level. Whatever they're bringing to you, you've got to first accept it.

NC: And it's a small group of students.

GS: We get six hundred applications a year and we get six to come, so at any given time there's eighteen up there: eighteen fiction students in the program and eighteen poets. So you get to know them pretty well over three years. You're part of this extended family. They're already great writers. So it's advanced mentoring. It's all-engaging for the teacher, too, because you can't phone it in. You have to be aware of the different arcs that a writer might go through. Like, she might be really pissed off for a year, or she might be disengaged for a year. And whatever she is, that's what you have to work with.

NC: In *Congratulations* you talk about today regretting the missed opportunity to be kind to a grade school classmate. Was kindness something that was valued in your home, your town, your neck of the woods? Where did you find kindness and why did it linger?

GS: Certainly, our family on both sides are just tender people, and always were. I had the feeling from both sets of grandparents, to whom I dedicated the book, that they were always happy to see you. They were just unreservedly there for you. Maybe you assume that, but I know that's not true for everybody. It felt really welcoming. I think when you're a little kid, your sense of the world comes from whoever is around you and what they think of you. So if someone is always happy to see you, then you're like, "OK, I'm alright," and you live as though things are basically benevolent.

Then, I went to a Catholic school, and the Catholic schools in Chicago at that time, the late '60s and early '70s, were also kind of wonderful. You could feel a lot of progressive Christian ideas, a kind of Dorothy Day approach. I got this sense that Jesus was supposed to be a real guy, a really active presence, and you were supposed to emulate him. Any idea of Jesus at that time was the most empathic, present, cool dude, who could be frank as anybody, he could make any situation work . . . just a real big-hearted person, really.

NC: A hip camp counselor.

GS: Even at that time, the so-called "virtue of kindness" wasn't this kind of wimpy, gauzy thing. In the Jesus story, kindness was something he was able to maintain even as he was dying on the cross, where he says, "Forgive them, Father, for they know not what they do." That seemed to me like it was, across the board, a virtue that one would want to have, and that it had active, masculine components to it. Lincoln. Lincoln was kind.

NC: Having the wherewithal to be tender was itself a form of willpower and control.

GS: Right. It was part of real strength. Lately that's gotten a bit downgraded. There's strength, power, aggression, succession, and then . . . yeah, kindness, gentleness . . . if you want. [*laughs*] After you've vanquished somebody, then you can be kind to them.

NC: On the subject of masculinity: during your [*Late Show with David*] *Letterman* appearance, you're telling a story about seeing the Chicago Bears play at Wrigley Field, and you offhandedly mention that your father was the most generous person you could ever meet.

GS: Yeah. He was a very tough guy. He'd been an errant youth as a kid in Chicago. Even now, he's got a powerful life force. But it's tempered by an incredible ability to sacrifice that or soften that as needed. These qualities were inseparable. In fact, as a kid, I felt: well, he can be gentle because he is so strong. Those things were tied together. And that was a great, great example.

NC: Just to refer back to your classmate you refer to as "Ellen" in this book, you say that she wore blue-rimmed cats-eye glasses that at the time only old ladies wore.

GS: Yes.

NC: For what it's worth, I've recently seen you in the media wearing blue glasses.

GS: They're blue, but they're not cats-eyes.

NC: So you would not consider yours to be feline.

GS: No. Hers were those kind that curved up. Actually, Flannery O'Connor used to wear those.

NC: But it's endearing to think that as we get older, there are fun things that we get to do, that maybe we were hesitant to do for fear of ridicule or standing out too much.

GS: That's a great advantage of being middle-aged, I can tell you in advance. You get away with a lot more. Because people look at you and they say, "Oh, he's an old dude," and then they just go, "Oh, alright, he's wearing a miniskirt; that's cool." But when you're younger, you're not quite sure who you are, and you're walking a tightrope of identity. And as you get older, especially after you have kids, you feel like, "Anybody who wants to disapprove of me, you're welcome to it."

NC: It does seem that in youth, you judge yourself by the standards of others. Other people are your mirror, and you're conditioned to believe that you need to blend in.

GS: Which I'm sure is totally Darwinian and natural. It makes sense that it would be the case. One of the things about [Ellen] that I remember is that she didn't have that sense. She didn't quite know where she was in relation to where she should have been. So that was one of the hidden things about that interaction. It wasn't like in a movie, where she's Emma Stone and becomes popular.

NC: If only she'd take off those overalls, suddenly she would be a model.

GS: Exactly. It wasn't like that. And also, because I think she had reenacted this pattern at several schools . . . she didn't really want to be engaged, even in a "helpful" way. She just wanted to be left alone, because she knew what that helpfulness could cost her.

NC: Reading some of your earliest work, I was drawn in particular to a story called "Offloading for Mrs. Schwartz," published over twenty years ago. It's about a man regretting his unkind words to his girlfriend, and then stumbling upon a rather fantastical tool to escape the memory of this unkindness. He wakes up with a note pinned to him that says, "Your heart has never been broken." It seems as though these moments in which we choose, consciously or unconsciously, to either be kind or pay the price, have been dramatic pivot points for you from the beginning.

GS: I remember always feeling really terrible if I hurt someone's feelings. Which was sometimes a nice quality, but sometimes it wasn't. Sometimes it was a form of being passive and a little bit egotistical. If you say something that's honest, and then you feel all kinds of worry about whether you hurt someone's feelings, it might indicate a certain reluctance to engage in conflict.

Kindness is a great virtue. But it also sometimes gets misunderstood as mere niceness, which is not necessarily a good thing. If somebody drives a spike through your head, and you go, "Oh, thanks for the opportunity," that achieves nothing.

["Offloading"] was funny, because the older woman in that story was based on somebody that I knew. My dad had a restaurant when we were in Chicago, and I used to do his deliveries for him. There was this really ancient woman who would order quite often from the company. You'd go to her home. She did really wonderful monologues, but was kind of excitable. She had been a silent movie organist, so she would play the organ for you. She was amazing, but she didn't really want you to leave once you got there. And there was a certain drill. You'd listen, and you'd start backing towards the door, and at some point you'd have to just leave. She'd still be talking usually, because you just couldn't escape. So one Christmas Eve this was going on, and I'd been there forty-five minutes, honestly, and we were about ready to close down, and just as I was about to go home, with one foot out the door, she said, "All right. Well, I love you, Georgie." And I didn't even realize that she knew my name. I was in for another forty-five minutes after that. But I had that woman in mind, in Mrs. Schwartz.

NC: You've been a fiction writer, a reporter, an oil exploration researcher, and held several other odd jobs. In all these gigs, you've been a world traveler. Do you think the concept of kindness, or what constitutes an act of kindness, differs among countries and cultures? Is there something different about the kindness that you observed in Kathmandu or Sumatra compared to the kindness of Chicago or Syracuse?

GS: Let me say parenthetically, this book has been a bit of a trap, because I'm not really an expert on kindness. But I will say that I think, in the big picture, no. In a given human body and mind, those things feel a certain way. But I know some cultures are comfortable with it as part of their national manners. Like, in Nepal, it's just part of what they do socially in the culture.

NC: It's probably in some ways universal in its nuances.

GS: The speech is eight minutes, so I telegraph kindness. "Kindness" actually is a suite of things. In any time and any place, the people who are the kindest had a certain relation to reality. I'll go that far.

NC: In *Tenth of December* and dating back to stories in your earlier books, you see these characters who, fairly or unfairly, believe that they will become kinder when they become wealthier.

GS: [*laughs*] Yeah.

NC: Even of your own young adult struggles to make a living, you've described realizing that "money forestalled disgrace." But in terms of finding a happy medium between security and pleasure, how in your estimation can we insure that money doesn't forestall kindness? How do we keep greed and materialism at bay? Does it come to charity, or simply self-awareness?

GS: [*laughs*] Oh boy. That's a big one. That's a big one, Nick. I don't know.

NC: What I'm saying is: please save us from ourselves.

GS: OK, let me just do it right here, over breakfast. When you were talking, I thought, you know: money does forestall disgrace. In my experience, you can imagine a path of a mountain, and let's say the top of the mountain is a really together person, somebody who is really just cool. My experience was, you get to a certain point on a mountain where money has put up a barricade. Especially in our culture. Money puts up a barricade, and you do get embarrassed and humiliated and kicked around by not having enough. Even if it's just that you have to work two or three jobs to get your family fed, OK, then, you've got to kind of pause there because the world has kind of kicked the shit out of you for a while.

NC: It's immensely trying on one's patience.

GS: Yeah, and on the body and everything else. That Terry Eagleton quote: "Capitalism plunders the sensuality of the body." As a kid, I didn't have it. Our family was doing really wonderfully, and my dad made a lot of money for where we lived and for his time. Then when I got out in my twenties, I kind of screwed up and pushed myself back down the hill, and had to get myself back up and hit that barricade. I wasn't in the Gulag, but

I felt it. Does money make you necessarily a terrible person? No. Does it present certain temptations? Yeah. Well, let me see if I'm telling the truth here. [*pauses*]

Chekhov wrote that every happy man should have an unhappy man in his closet with a hammer, to remind him by his constant tapping that not everyone is happy. That's a great danger of middle age. You start thinking: Well, since my job is great, it's great that everyone has great jobs. You move out of the swamp onto the high ground and you go, "It's so nice that they dried the swamps." It's human nature. But it's also how the aristocratic ruling class gets murdered in the street. That was the great Russian Tsarist delusion: since he felt everything was good, it was.

The materialism that we are in the middle of now is kind of catastrophic, because it's so beautiful. Even with the financial crunch, we're so affluent compared to almost all of the rest of history.

NC: Walking around here, within a block of the Plaza Hotel, Central Park, Trump Tower, and an Apple store that looks like a glass cathedral, it's a little jarring.

GS: It's unbelievable. In my view, that kind of thing-based materialism is problematic. But the deeper one is that when the material world is so good to you, you start to think somehow that everything is material. The universe just happens to be pitched in such a way that we totally get it. There's nothing that we can't perceive. I think that's hubris. It means a shutting down the spiritual dimension of life.

NC: Accumulation comes to be viewed as pure evolution, pure progress.

GS: And also that whatever we need to know, we know. Whatever is habitually obvious to us is what's true. That's a real sign of decadence, or degradation.

NC: In *Congratulations*, you acknowledge that at times in your life, kindness went on the back-burner. You say, "First let me finish this semester, this degree, this book." If I may ask what might be a fairly personal question: when are you unkind?

GS: [*laughs*] Tuesday is usually the big day when I try to get it all out of the way. That's when I do that. Ethnic cleansing on Tuesday.

NC: [*laughs*] But even on Wednesdays, what causes you to fall into those easy rationalizations of selfishness and pessimism? Perhaps a more beneficial question would be: How do you climb out of the hole?

GS: I think I've never been an un-nice person, and I try really hard to be considerate and all that. But for me, maybe because of biology or anxiety, on a normal day, life is going by about 20 percent faster than I can really manage. Not in a dysfunctional way, but somebody will be with me, and only later I'll go, "Oh, I wonder if I missed an opportunity?" or I said something I shouldn't have said, or I inadvertently said something that I didn't mean to. So for me, what I'm calling kindness in that speech is probably more accurately presence.

When I'm nervous, I'm kind of a wisecracking guy. I noticed a couple of times where I went a little too far. Didn't really even hurt somebody's feelings, but you know—that kind of thing. At this point in my life, at fifty-five, I'm not trashing hotel rooms. It's more just sort of subtle absences, where your mind is so consumed with your own anxiety or inadequacy that you totally missed the banquet.

When the speech came out, people responded. And I don't think they were saying that "We burned down an ancestral village; whoops, that was bad of us." It's usually about small things, where you look up and you think, "Oh, my friend was going through a rough time; I kind of missed it. I didn't even realize it." Or even just failures of functionality where "I know you're going through a hard time; I don't know what to do; I don't know how to respond." That to me is the real crossroads. Because this so-called kindness has got elements, of course, of courage, but also discernment. Almost that feeling of Kipling, when he says, "If you can keep your head when all about are losing theirs . . ." If you're in a situation where somebody just saw you in your moment of need and came to your rescue, that makes you want to be better.

I was in the airport the other day, and it looked to me like the line was here for something else, and my thing was here, and I went up, and this guy goes, "Hey, are you in a hurry?" It threw me off: my reality and his didn't match. And that happens, of course, a lot. If you're up teaching college and living in the Catskills in your quiet house, it doesn't happen that much. But if you're doing actual things in the world, it happens a lot. That moment of discomfort is really telling. How quickly do you rebound? How do you respond in that moment when somebody comes after you?

NC: You've received some accolades recently. How do you feel, in the midst of them, that you've changed as a writer? Do you find that there are more opportunities? More inspirations? That your self-esteem has grown? Or is praise something that has to be put aside once you're alone in front of a new blank page?

GS: I would agree with all of that, actually. I think the big mistake would be to think it didn't affect you. It's like if you ate a bunch of beans, and you say, "Beans don't affect me; I'm a good person."

But what I've noticed is that when you're in a period of public stuff and/ or success, your mind turns to you. In other words, you get up in the morning and you're like, "Oh, I hope there's more good news."

Also, I've been writing through this. The last two years have been really busy, but I've also been writing this new thing that's really hard. So that's good. You're out on the road and you're feeling pretty happy, and then you get home and that manuscript's glaring at you from the corner.

And teaching is amazing. You go out on the road and do a reading, or you get like an award, and then you go back and teach a Chekhov story. The world can respond how it will, but those great masters are there all the time. You do a gut-check against them, like, "Wow, I know where I stand in this pecking order, and it's really low." Then, if you have a love for craft, you go, "OK, fair enough; when I can, I'm going to come back and try to get higher on the pecking order."

NC: I think you should feel good about your pecking order placement. Although I am curious: your Chekhov analogy of the man tapping in the closet—where is that from?

GS: That's from a story called "Gooseberries." It's beautiful. What's really amazing about it is it's embedded in a whole speech. It's a beautiful speech about why we should be suspicious of happiness. It's probably Chekhov at his wisest, speaking from his heart. What he does in the story is, he puts that speech in this pompous guy's mouth, and it totally works. The guy is right and he's also wrong. He's made such a good case that happiness is suspect, and we go, "Yeah, I agree, but he's miserable!" He's in a group of people, and he's a drag. He tells this big, depressing story, and then that story ends with this great image of that guy sleeping in a bed beside his friend, and in the middle there's a table, and the guy who made the speech has put his smelly, uncleaned pipe there, and so his friend can't sleep. This great speech is undercut with real human things. That story is part of a trilogy called *About Love*: it's got a story called "A Man in a Case" and "Gooseberries," and ends with this beautiful story called "About Love."

NC: That seems a great distinction of the short story: its ability to distill.

GS: Those three stories taken as a trilogy might be one of the greatest things ever written. It has that Chekhovian quality where he never occupied just one seat. He's always moving around into the different characters' heads and subverting what you already think, and in the end it's this beautiful, resonating question. And you don't even know what the question is! When I was in grad school, Tobias Wolff was going to do a reading, and I think he was feeling under the weather, so he said, "Rather than read my own stuff,

I'm going to read some Chekhov," and he read us those three stories. That was one of the biggest moments in my education as a writer: how much he channeled all the different valences in Chekhov. They were funny, and they were severe, and lyrical. It all came through and was really magical.

NC: Talking about these powerful responses that rise from Chekhov's work and others: are you ever moved to physical emotion by your own stories, by your own words?

GS: Not so much. But every so often. I do a lot of moving around of stuff. So sometimes a joke will not be where I put it in the first place, and then it will hit funny. This is kind of weird, but it's almost like the awareness that if I wasn't so much in the middle of it, I would have been jolted. It's almost like a simulacrum feeling, like, "Well, a normal person would feel this at this point."

In *Tenth of December* there was one place that really surprised me. There's a speech that a guy makes in his head about his wife, about their marriage. I remember just going, "OK, he needs to think about his wife," and that came directly from my life.

NC: There are real varieties of poignancy in that book. You've got the very touching ending of "Victory Lap": the sentiment that is expressed in its very last line. You've got this bitter rationale of a character like Al Roosten, or this put-upon father in the "The Semplica Girl Diaries." Part of what distinguishes this book is not only that people are choking up, but that they're choking up for a variety of different reasons.

GS: Thanks. Sometimes I'll have these sections of alternating viewpoints, and you're kind of looking around, like, "OK, where is the doorway? How do I get out of this?" It would be nice to think, "If I feel emotion at this part, it's a keeper." But even that isn't really true. You have to feel emotion when you clear your mind and read the whole thing from the beginning to the end. Otherwise, you've got to cut it. Which hurts.

NC: Now that this commencement speech and *Tenth of December* have really resonated with people, do you find that members of your readership are seeking advice from you? Or that one curiosity of kindness is that those who are seeking it will often latch on to someone who they see as a provider? Have you had instances where people have reached out to you, either through correspondence, or in person, after readings, etc.? What are you able to give, and what do you have to withhold as a mere mortal?

GS: There is some of that. Actually, I would trace it back to that Joel Lovell piece which was in the *Times*, which was so generous, in terms of getting new readers. This will sound weird, but if I'm like, 60 percent nice, you get extra points because you're a public figure. You get inflation in that way. What I try to do is say, "Even if I can't see it right now, even if I'm kind of blind, that person is just as real and valid and there as I am."

I read something that said, "If you're talking to somebody and you're in a confrontation or in trouble, open your chest, like literally turn . . ." [*pulls chair out from table and adjusts himself to align his chest directly with Curley's*] That's actually hard to do.

NC: You're exposed. You're actually saying, like, "Go ahead, put the knife in me," or simply: "Here's all of me."

GS: Physiologically, yeah. You don't want to do that too much because you look like a crazy person. But I was hosting a Zen monk who had written a book, and he was an amazing person. I was hosting him for a dinner, and it was me and him and his assistant. We talked late into the night, and we went outside, downtown, and suddenly, out of nowhere, this homeless guy comes up: "You got any money?" Of course, my thing was to turn away. "No, I don't." Get to the car. This monk just turned to him, looked him right in the eye and said, "What's going on?" You could feel the energy change. The guy's tone changed and he stood up a little straighter, and he said, "Well, I'm having some bad luck." He goes, "What's happening with you?" He made the guy tell. Almost like magic, as this was happening, a young woman stepped out of the shadows. That was this homeless guy's girlfriend or whatever. By whatever was going on, she felt . . . Suddenly we're five people hanging out on the street. They told the story. He goes, "Oh, man, that's terrible."

NC: You're actually giving them a place in your world. You're saying, "You belong here as much as we do."

GS: Right. Also, what the monk did was, he just took that label that I just used, "Homeless Guy" . . . He's not a homeless guy; he's Jeff, or whoever he was. It was really startling to see that. Kind of like this thing in the speech with Ellen, I instantaneously observed my own shortcomings: my intuitive reaction, which was to get the hell out of there.

Then he said to his assistant, "Can you give me twenty dollars?" It was just a totally loving exchange. And it was because of something that this monk had going on. It wasn't a show. It wasn't fake. Totally natural. So that kind of thing is really educational.

This book [*Congratulations*] is a little scary. I make a little joke about it. "How to be kind? Well, I've only got three minutes." That was a purposeful evasion on my part, because it's very uncool to act like you have information in an area when you know you don't.

NC: You risk becoming not only the role model, but the public spokes-man for kindness . . .

GS: Yes, a facile guru. "Yeah, I wrote the book on kindness; hey, come to me with your kindness questions." That would be like a nightmare.

NC: [*laughs*] In that case, get ready for more kindness questions. This ties in nicely to the next one. I want [to] ask about the practice of Buddhism. As I understand it, there is a condition which translates to "loving-kindness," sometimes referred to as *metta*. It's a meditative practice in which you think kindly upon a variety of different people, different circles of your life. You think kindly upon your friends, your family, teachers, strangers, even ene-mies, in a series of outward expansions of goodwill. But the first person in this *metta* cycle to whom you must think kindly is yourself. Does this notion of self-kindness as the nucleus of generosity speak to you?

GS: I should say, too, that I'm a very novice Buddhist.

NC: I ask because in the speech, you do cite prayer, meditation, and establishing ourselves in some kind of spiritual tradition as practices that can "raise one's ambient levels of kindness."

GS: When you were asking the question, what occurred to me is that that's actually not a bad description of fiction, even. What you're doing is throwing down an imaginative view of life. Once you get your first draft down, you're then coming back to it to try to "improve it." But what you're really doing is trying to improve the quality of your imagination. So first, you're sort of puppeteering and mocking the character. Then with many drafts, you see him more clearly. I've found that eventually you've got to cut him some slack. You've got to imagine him, again, to be your equal—or close. Just mechanically, for the story to proceed, you have to give him the benefit of the doubt. If you caricature him too harshly, he can't go anywhere, and the story flatlines.

For me, maybe that was the first time I've ever had that experience of try-ing to change the way I thought about things, was through fiction. You have a crummy first draft, and you're like, "I don't really feel that way about the world." Or, "Here at this point in the story I'm being a little harsh." You cor-rect that. Then suddenly, you're making a model for yourself of how to think about the world. Like that example of the homeless guy. That Zen Master didn't see him the way I saw him. His mind skipped past "Homeless Guy" and saw a human being, which is sort of a fictive technique.

I don't know if that answers your question. You can see I'm going to skip around all the Buddhist questions, because I really don't know.

NC: I think in the past you've even commented that the magic in your Buddhist practice is to some degree that it's difficult to explain: the wonder *is* the value.

GS: It's difficult for me because I'm such a novice. That's really the truth. In the speech I talk about this spiritual tradition. I was trying to tread lightly there, because it was a graduation speech and you don't want to be preachy. But it does seem to me that if a kid felt that kindness was something in which he would like to improve, it's not like that's a new idea. In all the great spiritual traditions, if you find an authentic core, that's really what they're doing. There are traditions that are so vast and intelligent and beautifully reasoned and comprehensive . . . and they're just sitting there for us. These are thousand-year, even two thousand-year lineages of people who have been totally on top of this.

The one thing about being even a novice Buddhist is you get to meet people who aren't novice Buddhists, and you see that this stuff we're talking about is not abstract. Kind of like if you were out shooting free-throws, and suddenly Michael Jordan walked up, you'd be like, "Oh, so that's where this can go." That's probably the stage that I'm at, is just to go, "Damn, I wish I had known this when I was twenty." I really do wish I had known it.

NC: In the spirit of kindness, and to try to make this more of a community exercise, I put out a few feelers on Facebook, Twitter, and among friends, asking if anyone had any questions for you. Many people were willing to "Like" or "Favorite" this notion, but only two brave souls actually stepped up to the plate. The first brave soul was my high school classmate Katelyn Shanklin, who is an English teacher now living in Baltimore. Very simply, she wanted to know what your dreams are like. Interestingly, I've even heard you say that some of your stories have come from dreams.

GS: "The Semplica Girl Diaries" came out of a dream. "I Can Speak" [from *In Persuasion Nation*] came out of a dream. "Pastoralia" came out of a dream. What amazes me about dream life is that your subconscious is so amazingly detailed. We've all had the dream where your boss yells at you during the day and at night an elephant trumpets at you. But what's amazing is the complexity of the dream state. Not unrelated to writing. Kind of better. Your dream state is a better writer that comes up with amazing little strange twists and stuff like that. But Freud said something about that, the idea being that the dream has no responsibility to be coherent, to be organized or beautiful. It can be beautiful, but it has no responsibility to be coherent, whereas in the story, you use dream energy to make coherence.

NC: It speaks to the talent of someone like Chekhov as well, to recognize that there is beauty in ambiguity.

GS: Yes. So a lot of times it's just a matter of trying to tease out the coherence. Like, "Semplica Girl Diaries" was a beautiful image. Troubling. But it didn't have that quality of dream insanity. It was quite tidy.

NC: And it was simply that women from the third world were being used as decoration outside suburban homes?

GS: I saw it, yeah. And I saw the person in the dream who saw it, and that his reaction wasn't horror but gratitude. "I'm so lucky to finally be able to give this to my kids."

NC: Like having a really good Christmas tree.

GS: That's exactly what it was. "Look at that. I brought that home." Faulkner actually talks about that. I think *The Sound and the Fury* came not out of a dream but out of something he saw. He was driving by this house, and I think he saw this older brother boosting his sister up into the tree with the muddy hand on her panties, and he saw that and went, "OK, what's the world behind that?" Thanks to Katelyn for the question. This [is] like a call-in show without the technology. We're going to go to a commercial break now.

NC: The second came from Jaclyn Backhaus, a playwright from Brooklyn, New York, who writes: "Lately, there have been a lot of prominent artists and thinkers lamenting the increasing impracticality of living in New York. I am an artist trying to combat that feeling, primarily through the operation of a nonprofit arts community called Fresh Ground Pepper, which presents free evenings of new work across Manhattan and Brooklyn. Do you consider yourself part of any communities that work to maintain vitality in the arts? Are there organizations that have helped you, or whose programming or message you believe in?"

GS: The one organization that I still belong to is the Syracuse MFA program. That was an incredible elevator up to a higher level of artistry. That's my artistic community—my colleagues there, my students. Other than that . . . I'm not exactly disciplined enough to be a recluse, but that's my energy. Or maybe like a bit of a cannibal, in that when I need something, I'll come in to New York and get it—go to a museum or a show. For whatever reason, I've found for me to share work early, to talk about it, doesn't really help much. So I tend to kind of just pull up and work alone, and then at the very last minute give something to my wife. That's my real community, right there.

Now, I'm not disparaging community at all. But a lot of my twenties were spent in Denver and Amarillo, Texas . . . trying to find other artists, actually, at that time. I had a little group out in LA of close friends from engineering school who were also artists.

I think living in New York would be hard financially, but what an incredible trove of riches in terms of just being always surrounded by humanity and beauty. So I wish her luck with her group.

NC: I wanted to quote you a passage from the final edition of your column, "American Psyche," that you wrote years ago for the *Guardian*.

GS: [*laughs*] Oh boy. Thank you for bringing that up. I enjoyed it, but it was a real Zen exercise. You had to crank out something every week, so there was a lot of variety in those babies.

NC: In the final edition of the column, published nearly six years ago, just a couple of weeks before the election of President Obama, you wrote: "America is having an identity crisis. On one side, fear, aggression, banality, xenophobia. On the other, hopefulness, humor, confidence in human nature, critical thought. This battle is not being fought along party lines. It is not the case that one party or candidate holds a monopoly on these positive virtues. No, it is more existential, and every one of us is fighting it internally. Which country are we to be? The terrified, torturing, isolated bully, or the tolerant, slow-to-anger, naïve-but-bright protector of the poor? It's not altogether a new battle. The American heart—hell, maybe the human heart—has been divided along these lines for a long time. But here, in our time, it feels like the battle is heating up."

Well, the battle sure did heat up, and in many ways, the temperature is rising still. Six years later, are we any closer to figuring out whether we're the bully or the protector?

GS: The thing in there that strikes as true is that it's an internal battle, in every person. If you went back to the Neanderthal times, and there were two guys in a cave, and a third guy approached across the prairie, one of the guys would say, "Kill him! He's gonna fuck with us." And the other one would say, "Maybe he's got some new ideas; let's go ask him." And actually, both those guys might be right.

One thing is: I am getting so tired of the liberal-conservative wrestling match. It's become such a big-money thing now, and the media is so invested in it—media outlets and pundits and networks—that it's become a great business to be in. And they are fanning the flames. They are taking a cosmetic divide that exists within every one of us into this deep crevasse, and they are making the crevasse wider. I think the only reason is profit. I think if you follow the money, it's easy business . . . it's easy broadcasting, it's easy writing to those liberals, those conservatives. I think it's actually really eroding national culture.

Right now, that's fine. But it's almost like if you had a really dysfunctional family, a really dysfunctional marriage. If they're at the beach, no problem. But if suddenly they run out of gas in the middle of the desert, that lack of functionality becomes dangerous. My fear is that we haven't really gotten better. I think President Obama is an incredibly positive presence. What has maybe depressed me more than anything else recently is to see that good, incredibly intelligent guy getting stymied from time to time by this kind of bullheadedness. It actually isn't just the conservatives' fault. It's that this national mode of opposition has gotten so reflexive and so late-failed-marriage that nobody could fix it. Washington could come back, or Lincoln could come back, and they wouldn't be able to maneuver.

I talked to a really brilliant guy, Melvin McLeod at the *Shambhala Sun*. He suggested to me that, in his experience, sometime in the '80s, these things like gentleness and kindness got demoted to the second-tier . . . he used the phrase "feminine virtues." He didn't mean it in a gendered sense. But "masculine" would be power, aggression, success, certainty, and "feminine" would be tolerance, compassion. If you think of the country as a being, a being who only believed in strength would be a monster. "I can manage it. No problem. No matter what happens, I'm just going to roll right over it." That's a monster. That's not a human being. It's also a very brittle monster, because eventually the world is going to kick that monster's ass, through age or death or circumstance, and he's got no resources. But the being that has those so-called masculine and feminine virtues coexisting is really strong.

With this liberal-conservative thing, we're making ourselves weak by falling into a permanent posture of belligerence. You put on your cap, whether it's liberal or conservative, and then you don't have to think any more. You know the answers. All the really vexing questions of life don't really have answers. They're complicated. I think if you're looking at any human heart, you can find a liberal and a conservative fighting like crazy. It's almost like the more lively the liberal is, say, in the conservative, the more he's going to have to shout to keep it down. That's why so many homophobes are actually secretly gay. Same with liberals. I know so many liberal people who are just a half-turn away from fascists.

But here's the thing. Let's say, forget about all those labels, and take a little eight-year-old kid, somewhere. That kid develops a moral stance by being afraid, by noticing pain in himself or people he cares about, by clenching. You go out and life starts to instruct you. So that kid is going to notice that life is scary, that paucity sucks, that life is short—all these things that any kid knows.

Now, what does he do with that? Some kids become liberals. They say, "We've got to help each other and the government is there to help us do that." Whatever a liberal says. Some of them become conservatives, and they say, "The only way I got out of this was to really knuckle down and work" or whatever. Look at somebody like John Boehner, whose life story is very moving and very compassionate. Nobody disagrees on the fundamental condition of life, really, I don't think. But in the face of that early pain, we take harsh positions because it's so scary. The first time that your cage gets rattled, whether it happens when you're eight or twenty-two, you go, "Oh my God, that's not happening again," and politics kick in.

Look at gun control. On the surface, I'm a garden-variety liberal and I have my garden-variety liberal beliefs. But I love shooting guns. I also have a really deep paranoia that I can get at where, "I'd like to have a few guns, just in case."

NC: There's a gorgeous moment in your story for *GQ*, "Tent City, USA," that's not over-explained, where you notice some pruning shears have been left at a fence, and you casually walk over and bring them into your tent, as means of self-defense. It's such a simple yet dramatically ominous moment that you very subtly utilize.

GS: Oh, yeah. I remember that.

NC: I did want to ask you about that story. My girlfriend said, "If you're interviewing George Saunders, you have to read this story." I credit her for that.

GS: Thank you, girlfriend.

NC: Yes, thank you, Megan.

GS: Thank you, Megan. [*leans closer into microphone*] Thank you, Megan!

NC: In "Tent City," you traveled to Fresno to live for a week with a tent community of hundreds of homeless and displaced people. You write there about how those less fortunate can often be cruel, mean, stupid, grandly delusional. You say something that counters poisoned "makers and takers" political rhetoric: "But to love the unfortunate, it is not necessary to feel fond of them, or tenderness toward them. Our minds can be kind when our hearts cannot." I wonder if you could expand on what that idea means to you, that "our minds can be kind when our hearts cannot."

GS: Here's the thing. When I went into that, we thought it was going to be this Steinbeckian love fest.

NC: That you'd be suckling from a teat.

GS: That was the hope anyway. And a person would be playing guitar while it happened. But it was not that. It was at least two crack dealerships— gang-related crack dealerships. So it was really scary. The people in there were all over the board. Many of them had been institutionalized and re-leased. Many were addicts. Everyone was humiliated by being there, of course. And dirty and hot, and not-nice, not fun. The place was not nice or fun.

So I thought, "OK, now watch me rise to the occasion. Watch me be a loving presence here." And within a day, that was done. I was scared and tired myself, and irritated. People were harassing you, people were telling you repetitious, pointless stories. People were lying to you. Again: "Capitalism plunders the sensuality of the body." A homeless camp plunders the sensuality of the body. Everybody is reduced. It's very sad, because nobody wants to be there. Everyone wants to corner you and tell you why they're the exception to the rule, that they're the only sane person in the camp. So it starts to work on you. Pretty soon, I had to recognize that that was the whole point of the story, that Mister Compassion over here had gotten his butt kicked. I had quickly seen that my everyday niceness was just circumstantial. Here I am, in a nice restaurant, having breakfast with a nice person. Yeah, I'm nice right now. But when suddenly you're down in the dirt, and there's a guy who wants to beat you up if you don't give him five dollars . . . then suddenly it's different.

NC: In a moment of real frustration, you write something in your journal . . . I forget the exact wording, but it's reminiscent of Travis Bickle in *Taxi Driver*, where he says, "One day, a real rain will come and wash all this scum off the streets."

GS: It was "Exterminate the brutes," from *Heart of Darkness*. I'll tell you the feeling I had, which I can't remember if I put it in the piece or not. We have two daughters, and I had a sort of post-apocalyptic feeling, like, "If I wasn't who I am . . ." As it is, I could get out of here in a heartbeat, I could call in the troops basically . . . I could call *GQ*, get the police in here. I could get a lawsuit. All the power was mine. But I remember thinking if that was not the case, if all that was taken away, like for example after the Russian Revolution, where people like me were suddenly in the street for real . . . it's terrifying. Just kind of cowering in the tent, doing that thought experiment, I thought, "OK, if that was the case, what would you do?" My response was, "I'd get hold of a gun for sure." There's not any question about it.

I was trying my best to listen, and I actually made some friends in there, and met people who were really wonderful and were incredibly heroic, because considering where they were, to have as much humanity and kindness as they did was extraordinary.

It's like Twain said: "An untested virtue is not a virtue." So for me to be reckoning myself a kind, friendly, benevolent force—all right, good. But where are you a kind, friendly, benevolent force, and what conditions have to pertain in order for you to keep being that?

It was in an abandoned freight yard that the homeless had taken over, and they had once been evicted from there very violently a few years before. By the time the story came out, about two months later, the city moved them out in a really intelligent way. They had money for each person, and they had found a place to live for each person, and basically had given them two or three months of stable living. They had people interviewing them to see what kind of programs they should be in, and what kind of federal money they weren't getting. So I was there kind of in the last days of the place.

NC: Another amazing thing about that story that Megan pointed out to me is that you're reporting your emotions and reactions in real time: fear, uncertainty, amusement. You give your internal self the weight of reportage.

GS: I would thank Andy Ward for that at *GQ*. We had done a number of pieces like that, and he gradually made that more and more OK, like that was actually what I was supposed to be doing. He guided me through all those *GQ* pieces. I thought of it as kind of a gonzo journalism, but maybe slightly more New Age. In that piece, the mock-scientific voice was really key. Then you can say, "I was feeling so sad," but write it as, "He noted at that time a certain sadness manifesting . . ."

NC: In closing, for what it's worth, I wanted to mention my own George Saunders kindness story. We've actually met once before, very briefly. It was at the after-party of this year's National Book Awards. I nervously approached you, and began by saying that I know people have probably been coming up to you all night, singing your praises. You said something wonderfully candid, which was, "I could use some more."

GS: [*laughs*] Actually, I do remember that.

NC: Your tone in saying it was very funny, gracious, and human, especially given that, without digging the knife in, you had five minutes earlier . . . shall we say, not won the [National Book] Award [for Fiction].

GS: Yes, let's say it that way. You can't lose an award. You can just not win it.

NC: You very patiently listened to me sing those praises, and you also introduced me to your wife, Paula . . .

GS: Now I totally remember. I'm sorry I didn't remember earlier.

NC: It seemed particularly cool, because I've met some authors who treat their spouses like silent servants, and this was different. You were very present. And as I turned away, I felt this hand patting me on the back. Mysteriously, I don't know if it was you or someone from the dance floor trying to push me out of their way . . .

GS: [*laughs*] I was going for your wallet actually.

NC: [*laughs*] . . . or if this was some entirely imagined part of my own invention. But that was as a moment where I saw your kindness with my own eyes.

GS: Thanks, I'm glad! Actually, that night, I got a lesson in kindness from my wife. That event is kind of exciting. You're there with your editors and your agents, and it's really exciting. Then, when you don't win, you feel a bit like, "Oh God, I'm in public and I just didn't win." Just a little bit. But afterwards, my wife just said, "Let's dance." I went, "Well . . ." She says, "Yeah, come on. I got all dressed up. We're gonna dance."

NC: You can't ask for better than that.

GS: No, exactly. It was a physical cure to whatever whininess or hurt feelings I had, whatever was embarrassing and uncomfortable. She fixed it with this physical gesture of taking my hand. "Let's go dance." You dance for two minutes and you're like, "Yeah, we're happy." She used to be a ballet dancer, so her way of being in the world is very physical, very joyful. I remember thinking, "I don't want to dance; it's embarrassing; I'm not going to . . ." But then I couldn't say no. She looked so beautiful. I'm not going to say no to her. Within a couple of minutes, you're back to yourself again. And I didn't do that. She did it. So that's marriage. A good marriage.

A Conversation with George Saunders

W. Brett Wiley / 2016

From *Image: Art, Faith, Mystery*, no. 88 (Spring 2016): 57–68. Reprinted by permission of the author.

George Saunders is the author of four collections of short stories— *Civilwarland in Bad Decline* (1997), *Pastoralia* (2001), *In Persuasion Nation* (2007), and *Tenth of December* (2014)—as well as a book of essays, *The Brain-Dead Megaphone* (2007), and an award-winning children's book, *The Very Persistent Gappers of Frip* (2005). *Civilwarland in Bad Decline* was a finalist for the PEN/Hemingway Award and *Tenth of December* was a finalist for the National Book Award. His awards include a MacArthur Genius Grant, a Guggenheim Fellowship, and an Award in Literature from the American Academy of Arts and Letters. Born in Amarillo, Texas, Saunders grew up in Chicago; he received a degree from the Colorado School of Mines and worked as a geophysicist before completing an MFA at Syracuse University in 1988, where he is now professor of English and teaches in the creative writing program. He has regularly published articles and stories in the *New Yorker*, *GQ*, and *Harper's Magazine*, and has appeared in anthologies such as the *Best American Short Stories*, *Best American Nonrequired Reading*, and *Best American Travel Writing*. His first novel, *Lincoln in the Bardo*, will be published by Random House in January 2017. He was interviewed by W. Brett Wiley.

Brett Wiley: In our initial correspondence, when I asked about your adherence to Christian and Buddhist teachings, you wrote, "I don't see them separately at all, or just a little." Would you be willing to elaborate?

George Saunders: I was raised in parochial schools, in Chicago, no less. In the 1960s, no less. I think I've always had a need, because of that intense period, for mystery and metaphor and beauty—really because of the power of the Catholic Mass. Catholicism was central to my way of thinking and being in the world—a moral system and an aesthetic system. Then seventh grade happened, and my connection to the faith kind of dwindled. But I think that early generated need is constant. Once a person has a glimpse of mystery, he's always going to be seeking that. Many years later we had our kids, and we started to attend an Episcopal church, and I felt that need being both reawakened and addressed there.

So, no, I don't see Christianity and Buddhism as separate; in fact, for me, one picked up where the other left off. My wife and I had started to feel that Christianity did a lot of urging one to be good but didn't tell one much about how to accomplish that—how to change, how to convert one's way of thinking and being in the world. And then we encountered Tibetan Buddhism and found a tradition that offered real practices that a person could do every day, and almost immediately I could feel myself changing. I actually felt parts of my mind reengage—parts that had been dormant since I left the Catholic Church circa 1972.

BW: Things lined up in your mind?

GS: Things didn't necessarily line up, but it felt like the practices were addressing exactly the things that were concerning me at that time: "How can I become more patient? How can I disrupt these decades-long habits I seem to have acquired? Is it possible to increase one's ability to love? How can I see situations more clearly?" The other exciting thing was that, as I did more meditation, I realized I'd been doing it all along, while writing. And, in fact, I'd been doing a kind of meditation during all those blissful years as a kid sitting in church. I had thought my mind was just drifting, but I was meditating.

Another similarity, and something I really responded to, is that Buddhism and Catholicism are both very rich in metaphor and symbol and ceremony: incense, bells, chant, intense color patterning in vestments. They both use symbolic deities and share the notion that there are realms of knowing that are not conceptual or literal and are only accessible experientially, and may not be subject to reduction. (And, of course, they share this belief with the arts.)

Also, from the time I was a little kid, I've had a probably overactive moral or ethical sense, an awareness of right and wrong—and I think that led me to find a home first in Catholicism, then in fiction, and then in Buddhism. I had a sense that we ought to be urgently seeking, because we are in some trouble down here: life is rough and death is coming.

I feel that our purpose here on earth is to move from a position of strong belief in self (strong ego, anxiety, fear, a sense of permanence) to a Christ- or Buddha-like position of unconditional love and erasure of self and acceptance of the conditionality of all things. Personally, I am a long way from that. My sense of self seems to get stronger every year, even as I get less attractive and more absent-minded.

One doesn't get rid of the self easily. The more practice I've done, the more amazed I've become at how stubborn and clever the self is. But along the way, I think we might be afforded little sneak previews, glimpses of something vast and deep and eternal in us. To me, religious and artistic practices are about what Buddhists call "accumulating merit." You do certain things as a way of taking baby steps towards that desired position of selflessness. The goal is to see all positive activities as part of the same greater positive activity: when you are meditating, praying, or writing, you are trying to get some clarity, to move yourself, even incrementally, in the right direction.

Right after I finished a story called "The Falls," I read an article about a phenomenon where a person will see somebody in distress and suddenly, instinctively, rush off to save them, and in that process, as they describe it later, their self momentarily disappears. I remember reading the testimony of a guy who leapt into the Potomac back in the 1980s, when a plane had crashed there, and he mentioned this: there was suddenly no distinction between himself and the drowning person. That's a powerful notion, that we are capable of that sort of feeling.

Our habitual way of thinking about those moments is that they are either miraculous or freaky, i.e., not real. But they occur in every culture. Maybe we are like eggs, with our shells made of habit and ego, but every now and then little cracks appear and some light comes in and we get a glimpse of how things actually are.

Most moments, we are trapped within our usual way of thinking (probably for good, Darwinian reasons). But it would be very strange if what we could feel at any given moment was exactly equal to what the universe actually is. Every now and then we get a brief glimpse of our own limitedness—which is, of course, also a glimpse of our limitlessness.

There's a wonderful book by Patricia Pearson, *Opening Heaven's Door*, in which she describes how, when her father was dying, he came to her sister in a dream on the very night he died and said, by way of a long and beautiful and future-revealing dream, "It's all okay." He had died unexpectedly, and this sister had the dream not yet knowing he'd passed away. Pearson, who is a journalist, got curious. She started interviewing hospice nurses and other people who'd had these sorts of experiences, and in the end something like half the people she interviewed reported having had communication from the dead or dying. We tend to treat these things as kooky, but speaking scientifically, if 50 percent of a data pool reports something, we ought to consider that. Pearson asks whether the Enlightenment pendulum has swung too far to the logical side, and whether now we are actually being anti-scientific by ignoring this sort of data.

I find all of this fascinating and hopeful—indicating, as it does, that we are not just these bodies and that the truth, whatever it is, is not limited to what we can perceive and prove.

Of course, you have to be careful, or you may find yourself in some small cult that believes penguins are actually aliens.

BW: You've said of your move toward Buddhism, "It wasn't a rejection and then an adoption." Rather, you're putting these two things together, borrowing from each and allowing them to bounce off of one another. Do you think of your experience with religion in that way, as syncretic?

GS: First, it's important to note that my initial experiences with Catholicism and Buddhism were separated by many years. But here's what Catholicism, Buddhism, and writing have in common for me: when I was young, though I couldn't ever articulate it, I was moved by the idea of Jesus as this incredibly present, accepting being who was also able to *roll* with things. He would say, "So, you're a prostitute? Cool, no problem, I accept you." I've always felt that if you had that kind of unconditional love for everyone and everything, you would be *so* powerful. That model of personhood was in my mind: with Jesus everything was workable because everything was loved.

In writing, it's the same. It finally came to seem, after years of writing, that there's never really an unworkable problem in prose, if we *abide*. If there is an issue, the prose itself can rise up to address it. That's what storytelling is. I was writing a story called "The Barber's Unhappiness," which at one point just locked right up. I kept writing the same scene over and over, although set in different places. And it finally occurred to me that my feelings toward that character (who was sort of a bad, sexist dope) were static. I'd already decided what he was. The story didn't like that and, like a dog on a leash, refused to be pulled along. So I started looking closer at the existing prose, asking myself if I could find any place to humanize the guy. And, seeing it that way, I found a few clunky places, where the prose was a little awkward and unformed, and by coming back to these, found out a few new things about him, things that made it possible to feel for him. The story opened up again, and I finished it. This is a very strange thing in writing—when the prose goes bad or vague or tepid, the story is concealing a treasure, sort of saying, "Dig here!"

So the stance is one of abiding with the text, of having faith in its essential goodness. The text isn't rotten; you just haven't looked deep enough yet.

In Buddhism I found the same notion. Meditation is really just the mind watching the mind, accepting whatever is found there, generously, curiously. Not judging, just looking.

In all three activities, I also loved the urgency—the sense that we are engaged in a serious endeavor and mustn't spend our time with our eyes averted from what is real: we are temporary. We love, but the objects of our love are also temporary. We can't seem to fully live into our love, and that is frustrating and sometimes tragic. Now, what can we do about it?

One thing I enjoyed about my early experiences in Catholicism: those nuns and priests were not fucking around. They had a sense that all of this mattered, very much, and they would be happy, even obligated, to kick your ass to help you see that too. Years later, I saw a priest at the funeral of a young person, an unexpected death, and he was walking around saying something like, "Is this surprising to you people? Why is this surprising?" It was like a lightning bolt, that directness.

BW: You've described an intensely ecstatic experience you had at twelve or thirteen, and how you longed for it to continue, though you knew it had to end. How does that fit alongside the regret you describe in "Congratulations, by the way," the now famous talk on kindness you gave to Syracuse graduates in 2013?

GS: I was in Friday-night Mass and had this feeling of what I'd describe as loving lineage—I felt part of a long line of Catholic practitioners ("Hi, Peter! Hi, Paul!") and felt a kind of ecstatic uplift at that brotherhood. And I felt it would be so beautiful if this feeling could be sustained. But alas.

I think those ecstatic experiences are favors God does you, in order to say, "You're not ready for this yet. You can't do it, but I'm not kidding—this state is real and valid." I still remember the clarity and power of those feelings. I felt this great and overwhelming affection for everything and everybody. But then I could feel it waning over the course of the regular-old Friday evening that followed. It was like a drug buzz: you're feeling this way because it's in your veins, but metabolically it can't stay there.

I was an earnest little kid. A little bit neurotic, but also very earnest. I remember going to first confession, which to me meant I was going to be pure for the first time in my life. And I remember feeling that purity, loving it, and then, walking out, knowing that my mind would think something perverse or I'd do something bad. And as soon as you think, "I might think something bad," your mind supplies some bad thing, and there you are, sullied again. When I look back, it seems sweet, how hard I tried to be good. At the time, I thought it was my fault that those feelings of purity and ecstasy went away. But I can also remember thinking, "You are the guy that had that experience and is now losing it and is worried about it, but you're okay. You're still all right. If it's real, it will come back."

I remember, at the end of the service, we'd always sing, "The Mass has ended. All go in peace. We must diminish and Christ increase." I really felt that happen to me, that once.

BW: Did you ever read the Catholic mystics?

GS: Years later. It was really too bad that wasn't part of my experience growing up. Although it did seem part of it organically. That is, some of that mystical experience came through the Mass—through its structure and so on. But I don't think we were overtly taught those things. We didn't read Saint Teresa or Merton or anybody like that, that I can recall.

Anyway, once you've had that experience as a young person, it's real to you forevermore. It's not trivial. It's not laughable. And you have a hunger for it thereafter. You could say, "Oh, I was just a crazy little hallucinator," but you know in your heart that isn't true. To me, that's one of the beautiful things about that tradition. At that time, it was not gentle, it was not ambiguous, and it was not touchy-feely—it was radical. Of course the radicalness, the extremity, produced a lot of bad side effects—but it also produced things that were profound.

For a couple of years when I was quite young, the Mass was still done in Latin, and my mom tells me I could say it from memory, beginning to end. Artistic things were going on there. Every day the altar would be decorated differently, in different colors, for different holy days and so on, and I remember being really interested in that—in the care that was taken in the visual display. And there were things about the Mass itself that were powerful training for a would-be artist. The Mass is a beautiful, big metaphor, and one thing a kid could learn by going to Mass over and over was that meaning can be conveyed in various ways, including sublingually and subconceptually, through metaphor and repetition and what is not said. That's great training for an artist—the idea that even if you can't articulate a certain effect, it can still be happening. Once that notion gets into you, you're hungry for it the rest of your life. I'm grateful for all those things: For the idea that you can be more than you think you are. For the idea of Christ blessing the unfortunate with his un-judging attention. That was powerful, and I'd say that was the beginning of political thinking for me.

As a kid I had this skin condition where I'd get cuts really easily, and I played football. My knees and ankles were always open wounds. We'd do the Stations of the Cross, and you'd have to kneel for a long time, and these sores would open up and start to ooze and sting. Very uncomfortable, very embarrassing. I remember talking with a nun about this problem, and her advice was, "Offer it up to the Lord." At the time I thought it was a bunch of bull, but I did it, and afterward I found I had discovered a way to sort of play through pain, so to speak. I remember thinking, "This hurts, yes . . . but what is hurt? Where is it located?" Which, in hindsight, I can see was a form of meditative experience. So I think that ungentle style of Catholicism led me to certain meditative insights I wouldn't have had otherwise.

This was helpful in later periods when a certain result wasn't coming to me as quickly as I would have liked, for example, in engineering school, or writing my first book. Immersed in what is starting to feel like a negative experience, you can slightly turn the mind and say, "This experience of failure is also part of this thing I'm trying to do." Rigor, and even harshness, are one way of forcing a person to explore the outer boundaries of who he is.

BW: It is not unusual for characters in your stories to pray. The narrators of "Offloading for Mrs. Schwartz" and "My Flamboyant Grandson" pray, as well as Don Eber in "Tenth of December," and there are more. What role does prayer play in your stories or for your characters?

GS: Let me start with a disclaimer: there can be years separating the composition of these stories, and when I write them, I'm just in the story trying to figure it out, just doing what I have to do. So the honest answer would be that I never really think about the role of prayer in my stories. So this is going to be a constructed answer.

But, when are you more honest than when you are praying? Narratively, prayer is handy, in the same way a Greek chorus is handy, because it lets you have a character speak directly to the camera. It's a way to let a character say, essentially: "Here's my truth, as well as I can tell it."

BW: Prayer rather than soliloquy.

GS: Yes. Or prayer *as* soliloquy. Because, really, what's the difference? A soliloquy is just some very honest, eloquent talking. So is prayer, but the honesty and eloquence are for God's benefit.

Often when I do something strange in a story it's just an attempt to find a natural-seeming way of doing something theatrical. So, for example, when

I have a ghost appear, that's a way of objectifying something that's actually rhetorical. We need a certain point of view represented. For example, in "The Wavemaker Falters," this guy has accidentally killed a kid, and I needed some way to make that tragedy more palpable. So I let the dead kid show up and earnestly kvetch about all he was missing out on.

BW: But for a reader, the presence of ghosts and prayer and so on seems to suggest that life is more than just what is evident in the material realm. Is this something you are thinking about when you're writing?

GS: Well, as I mentioned, my sense is that we live in an incredibly material time. We like stuff, yes, but we are also inclined to think that whatever is, is *all* there is. Whatever we feel is sufficient. Whatever we habitually think is right. That's a weird contemporary trait, that we could be so arrogant as to think that it just so happens that in this generation we are fully equipped to know all that there is, and that we can know it logically and via the senses, period. And this inclination leads us to be very rational and data-reliant and pragmatic and mystery-denying—and yet mystery is real. We have no satisfactory answers for any of the biggest questions.

For me, spirituality is the more intelligent part of me asking, "What are the odds that you, a little created cellular creature, just happen to be ideally suited to understand all of this?" Smarter generations have known that we are just sensing little bits of whatever the ultimate reality is. They treasured those little bits, and they didn't overanalyze them or discount them. The spiritual life acknowledges that those little glimpses are real. I can't get back to them all the time, but I can at least not forget that they exist. That would basically be my definition of the sacred: those little traces of that greater knowledge that extend beyond our everyday ability to grasp it—and then the spiritual life is just that set of rituals or practices that serve to remind us of the reality of those glimpses.

Any moment in which you say to yourself, "All right, stop bullshitting, please," or turn your mind to your actual fears, or are shaken out of your usual position of clinging to certain things for comfort (your success, your position, your unerring goodness)—that is a moment of prayer. Prayer is truth, or is steering oneself toward truth. Prayer is briefly getting free of our habit of denial, maybe. Sometimes I think it's just taking a moment to ask, "Where am I?" and then answering that as honestly as you can. The convention is that we pray "to" God—but it reduces to the same thing, I think.

BW: So prayer reminds us of the truth, of something that is significant, even if you aren't feeling it at present?

GS: Yes. Maybe, too, that's what devotion is: a habit of trying to remind yourself that your current state of normalcy is not necessarily accurate. It's as if you were a blind person who periodically saw. Each time, you'd ask yourself, "Was that a hallucination?" And the right answer would be: "No. Sight is real, but it just isn't available to me right now."

BW: You've talked about writing as a means of praying, as a sort of functional praying.

GS: I think real praying is something different. I don't want to be the guy who says, "I don't pray because I write." How convenient! I do think there are some similarities between, say, the level of concentration in writing and meditating—but I don't know. Better to do both.

BW: You have a number of characters who self-identify as Christian, such as Giff in "CommComm," who belongs to the ChristLife Reënactors group (they stage events from the life of Jesus). Despite the comedy, your depiction of religious characters, church characters, is not sarcastic or critical. You don't poke fun. As silly or misguided as they can be, they seem to be played straight. That's not entirely atypical in this literary moment, but I've found your depictions somehow different.

GS: Part of it is that, having had a real experience, I'm less prone to throw it under the bus. But it also comes from the way stories evolve. In a first draft, the characters are poorly made; they're crude, cartoonish puppets. As you revise, they get facial features, they start to move in particular ways. And always, you are trying to make the character be his or her most intense and interesting self. Through the revision process, that is.

I started "CommComm" mostly because of a guy, a nice guy, an old friend, who was giving me the spiel that the Iraq war was a just war, per Saint Augustine. Somehow the way he was doing it was disappointing to me, because he was overriding all those other Christian teachings about not killing. Sometimes as I start a story, I think, "I'll correct that guy, or parody that viewpoint." A good place to start, often.

But the beautiful thing about revision is that after a couple of months, the story starts getting tired of being so tightly controlled. It wants to mean what it wants to mean, and your original conception is cramping its style. So at that point you have a choice: cling to your original conception, and have a boring or unfinishable story, or give the story some rope. In this case, that meant saying, "Okay, I started out playing mock the fundamentalist, but the story seems to want me to take him somewhat seriously." Then it gets interesting. You think, "Well, I've said he is a fundamentalist and that's bad. And I demonstrated that. But what *else* is he? What if he not only believes, but will put his money where his mouth is?" In this case, Giff started to be sort of honorable, or at least considerable, in the purity of his belief, and in the lengths he would go to in order to live them out. He didn't want to be a cardboard cutout—he wanted to be a person.

You go into writing a story with a certain static view, and then the fictive process destabilizes it. This tends to push the narrative toward empathy. I honestly don't know why this should be the case, but I've seen it time and again.

This motion has more to do with technique than religion. There's a certain stance toward religion that your cookie-cutter liberal agnostic or atheist will take, and I don't really like that. It's the same with politics. I don't like it when people simply mock; that isn't that interesting, and as a fictive technique it doesn't stand up. But attention to technique—to truth, and velocity, and logic—will often force you out of your lazy, received beliefs and into something much fresher, which is sometimes even a little scary.

BW: Does some of that come out of your own desire to be kind?

GS: It's the other way around, actually. Writing, I think, can train us to be kind, or kinder anyway—to look twice at the people we are making and cut them a little slack.

My natural disposition is to be willing to look a little closer at odd people—probably because I was raised on the South Side of Chicago. It was a funny, crazy, lovely world, and I had affection for so many different kinds of people. Dispositionally, I like fiction in which people are shown to be multivalent. I try to write those kind of stories.

The downside of this is—and I've been thinking about this a lot lately—you internalize this technique, or you have this aspiration to kindness. But is all this a function of my nice life? If you're a tenured, well-paid professor at a nice university in America—in that world, kindness works great. But what about in Syria, or somewhere else where circumstances are different? What would kindness look like there? Not just smiling all the time, or holding the door open for people.

BW: In other interviews, you've mentioned Anton Chekov, Raymond Carver, and Ernest Hemingway as influences. Are writers like Nathaniel Hawthorne or Flannery O'Connor, who write violent and religious stories, also influences? There is a good deal of violence in your stories.

GS: I love what O'Connor says: "The writer can choose what he writes about but he cannot choose what he is able to make live." That has been like a mantra for me, and it's sometimes heartbreaking. I don't particularly like writing violent, off-color stuff, but if I don't, somehow the thing stays dead on the page. When you begin, you're trying desperately not to have your story be dead on arrival, and you do this by any means necessary. Be a clown? Sure! Exaggerated violence? If that's what it takes. Because without energy, fiction is and does nothing. It conveys no moral stance, no thematic content. As soon as somebody shuts the book, the story's active period—the period during which it can actually cause something out in the world—is over.

Why would it be that, for me, darkness conveys power? I have a bunch of responses, because I don't really know the answer. My main argument is that if you are going to write about kindness, you'd better do it in a test layout that isn't *de facto* invalid. I think fiction is a scale model of reality. In reality, there's good and there's evil. In order for a story to be a valid experiment, good and evil have to be about the same size, like in the real world, and then they have to be allowed to fight. So that's why (I sometimes say) I put violence in.

But do I have to put in quite so much? As a kid I watched a lot of television, and we always played violently. My guess is that it's also something neurological, the way violence interests me and has animated my imagination.

BW: You often use two point-of-view characters within a story—as in "The Falls," "Victory Lap," and "Tenth of December," among others. What does that offer you? Is there something intentional in that?

GS: "Necessity is the mother of invention" is amazingly true in fiction. When I wrote "The Falls," I had just finished a first book, and I was so sick of first-person. I almost got to the point where I couldn't do first-person without self-imitating. I had to write something else, anything else. My thought at the time was that third person can have a freer diction than I had allowed myself in that first book, and so I was drawn to that. I just had to get out of those tight first-person clothes. In that first section of "The Falls," I had so much fun with the neurotic character. I knew somebody like that. I had that section around for a long time, and I took a break for about six months to read and try to catch up at work after writing that first book. And then I did another free-write that turned out to be the other guy. The trick was just to make two voices that were not the same. And then, I thought it would be cool to put those two guys in the same story.

Other times, a story wouldn't move forward, or agree to be finished, in just one voice. So then you turn to a second narrator as a kind of Hail Mary move. "Can you, second narrator, help us out of this bind we find ourselves in?"

I think what I like about having two narrators is that it's true to my way of seeing things. What's happening in this room right now? A bunch of molecules are spinning around—that's all. But also, *that* set of molecules over there—you—has a consciousness. And I've got a consciousness, too. There are two incredible monologues going on inside our heads, and, now and then—like if you were to try and steal my wallet, say—they intersect a little bit. That's life. When I write those stories, I'm being truthful. And then the story can arise, very naturally, out of some small conflict or interaction between those created minds. It lets me put aside all of those messy, inhibiting thoughts about plot and theme and so on.

BW: While you aren't writing science fiction per se, your stories include elements of that genre. When I've described your writing to friends, I've said, "He's not writing stories set fifty years in the future; he's writing about tomorrow." There is something very familiar in your futuristic stories, even when they incorporate elements like virtual reality or, in a story like "The Semplica-Girl Diaries," when people are used as outdoor decorations. Do you see your stories as science fiction?

GS: My feeling is, the gateway to any story is energy. You have to have some way of getting things going—something that excites you, something that makes you confident enough and interested enough to generate prose. Sometimes you do something because it makes cool sentences. For me, introducing some sort of science fiction element is often just a way of getting myself interested. I work on the assumption that it doesn't really matter what I start with—a genre conceit, a monologue, a realistic description of a mall. Whatever I have to say will get said if I only (1) start and (2) revise like crazy. If you take any system of symbols and obsess about it for three years, eventually some light will come off it. (Unless you know too well what light you want to come off it. If it's over-managed, the light won't come.)

The idea for the "The Semplica-Girl Diaries" came to me in a dream. And I thought, "Well, that's edgy. I'm interested in that, so we can go ahead." I'm working on a book now that started with an image that came to me twenty years ago that I have not been able to shake. I thought, "All right, if you can hold my interest for twenty years, I'm going to pay some attention to you."

I have a tendency to become a banal realist if I'm not careful. By putting these weird elements in, I guarantee that that won't happen. Putting something ugly or ungainly or futuristic in a story might be a form of pre-compensation. I have a tendency to be sentimental and overly lyrical, and if I put in some science fiction shit, it destabilizes everything sufficiently that I can't drift back to that banal mode. Even if my kneejerk tendency toward sentimentality tries to assert itself, a story reads differently once we have some nympho robots wandering around.

BW: I've been fascinated by the names you give your characters and places. How do these names come to you—as you're writing, or do you think of them beforehand?

GS: If they don't come at-speed, as I'm writing the story, they are false. They have to make sonic sense, given their location in the sentence.

When you're inside the world of a story, there's an incredible swirl of meanings, and your mind is working at a very high level, very intuitively. The right name will often just pop out. I never liked the idea of having a character's name reflect his character, like having an impotent guy be called Mr. Limp. It seems somehow unfair.

But anything can work. There was a time when our daughter was little and I would shout into the next room, "Sweetie, character name!" and she'd say something like, "Gil Fern!" and I'd shout back, "Thank you," and put it right in.

Those were the days. Now I have to call her in Chicago.

Interview with George Saunders

Aidan Ryan / 2016

From the *White Review*, June 2016. http://www.thewhitereview.org/feature/interview-with
-george-saunders/. Reprinted by permission of the author.

The American short story writer George Saunders has the kind of reputation that makes one hesitate before typing his email into an address line. It's
not really his outsize presence in the contemporary literary world, though
this is staggering: he is the winner of Guggenheim and MacArthur fellowships, while Mary Karr called him "the best" short story writer working
in English when *Time* picked him as one of the most influential people of
2013, the same year his latest collection, *Tenth of December*, won universal
acclaim for its blend of emotional immediacy, familiar absurdity, and ethical
complexity. What gave me pause, though, was his reputation for *kindness*,
the theme of his (now viral) 2013 commencement address at Syracuse University. Presenting himself with typical humility as "some old fart, his best
years behind him," Saunders used the occasion to tell his audience (and
within days, the world) about his regrets. All, he said, were "failures of kindness." "Try to be kinder" is the speech's title and its soundbite: Saunders
admits that it's facile, but he also reminds us that as a maxim it can be really,
really *hard*.

His stories are violent, hilarious, confusing—but I've always felt behind
them an animating spirit that was essentially, unfalteringly benevolent. Mechanically, too, his stories feature characters striving to be kinder (and often
failing): fathers struggling to provide for their kids, kid-veterans seeking
stable definitions of "family" and "home," or wearied workers wandering
clumsily through worlds strange but too much like our own to be labeled,
comfortably, "the future."

Consciously or not, Saunders never presents himself as the artist-as-
intellectual, artist-as-culture-hero, or artist-as-formidable-genius (though
he is all these things). His writer-persona is the artist-as-gentle-craftsman,

and his answers, as he explains his craft, are surprising, resourceful, cordial, given weight by the gravity of one preternaturally awake to wonder. In the interview below, Saunders uses whatever tool comes to hand: metaphor, confession, concession, contradiction; touchpoints in his generous answers include Gerald Stern and David Hickey, Dylan and Chekhov, Buddhist thought and black boxes.

Working on a Master's dissertation triangulating Saunders among the post-postmodernists, I caught George at a busy time, and it wouldn't have tarnished his reputation for kindness if he'd refused my questions. But he accepted. "I'm in the throes of finishing up a new thing but would be open to an email exchange," he wrote (perhaps referencing the long-awaited first novel, which he recently hinted in conversation with Jennifer Egan would be set in a Saundersised nineteenth century). "Fire when ready." Reading and rereading his answers, one feeling remained an undertone, constant through each new discovery. How grateful we must be, I thought, for this man's "throes."

Aidan Ryan: Ben Marcus offers one of my favorite descriptions of your work in his introduction to your 2004 *Believer* interview: "The Suits call his writing 'stories,' but they are really soft bodies to wear for a larger experience of life, hollowcore person-shapes that one can slip on in order to attain amazement." But his description, like your stories, might be deceptively simple, because while we "slip on" these fictional bodies, they aren't always easy acts of empathy. Your stories seem to hold a challenge to the reader like the one implied by the narrator, a returning veteran, to his family, in your story "Home": Empathize with me.

George Saunders: Sure, yes. I think this is what all fiction does, really, or tries to do—encourages us to step out of ourselves and into someone else, temporarily. Which, in my view, is *de facto* a moral experience. What might take a given story out of facile advocacy ("Be nicer, everyone!") is its complexity and particularity. I guess I believe in the idea that love equals attention and vice versa—so if we pay enough attention to a fictional character, even if he's a total shmuck, the resulting piece of prose will be an act of love (in its highest and best sense) toward him.

And yes—I always say I try not to write with a definite intention, and that is true. But lately it's occurred to me that one of the reasons I'm so emphatic about that is to counterbalance my very natural tendency to write with a definite (dogmatic) intention, i.e., to know too well where I'm going. It's sort of an autocorrect I'm doing on myself to counteract what I know is a lazy or preachy tendency, that doomed a lot of my apprentice stories to lying flat on the page.

Or: because I take it as a given that stories are about highly charged moral situations, I have to work against making the situations too didactic or easily solved—have to force the fictional universe to push back against my lazy assumptions and habitual moral stances.

AR: I notice that while your characters may find difficult redemption within these "highly charged moral situations," I can't find any instances of broader, lasting social or structural change. *The Brief and Frightening Reign of Phil* might be representative, as it ends with a pretty strong hint that peace won't last, that demagogues are as inevitable as the human tendency to invent difference, and pull from difference suspicion, and then hate . . . You've mentioned didactic tendencies: do you ever feel drawn to use fiction as a field to test visions of a better world?

GS: I'm not sure how that would work. I mean, if, in a piece of fiction, you "show" a certain type of social action working successfully, what have you done? What have you actually proven? You are working in Jello, essentially. If I show "my" solution working, no doubt I've loaded the deck somehow, if you see what I mean. When I say that fiction shouldn't be didactic, I don't mean that it shouldn't or can't have political or moral-ethical heft. I'm saying that stories shouldn't exist as too-easy proofs for one's pre-existing beliefs. And this isn't really a moral statement by me, or an aesthetic credo—it's more owner's-manual stuff: a story like that simply won't work. It's proceeding by methods which are counter to the physics of the form.

When we think of how "solutions" might be presented or represented in a fictive setting, we might want to remember Chekhov's admonition that art doesn't have to solve problems, it just has to formulate them correctly. Fiction writing is pattern-making. We aim to make beautiful patterns, but how to do that is not rigorously known, since each pattern's beauty has to do with the extent to which the pattern is aware of, and referring to, itself. In a fictive space, the mere suggestion of an impulse is often enough. The fact that some people in "Bounty" are trying to revolt is meaningful. The small motion the "Semplica Girl Diaries" narrator has made toward awareness, imperfect as it is, indicates that change is possible. Eva's existence indicates the notion that "good people can exist." So if we see fiction as a scale-model, you only need one railroad car to suggest a national transportation system, and one of the pleasures of the fictive scale model is that sense that everything is present and accounted for and in some sort of pleasing proportion. Whatever might move a human being towards perfection or enlightenment can be shown in a story—maybe fleetingly, maybe through its absence—but I don't think we need to worry about solutions.

If, as Marcus suggested, art can be hollowcore person-shapes that one can slip on in order to attain amazement—well, then, that would be, in and of itself, an incredible moral-ethical (i.e., political) accomplishment. Like, if a song, whose lyrics you couldn't quite make out, made you fall in love with the world and resolve to be smarter and more alert—that, I'd say, is a moral accomplishment. It's a thing-that-is-doing-something, rather than a rational statement or piece of advice. And as such, might need to be supra- or anti-logical . . .

AR: Is the act of writing an inherently ethical undertaking, for you, then? And do you see your narratives as fictional ethics?

GS: Well . . . I think I'm going to say yes. While writing, I'm always trying to imagine that the character is as real as me and as engaged and heartful and smart. With maybe a few flaws or intentional differences from me—me on a different day. And then I want the character to proceed in a roughly sensible way (i.e., the way you or I would). So I guess that's an ethical approach. But there are real limits to this, since, as mentioned above, I am controlling all the variables.

My go-to model for my stories—a model that actually helps me write them—is that a story is a black box, into which the reader goes, and something happens. Something big and breathtaking and non-trivial. I don't have to know what that thing is beforehand—it's going to reveal itself to me at speed and I don't need to be able to pithily reduce it. I just have to micromanage the machinery inside the box so as to maximize the various effects—to sharpen the curves, so to speak. Now, mysteriously, thinking of stories this way does tend to produce themes and ethical resonance and all of that—how, I don't know. But I'm okay with not knowing. I just want to get better at the doing.

I think people consider my stories political because they tend to be morally intense: people are put in fictive situations where what they do matters. That is: in situations where life is made to seem valuable and precious and fraught. I write those kinds of stories just because . . . those are the kinds of stories that got me interested in writing fiction in the first place. I want fiction to do emotional work, or why bother? The difference between one writer and another might just be the means he or she applies to achieve that end—one's view of the world will tell one how best to go for the throat. What I've found over my years of writing is that straightforward realism doesn't get me where I want to go. I don't have that gift. My realist writing feels too safe and reactionary—I feel more outrage in day-to-day living than a realist approach allows me to express. Or: when I think of what's actually going on here—the briefness of life vs the "normalized" way we go through our days (denying death, planning very sanely for everything, as if we're going to live forever)—it feels that conventional narrative is insufficient. It's kind of like, if you see a snake and it scares the shit out of you, typing, "Suddenly I saw a snake" doesn't get it—has nothing to do with what you felt in that instant. How to use or exploit or get at that (having-seen-snake) energy? The energy of what you actually felt in that instant? That's the question. And the answer—the prose that could achieve that—might have fuck-all to do with snakes, if you see what I mean.

But having said all of this—I think we have to be a little careful when we start talking about fiction-as-ethics and all of that. A story based on that idea can turn out awfully facile and thin. Mainly because fiction is an argumentative system with movable parameters, supplied by the author. Any meaning that comes of a story is not related to the outcome of the events in the story—or, let's say, is only related to the extent that the system is fair and rigorous. It's the *internal dynamics* of the story that cause meaning. The way that A opposes B, and so on. The existence of C in the same story as D, and the way they push off one another.

So that's why I'm a little uncomfortable with talk about "moral fiction." I do think art does moral work, but that work has more to do with destabilizing us and making us re-examine whatever position we are holding—humbling us, as it were. That's a moral position but not a position of "knowing" or advocacy.

So I don't think fiction exists to demonstrate ethics, or advocate for certain actions. I think it exists to remind us of the complexity of living. And the beauty. And the horror. My favorite English phrase is "on the other hand." Fiction does a lot of that. It "on-the-other-hand"s us into a state of confusion and uncertainty that is very holy and very hard to achieve or sustain.

AR: How do you know when a story is "finished"? When it resists your writerly/readerly attempts to draw out an easy meaning, a rationale?

GS: Well, for me, this is something that happens continuously along the way. You keep creating too-easy meanings and then complicating them. And that has to do with keeping my attention on the line-to-line energy. Improving that improves everything. It undercuts the too-easy ideas and intentionality, it raises the ambient intelligence of the piece, etc.

So you start out and try not to have any intentions and so on, but then, partway through (you can't deny it) there's some "meaning" appearing. Then your job is to be skeptical and interrogate that meaning (by these

line-to-line methods). Or, to continually ask yourself if the apparent meaning of the story is more facile than what the eventual meaning might turn
out to be.

If the story wants to go in a new direction, you let it. If a line is good but
it doesn't fit with your plan, keep the line, kill (amend) the plan. I always
quote that Gerald Stern bit: "If you start out to write a poem about two dogs
fucking, and you write a poem about two dogs fucking—then you wrote a
poem about two dogs fucking." Along with Einstein's bit: "No worthy problem is ever solved in the plane of its original conception." Those two quotes
are the essence of this approach. Let the story lead you.

All of this is based on the idea that the subconscious (or whatever the
correct term is for that great under-intelligence we all have that comes to
the surface now and then) is vastly powerful—much smarter and wisdom-
infused than our everyday minds.

At the end I know *where* the story has energy and know that I have inves-
tigated every possible change and wouldn't change a line—but I might not
"know" what it means in terms of being able to reduce it to a pithy statement. Three things to remember in this context: first, a story always means
beyond its thematic valence. The "how it proceeds" is why we love it, more
than the "what it means." Second, the goal is for that meaning to be complex and irreducible. Third, the meaning will, often, show up very late in the
game, without me expecting it or seeing it coming. It's like a new or more
complex meaning sort of falls into place, because I change a line or add a
line or invert a couple of sections or something. And those changes came in
response to close, intuitive line work—often what I'd consider an "ear thing."
Something sounds better, or two sections work better if transposed, or the
addition of a new section suddenly lifts the whole thing up. But all of those
changes occur via intuition, at speed. So it goes: make a move, notice related
change in meaning.

AR: Do you ever worry you've written a character that might be beyond
a reader's powers of empathy—or wonder if you could?

GS: I don't think that's possible. If I genuinely revised myself into a position of empathy, then the reader will follow. If I don't feel empathy (or if I
force a fake empathy) that will be felt in the prose, and the reader will depart
from me. (And hopefully I'll have caught that in the revision process, and
disallowed it.) So your question is, to my mind, more a technical question
than an ethical or aesthetic one. In stories like "The Barber's Unhappiness"
or "Al Roosten," I started out disliking the character, feeling mostly scorn,

but then the process of revision forced me to a better, richer understanding of these guys. I had to gain that new understanding or the story would continue to be moribund. Improving lines and transitions and the internal logic is exactly equal, strangely, to improving one's ability to empathize with the (unlikeable) main character. It's like compassion training wheels: a slow-motion opportunity to improve one's way of regarding other people, through close attention to one's prose.

But maybe what you're asking has to do with another question that's been on my mind lately—there must be people/characters for whom empathy is not the right approach. Let's call these "real dicks." (Or, we might say, conventional touchy-feely kindness/empathy isn't what's needed—to apply that would be a form of what Buddhists call "idiot compassion.") How are these people to be regarded and represented in fiction? There's something lame about auto-applying the same kind of soft empathy to everybody. There are people who are manifesting zero good traits and have very little hope of ever doing so: sociopaths, brutal dictators, etc. Again, here, for my answer, I guess I'd turn to the "attention = love" trope. If we paid very close attention to the specifics of, say, Hitler's life, we might feel the judgment ("Hitler sucked!") fall away and get replaced (or supplemented) by . . . something else. A sort of plain seeing—a kind of cold understanding, let's call it. We might be able to grasp what the world looked like to him. That is powerful. We would have a better handle on what "evil" really was. (That is, it doesn't look like evil to the person manifesting it.) If you want to eliminate or transform (insert name of evil entity), then endeavor to understand (insert name of evil entity), and even to sympathetically, *generously* understand (insert name of evil entity).

Also—the story form, as I've experienced, is meant to represent those for whom change is possible and imminent—so maybe Hitler just doesn't belong in a short story. If someone really couldn't change (and there are certainly real people in that category) then it would be hard to construct a story around them, unless that story was, "Craig, a total a-hole, should have changed on that day, and almost did—but didn't." And that could be a story, for sure.

AR: "Ethical critics" like Wayne Booth and Martha Nussbaum argue that fiction's quality of encouraging empathy is a unique moral tool, while aesthetes like Richard Posner say that this cheapens fiction, that empathy is an amoral act—citing for example our empathy with Shakespeare's villains. You shared your own discomfort with fiction as a vessel for "ideas" (especially moral or political ideas) with David Sedaris, but do you think there's an inherent ethical value in fiction's power to encourage empathy, no matter the work or character in question?

GS: But villains should be empathized with—what's the harm? We don't want to confuse "empathy" with "forgiveness" or "apathy." As I started to say above, if we understand empathy not to be something warm and fuzzy or New Age but, rather, let's say: "seeing, shorn of projection"—then it is amoral, in the sense that it just lets us see what is. Which, you could argue, helps us act efficiently, when action is necessary, and also helps us defer action, so as not to make stupid mistakes. So if we have some perceived enemy and work ourselves into a froth and project all of our shit onto him, we will be inclined to make dumb decisions, as we try to change him. Whereas if we look at the world from his viewpoint (and again, not with the aspiration of feeling warm-and-fuzzy towards him, but just of really seeing him, or seeing things from his POV) then anything we do will just be more on point. It will be based on the way things really are.

But having said that, I think we have to be careful. The more we talk about the moral aims and abilities of fiction, the more we paint ourselves into a certain corner. The critic Dave Hickey has written about this—how, if we say what art should or can do, this can get twisted and misunderstood as saying what art *must* do—which can become good ammo for anti-art reactionaries. Art is, or should be, a place of total freedom, and we don't know what it does, precisely, or why, or how. We don't need to know and don't want to. Each work does something new, or tries to.

When I talk about empathy, I'm talking about a space the reader and writer agree to participate in together, within the playing field of a work of prose—in which they agree to make up a person and, together, go, "What would it be like to be her? How does she think? From what valid impulse do her mistakes stem?" And so on. And actually, the real love or empathy in a work of fiction is not only writer loving character, but also writer loving reader—manifesting respect in each line and so on. We always think of empathy in fiction as going from reader towards character—but I think the reason fiction moves us has to do as much with the notion that somebody out there (the writer) thinks well of us, and is regarding us as his equal and so on . . .

AR: I'm interested in the role naïveté plays in your fiction. The almost-fifteen-year-old Alison in "Victory Lap" is one example: she says, "To do good, you just have to decide to do good." As you said on the *Organist* podcast, she believes it, you believe she believes it, you kind of like her for believing it, but you have to be skeptical, you have to test it. And then in "Semplica Girl Diaries," the daughter Eva's complete naïveté acts like the family's conscience—"If we want to help them, why can't we just give them the money?"

Your fiction always shows that it's so, so much harder than that—but it seems that to be able really to test these expressions of naïveté one has to be able to entertain them, so the reader recognizes the legitimate impulse behind that naïveté, without ultimately accepting the viewpoint.

GS: Right. I always think of a thing Dylan said in his book, something like, "Sometimes I write what I know to be true; sometimes I write what I know to be false; sometimes I write something and don't know whether it's true or false." So if I have a character say, "It's terrible that children are starving in India when I have just eaten three Big Macs"—well, that's true. But it's also a little smug, showboaty. It would be bad writing, I suppose, if you felt that I, the author, very simply agreed with that statement—that I didn't know that the person saying that is being a little naïve or unrealistic or self-satisfied or whatever. I can communicate my knowingness by having someone else say, "Well, why don't you FedEx three Big Macs over there, dumbass?" or I can have that character do or say something else that, taken with that statement, presents him in full, or challenges him, or penalizes him, or "shows" that I do not consider him 100 percent right. I think here of Chekhov's story "Gooseberries," which has this beautiful and very passionate and naïve speech, in which the character urges some friends to do good, eschew happiness, etc.—it's too late for him, but they should live more purely. And Chekhov does this really brilliant thing of making that guy's speeches incredibly persuasive and intelligent—you can't deny that what he is saying is basically correct. And the reader goes, "Hell yes, I agree with that guy." But then Chekhov has the friends be bored by this (didactic) speech, and that night, when the speech-giver goes to bed, he leaves his smelly pipe on the nightstand, and the pipe keeps one of his friends awake all night with its bad odor. So instead of being a one-dimensional propaganda piece (a tract on self-denial and do-goodery, with which we might mostly agree) it becomes a beautifully complicated reflection on the role of pleasure and happiness in our lives. Now, I'd contend that this story is a furious and wonderful moral-ethical object—it's moving and disturbing and it brings forth all of one's feelings about happiness and decadence and how we privileged few should live in the world, given that there's so much suffering—but I don't think it "advises" anything. It sets the problem on its feet and says, "Huh, look at this." And whatever "moral" work the story might do, it does in that ambiguity—in the holy confusion it makes—which would, I think, make one slower to act and less confident about moral tidiness. You walk away thinking not "Now I see what's right" but "Ah, yes, it's like that, isn't it? Complicated."

So the writer might be seen as an idea-generator. The job is to generate these in a vivid way, so that they come to life. It doesn't matter which idea the writer "believes." His job is not to argue or persuade but to be really good at making living breathing beings, who run around saying interesting and convincing things, and then the writer runs over to the other side of the table and makes a living breathing being who says some interesting and convincing things that totally contradict the other guy.

That's where fiction grows out of being mere polemic and starts being beautiful art. Stories as dynamic systems of contradiction, the upshot of which is something like: (1) don't be too sure, and (2) love the world.

AR: Often your fiction seems like a fulfillment of what David Foster Wallace said in 1993, at the end of his essay "E Unibus Pluram." He predicts the next literary "rebels" will toss out irony and maybe even embrace naïveté, risk even sentimentality, melodrama, credulity. (The critic Adam Kelly puts Wallace at the vanguard of this movement, calling it "The New Sincerity.") So, you haven't tossed out irony, but you've resisted the postmodern impulse to sneer—and without that drone note, the reader can hear more voices (representing overlapping worldviews). Did you ever see sentimentality as a risk? What about too much irony?

GS: Well, the thing is, this is what literary rebels have always been doing, including Shakespeare, Gogol, et al. (becoming "skeptical of irony" or skeptical of "mere" irony).

For me, the main thing was (and is) to not make trivial work—work that poses too-easy answers to not-critical questions. We're here, we're living, loving, but won't be for long—so I want my stories to somehow urgently acknowledge all of that. So I don't think we'd want to risk sentimentality, if we define sentimentality as "causing unearned emotion." I think we'd want to risk earned emotion. But to do that—to risk earned emotion—we might have to pioneer new techniques. Or depart from regular old realism as necessary (as storytellers have always done, going even back to the cavemen and so on).

But actually—let me go a little further, and contradict myself, and say, yes, we could even theoretically evoke genuine emotion via sentimentality or melodrama—or whatever. There are no limits to the way we can evoke genuine emotion. That is the big principle of art. Maybe the emotion gets evoked in the reader when he notes the author stretching a given form, working it beyond its usual limits. To say it another way: a story is a dynamic system and we perceive meaning and delight via the way the thing moves internally. Here I'm thinking of a couple of experiments I tried—"In Persuasion Nation" and "Brad Carrigan, American." They were overtly 'ironic' and used a sort of easy satirizing of pop-culture and advertising, and so the experiment was: could I get that soufflé to rise, i.e., could I get the stories to evoke emotion, even though their materials were designed for mockery? I felt that, in the end, the answer with both was, yes, sort of. But that led me to believe that a work of art makes us feel things to the extent that (1) we don't know what we're trying to do or how it's going to get done, and (2) we keep working toward more and more intensity of form (maybe it's that intensification of, or within, a given form or constraint that causes the reader to feel something).

AR: How do you feel about reviewers still calling you a satirist, then? I've only read a handful (Sam Lipsyte comes to mind) who've challenged this, but it's on the book jackets, it's in most newspaper reviews: "Savage satirist." The genre's associated with scorn, with moral surety—things that have no place in the kind of tense ambiguity you just described.

GS: Honestly, I've just learned to accept it, inaccurate as I feel it might be. To me, satire is more one-dimensional and sure of its relation to its subject. I've always—always—thought of myself as a fiction writer with comic inclinations. So this recurring identification as a satirist doesn't really bother me but I can't do much with it.

Sometimes I use that question as an occasion to make a distinction between satire and the comic. Or I might acknowledge that there are satirical elements within my stories—places where I seem to be satirizing, you know, advertising or corporations. But if someone feels that's all I'm doing—that that's the primary mission—then I've failed.

It's just much cleaner to go: I'm a fiction writer. I use any- and everything I need to get certain effects that I'd describe as "emotional effects"—to do the good old aesthetic work that stories do. So, in other words, as a producer of art, I try to keep things as simple as I can, i.e., the questions of my place within satire, or satire's place within the broader cultural project, don't interest me that much—aren't necessary for me to do what I do and might (might) even be harmful. Because if I decide X about my role, or my style, or whatever, and then venture into a story where clinging to X is causing me to miss the actual energy of the story—well, then shame on me. So I think originality would be related to one's ability to resist self-labelling and the related self-policing. Steer toward the energy, no matter what. Hope that you somehow break a mold or two, intentionally or not.

AR: You've mentioned conversations with Wallace, Jonathan Franzen, Ben Marcus, in the early 1990s, when you talked about the challenge of writing emotionally honest fiction. What were their hang-ups and what were yours? Have you (singular; collective) succeeded?

GS: My memory of those talks is just that, under the surface, each of us was struggling with a sort of inherited idea that art had to have edge and mustn't be too realistic or emotional or mushy . . . a suite of ideas, the ones Dave was talking about in his essay. And these ideas were sort of roping us off from what fiction has always strived to do—we were sort of prisoners of our own inherited idea of the necessary level of hipness or something. And each had, in his own way, hit a sort of ceiling with that outlook. It was the struggle to retain a kind of newness in the prose and the approach (in order to serve the eternal newness of the world, or the weirdness of our particular time) but without sacrificing heart and/or the old honorable work of fiction—the part about engaging the big moral questions and so on.

My arc has been, basically: a very traditional writer and thinker (traditional by default because he was a rube who, when younger, didn't read much contemporary fiction) finally lived enough to wear out his attempts to imitate older writers (Hemingway, Kerouac). When I was around twenty-five, I read Stuart Dybek's "Hot Ice" and that threw open a lot of doors, because it was very moving and was set in a place I knew (South Side of Chicago) and also was just magical and mythic and it seemed that nothing was disallowed. It was also emotionally true to what my teenaged life in Chicago had felt like and sounded like and so on. But it wasn't straightforward realism. Anything went. So that was interesting, to see what a piece of fiction that was coming out of "my" world sounded like and what it made bold to include.

Reading Dybek was the beginning of a long schlep, to try to find a way to express some truths I was discovering, about what life in America was like when a person found himself in a state of paucity, under financial duress. I read Carver, and that was eye-opening. I loved the severity of his style and the fact that he was taking on class issues and so on. I read the postmodern guys and didn't really quite get it—they seemed too removed from what I was going through. My problem was, I found I couldn't get much heat going in straightforward realism—even in Carveresque realism—and

I wasn't intellectually sophisticated enough to really understand postmodern writers like Barth, Coover, Barthelme, etc. I'd had little intimations that I could be weird and funny, and that I responded to a certain sort of absurdism in art (Monty Python loomed large) but I didn't feel this strange stuff was "literature" (i.e., it wasn't 'real' enough). Around 1986 I'd had a mini-breakthrough with a story called "A Lack of Order in the Floating Object Room" that was very much like what *CivilWarLand in Bad Decline* would be, later, but because I couldn't quite intellectually justify it or understand it (and couldn't sustain it)—I sort of froze there and went back to imitating Hemingway et al.

Anyway, years later, when we'd had both our kids, something snapped into place: the idea that there was no difference, at all, between so-called experimental writing and emotional writing. You did the "experiments" in order to go to the wall emotionally. There was no other reason to do it. An "experiment" was just whatever was necessary to get the desired energy into your work. So the dichotomy cleared up: do whatever it takes. Steer toward the energy. Don't worry about being edgy or not being edgy or being soppy—if the emotion of the story is real and earned, it sort of retroactively justifies whatever form you've used.

AR: If your aim suggests continuity—to do what the best fiction has always done, but for your time—do you see your writing (and that of Wallace et al.) as in any essential way different from what came immediately before?

GS: Honestly, I struggle to answer this. Mainly because I think the answer lies in the future doing. I am trying my best to do something new and non-trivial and bold. It helps me to read what came before—and then react to or against that, intuitively. To think conceptually about it doesn't help me much, I've found. Read, live, react. Revise. That's really it for me, in a nutshell. And I don't mean that as an anti-intellectual position—but a revved-up form of intellectuality, that includes intuition as a legit arrow in the quiver. What's going to make my work vital and new is my taste, applied maniacally, over sufficient time.

It's not that I don't think about this sort of thing—I spend a lot of time mentally kvetching about culture and old forms of art and other writers and so on, and what America is becoming, and all of that—but I don't articulate the results very well, because they are essentially inarticulable. When a hitter is up against a great pitcher, how does he get better at hitting the guy? Some thinking, some study—but mostly via thousands of muscular and mental micro-adjustments that happen faster than language. Writing is similar, I think. Sometimes criticism seems uncomfortable with this aspect of art but in my experience, it is 99 percent of the game. Criticism tends to put, in my view, an undue emphasis on intentionality—as if the writer had it all planned out in advance and as if his main goal was to "demonstrate" or "prove" something. I really want to play, and discover the internal dynamics of the story—find out, via intuition, what thrills the story wants to deliver.

George Saunders

Zadie Smith / 2017

From *Interview Magazine*, February 15, 2017. https://www.interviewmagazine.com/culture /george-saunders. Reprinted by permission of *Interview Magazine*.

Some writers work within a tradition, and some create a world from whole cloth. There aren't many who can do the whole-cloth bit, but George is one of them. Within the universe of American writing, there really is a continent called GeorgeSaunders-Land, where the people speak funny, and the social contract has either broken down or been bent out of all recognition, and our most intimate lives feel like reenactments of something we maybe saw on TV. If he were just a vicious satirist, he would still be hugely enjoyable, but what sets him apart is his willingness not only to go into the heart of darkness but to suggest possible routes out. The cool kids don't *dare* do that, but George always has, and without sanctimony or even a hint of righteousness. I once heard him describe satire as "the inverse praise of good things." Seen from this perspective, George's career has been a twenty-year praise-song to the power of language, the grandeur of the visible world, and the awesome possibility of genuine enlightenment. That we can even see this through the parade of holy fools, venal idiots, smiling demagogues, degraded environments, and twisted corporate spaces he has presented us over the years is a testament to his extraordinary skill.

But in *Lincoln in the Bardo*, in my view, something more has happened, though I'm finding it very hard to verbalize. Good luck, reviewers! To me, it felt like reading my favorite bits of Kierkegaard or listening to Lauryn Hill take 1 Corinthians and turn it into that exquisite song "Tell Him" . . . It is a work that recreates within you the emotional and mental processes it describes. It is not a "reading about x," it is a *going-through*. *Lincoln* is about, among other things, grief and rebirth, and it goes through you that way: you shed one way of looking at the world and emerge with another. I always thought George was among the greatest American novelists, but until

Lincoln—having never actually written a novel—he wasn't exactly helping my case. Now the Nobel folks have no excuse. Not that work this good even needs gongs from Sweden. It is better than the somewhat shabby world it finds itself in—it is the thing in itself—and any attentive reader will find its wonder for themselves.

Zadie Smith: I'm a little anxious. It's hard to know where to start.

George Saunders: I feel nervous because I revere you so much. I don't want to be stupid. If I say something stupid, just interrupt me.

ZS: I will immediately. [*Saunders laughs*] First of all, when I was reading your book, the pages weren't even connected by a staple. You sent the pages to me wrapped in an elastic band.

GS: That's how I like it. That's most ideal.

ZS: And because I didn't want to carry the weight of it in my bag, I would read a page and then scrunch it up and put it in the trash. [*Saunders laughs*] So I finished the novel and had this tremendous emotional reaction but with nothing to show for it. I couldn't show it to Nick [Laird, Smith's husband] or to any of my friends. It was like a kind of dream that I'd had. It was a very odd experience.

GS: That's perfect.

ZS: It vanished in the act of reading it. I went onto Goodreads because I wanted to find somebody else who had read this book. There were only eight or nine people who had at that time, and they were having a kind of spiritual convening. Normally, it's thirty people on there bitching about a book. But this was like a church meeting. It was very moving. And finishing it, I'd become part of this small community of readers.

GS: Well, I hate to disappoint you, but seven of those were my mother. [*both laugh*]

ZS: My first question is about the ending. The last page of this book—without giving too much away—involves somebody entering somebody else. Not in a sexual way. But it says one of the simplest things you could ever say, which is that we must try and be inside each other. We must have some kind of feeling for each other and enter into each other's experience. Novels and stories are sometimes very complex staging grounds to say, in fact, very simple things. Things impossible to say otherwise because they are repeated in so many exploitative contexts—adverts and TV shows and political speeches.

GS: To say a factoid is one thing and to demonstrate it by embodiment is a different thing altogether. And we've become very, very addicted to the first thing. I have a lot of theories about the beneficial effects of fiction, but I'm always trying to get away from them a little bit because—

ZS: Because they're really unfashionable.

GS: Yeah. We watched a documentary last night about the immigrant crisis around the world. And it does make you blush at all the times you've stood up on the stage and given your speech about the healing power of fiction. But as the writer of this book, what I loved was the feeling of having so many surprises come at the end that I hadn't really planned or planted. Just through the process of trying to make the living and the dead feel real, all these little benefits came out. And these benefits turned out to be much more articulate statements of what I really believe. And somehow they were more convincing because they were arrived at at such length. Does that make sense?

ZS: One thing you learn about the novel as a form is that it's always smarter than you are. The novel leads you places that you never could have gotten to otherwise. Not that I'm saying you're an idiot, George.

GS: [*laughs*] No, you're right. And that's also the pleasure of the novel. I have an idea why that happens, but I want to hear why you think so.

ZS: My opinion has changed. When I was young, I was very technical about these things. I didn't like to admit to any intimate relation with what I was writing. [*both laugh*] It seems to me now that the deep structures are often subconscious and set in childhood. For me, it might be something very simply to do with the split in my family. That's why I'm always thinking about opposites. It's so childish, really, but that might be simply what it is. What about your deep structures? Where do you think they come from?

GS: My only take on that idea is that, for me, it all happens in revision. And it happens best if I'm not thinking in any big thematic or conceptual terms—especially in this book when I was trying to make the voices more active, more energetic. A lot of the decision-making had to do with things like: "Well, what should abut against what? What transition is more meaningful? If I cut these three lines out of this speech, how does it rest against the following speech?"

ZS: There's a little interview in the back of the book where you talk about thinking of the role of the novelist—in the case of your novel—as a kind of curator. But to me that's what novelists *always* are. I never bought the idea of individual genius from which the novel spews forth. It's always an act of curation. But you orchestrated this novel in a particularly fascinating way.

GS: Yes, whole swaths of the book are made up of verbatim quotes from various historical sources, which I cut up and rearranged to form part of the narrative. This was the only way I could get in some (what felt to me) necessary historical facts. But I resisted this at first, because I had this sort of prideful, juvenile idea—it might be a male thing—that every line had to shine with my inventiveness. And actually it was funny . . . There was one sequence of days when I had halfway decided to use the historical nuggets, but I wasn't quite sure it would work. I'd be in my room for six or seven hours, cutting up bits of paper with quotes and arranging them on the floor, with this little voice in my head saying, "Hey, this isn't writing!" But at the end of that day, I felt that the resulting section was doing important emotional work. Later, I went one step further, by putting in some invented "historical" bits. And reading those alongside the actual historical bits was like looking into a sort of a painful mirror, because "my" parts were so show-offy at first. They stood out because they were so flamboyant. So I had to go in and do the work of toning them down in order to make them fit. It's like if you're an actor and you're always overacting, well, you're a bad actor. But if you're an actor who subdues yourself to the extent that's necessary, then you're really acting.

ZS: I know a lot of people who read you think: "George is so much fun." There's no denying you're fun to read, but as a writer I think of you as, in fact, not a fun and freewheeling type but really an obsessive control artist. You're very precise about what you're doing. There isn't a thing left to chance. So when you decided to write a novel, I was very curious how that precision would translate because there's a perception that novels can't usually allow for your kind of absolute attention to detail.

GS: It's not a long book. And that meant I could obsess over it and live in it both backwards and forwards and hyper-control everything. The beginning is strange, and I did a lot of work calibrating that so that a reader with a certain level of patience would get through it and in the nick of time start to figure out what was going on. In a short book, you can do that. I sometimes think that I can't do the bigger thing that you do so beautifully, as in *Swing Time*, with so much world in it and so much rapturous paint thrown around. I don't think it would be possible to write a book on that scale with as much OCD as I have.

ZS: I was thinking about the generation before us—a bit before us, I suppose—like John Barth and all of those pomo dudes who had that idea of, instead of hiding the structure and making it look organic and natural, we're going to put the structure on the outside. But most of the time, at least for me, all I could attend to was that act of structural self-consciousness. Now, what you've done here is put the structure on the outside, but it's created a deeper fiction. It's more emotionally intense.

GS: From the beginning, I actually had it in mind not to write a novel. I'd kind of gotten past that point where I felt bad for never having written a novel, even to where I felt really good about it, like I was a real purist. And then this material was around and I approached it, but almost warning it, like, "Do not try to bloat up on me because we're not doing that; we're not writing a novel. We're not going to suspend all the usual rules of composition that I have accrued over the years just to get past the 130-page mark." There were several points where I would kind of turn to the book and say, "Get thee behind me." I don't think real novelists do that. But I make a distinction between prose that's very efficiency-minded (like, the minimum I can get away with), versus loosening the screws and letting the words spill out beautifully and so on. I don't really write beautifully naturally, unlike some people in this conversation. I don't feel like I have the intelligence to really inhabit a consistently high level of prose. I have to really squeeze it to make it into something. It blew my mind, reading *Swing Time*, that I could take any sentence in the book, and it was one of the most beautiful sentences written in English, and you grafted all those sentences into this incredible, multi-continent, epic. Such a vast and expansive book. It made me a feel a little bit like when I used to read David [Foster] Wallace. Like, "I can't play that game. I wish I could, but I can't do it."

ZS: The young people have a phrase for this now, which is "slay in your lane." [*both laugh*] That's a very important principle of writing. You have to work out what it is you can't do, obscure it, and focus on what works.

GS: Yeah, that was the first forty years of my life. But what was fun for me with this book was to start out with the principle that went, "We're going to fight every day to make this not a novel; make it *too short* to be a novel." And then with that principle in place, the book sort of starts to say, "Okay, but I really need this. I really need some historical nuggets." And you're like, "All right, but keep it under control." Or the book says, "I really need this sci-fi device of a ghost inhabiting another person." You say okay kind of begrudgingly. So the structure seemed informed by need and efficiency. There's not a lot of whimsicality in the form, not a lot of indulgence allowed. Like when I was younger, I would sometimes go, "Oh, every other section will be narrated by a chair." [*Smith laughs*] Or, "It will be a double helix shape!" That never really worked. I guess what I'm trying to say is that whatever weirdness was going to be in there, I felt, had to be earned. And it had to be required by the emotional needs of the book.

ZS: What interests me in it is a slight perverse balance between the sublime and the grotesque. Like you could have landed only on the sublime. But my argument is that the sublime couldn't exist without this other half. For example, you have these grotesque, hilarious, profane ghosts in the book. Even the concept of talking ghosts is, from an aesthetic point of view, grotesque. It's not in good taste to have talking ghosts in a grown-up novel. [*Saunders laughs*] But you seem compelled by that risk in order to get to the other end of the equation.

GS: I think it's also a kind of a psychological thing. As a kid, I had a real fascination with perverse, off-color, and kind of risky things, and I also had a very sanctimonious Catholic, purist side. For me, things were either very sullied or very pure, very controlled or very under-controlled. One of the big breakthrough moments was to realize that you aren't going to be able to excise one of those. But you are going to be able to use them against one another or in support of one another—almost like two people on a motorcycle. One tendency has to aid and abet the other, in a certain way. So if I find myself being too earnest and sentimental and hyperbolic and simplistic, which is definitely a tendency I have, then I bring in this perverse henchman.

ZS: There's something very Catholic about that.

GS: Right. And in my personal and spiritual life, I reject that. I don't believe in that. I'm always trying to get my mind into a less judgmental place, making less rigid judgments about things like "perverse" versus "pure." But in terms of prose, those sorts of oppositions seem to work. This book scared the shit out of me for many years because it seemed to me not all that open to the perverse or funny or naughty. And I knew if I evoked that stuff too easily or gratuitously, as a way of assuaging my fears of not being edgy or whatever, the writing would fall apart. This book was going to have to have some earnestness in it.

ZS: I have a spiritual question, and it's going to come in a minute. But I want to ask first about *A Christmas Carol*, which I know from speaking to you about it is an important childhood influence on you. It was on me, too. Since Christmas Eve, I've watched four versions of it because my children are slightly obsessive, ending with *The Muppet Christmas Carol*.

GS: Did you watch the George C. Scott version?

ZS: Yes, and the Jim Carrey. And I watched a terrible, early '80s cartoon version. And then I read it to them in a slightly desperate attempt to bring some meaning to the gift parade they'd had the past few days. Anyway, I was thinking about the legacy of ghosts in fiction, and specifically the moral power of those Dickensian ghosts. Because a ghost can be a very powerful but also manipulative element. For example, I do find the values in *A Christmas Carol* significant. It is important not to be mean and stingy and not to give up love for money. All true. But by the end of it, you could also see that there's also a kind of a sentimental protection of capital, right? Because in the end, everybody gets to keep their money. The poor stay poor. Scrooge just gets to feel better about himself. And all is right with the world. I bring this up because I feel like your anxiety of fiction and certainly mine is exactly the limits of it, right?

GS: Yeah.

ZS: That it has historically been a comfort for the bourgeois and that you can read the most extreme books and not change. You can read *A Christmas Carol* and not change in any way.

GS: Yes. A lot of books can probably even help you not to change.

ZS: But something in me was changed by *Lincoln in the Bardo*, and the great sublime/grotesque risk of your ghosts was a part of it. Are you writing fiction with the intention of creating some change inside a person?

GS: Well, first, the one thing about *A Christmas Carol* that always bothers me is that Cratchit is so sweet and perfect. He's like an Ivy League kid who just is labeled "poor." He doesn't have any bad habits. He's never cranky with his kids. But I was thinking about something I heard you say recently, about multiplicity. That meant a lot to me. When I think about what fiction does morally, I'm happier thinking of a person full of multiplicities—sort of fragmented. Maybe you could even think 100,000 people are inside each human being. And you drop a novel on that person, and a certain number of those sub-people come alive or get reenergized for some finite time. It's maybe just for a few days even, depending on the book. Although there are books that I read years ago that enlivened things in me that haven't died yet.

ZS: I think we understand this experience more from being readers than writers.

GS: Yes, that's right. I remember reading *The Bluest Eye* when I was a young parent, and something opened in me. That's the highest aspiration. So *A Christmas Carol* would enliven a certain subset of those 100,000 internal people. And you come out of it crying and saying, "Fuck, that's beautiful." And yet, like we've said, there are some things fundamentally off about the stance of the book. And maybe that's okay; maybe every book is flawed, and great books, as flawed as they might be, articulate a moral argument that the reader then carries forward. The critique to this model is, of course, to ask: Should a book be ever so perfect that you come out of it with complete moral agreement that can be sustained? If that's the case, wa-hoo, you know? Wa-hoo.

ZS: I have some questions about the bardo.

GS: Well, you're speaking to the right person.

ZS: Do you, George Saunders, individual citizen, actually believe in the extension of consciousness after death?

GS: Yes, I do. Not for any particular reason, and I don't know how long that state would last. Do you, Zadie Smith, citizen?

ZS: I don't. For me, your novel is about a problem of pain. I have a natural tendency to feel well about the world, I suppose, one way or another. But then there is the problem of pain. There are things like Lincoln's beloved little boy dying. Children with cancer; that's a classic one, too. To me, these kind of everyday miseries act as a fatal disqualifier. My sunniest beliefs are basically contingent on the fact that my child is not dying of cancer right now.

GS: Yes, that's true.

ZS: So those beliefs about the essential goodness or beauty of the world are fundamentally paper-thin bullshit. There's not an essential belief that isn't a contingent belief. It could all be destroyed in a second, at any second. And I have an issue with that.

GS: Yeah. I do, too. But maybe it's the scientist in me that says, "Okay, if we want to have the most expansive vision of things, then we'd have to imagine the world to be made of billions of contingent moments." And certainly we're always rooting for our particular contingent moment to be a great one. Pain-free. But the more expansive vision has to include the idea that, even for us, sometimes our particular contingent moment is going to be horrific. So then the big moral question is: how do I live with that terrible truth? I keep thinking of Robert Stone making the distinction between the word *sublime* and the word *beautiful*. He described being in a battle as sublime. Because even though people were dying, it was such a huge sensory experience that it became sublime. The other thing that's useful for me is this notion of the absolute versus the relative; like in a relative sense, yes, if we walk out and it's a beautiful morning, it's only a beautiful morning because we don't have a broken leg or hemorrhoids or something. But then in the absolute sense—kind of from the God's-eye view—God might feel like, "I made this thing that has all of that in it, all the horror and all the beauty." So in a certain way, we're always toggling back and forth between the absolute and the relative, if that makes sense.

ZS: I used to take that God's-eye view as a comfort when I was a child. I'd think, "Well, we couldn't find the world meaningful at all if it weren't for death." Of course, that is the smuggest and most intolerable of all perspectives because I'm not suffering from the death or the pain. Yet when I was thirteen, I really used to skip down the street, happy in thinking, "Oh, well, someone's suffering pain in order for me to feel this pleasure."

GS: [*laughs*] I know what you mean. And I laugh because I'm such a baby if I even get a flu. I had an experience a few years ago where I was on a plane in which one of the engines went out. And, oh boy, you talk about seeing your philosophy fly out the window. I couldn't even remember my name. I was just repeating the word no over and over. But the reason that the contrast between the absolute and the relative is so terrible is because we believe so fully in ourselves as permanent, continuous, and central. I feel insane saying this, but if one weren't so deluded about the permanent reality of the self, a lot of this pain would actually lessen. In other words, if you could press a button and your ego investment was less, the toothache would be less. Or less tragic at least.

ZS: But the belief that consciousness extends beyond death is surely to put more belief in the permanence of self, not less. That seems to me a comfort that you're allowing yourself.

GS: Yeah. But I think the idea is that what extends is not identical to self. I'm no expert. (I have this tendency to take a little bit of questionable knowledge and riff on it.) But one of the ideas that runs through this book is this Buddhist notion that the mind is incredibly powerful; not the brain but the mind. Let's say there's something operating in you called Mind. It's very powerful, but it's dampened by the body, by physicality. When you die, that tether gets cut and off the mind goes with incredible power. And some of these Buddhist texts say that, in the moment after you die, you think of New Jersey and you go to New Jersey or you think of 1820 and you go to 1820. Also, all your sort of inner-symbology gets writ large. So, if you're a Christian, you see Christian iconography.

ZS: Well, that's very *Christmas Carol*-y of you.

GS: Yes. Or you might see the Kardashians if you're a big TV viewer. That whole idea is really intriguing to me. If you took snapshots of ourselves throughout the day, the way that our mind is twisting and turning, then at the moment of death, the mind would be twisting and turning in the same way. But the Buddhists say it's super-sized because there's no bodily damper on it.

ZS: There's no impediment.

GS: Yeah. That's how I approached these ghosts in the book. What do the ghosts do? Well, they do the same thing they always did, but more of it.

ZS: You mentioned in an interview a quote from the Gnostic Gospels: "If you bring forth what is within you, it will save you. If you do not bring it forth, it will destroy you." I was thinking about that. What that has to include is the belief that people have something essential inside of them that they carry with themselves always. And I guess I've always written more from the opposite perspective, that kind of existentialist perspective which argues that existence precedes essence. And there really isn't anything essential in there—you're the product of your actions, which can always change. And they retrospectively make you one way or another.

GS: But what do you make then of habit of mind?

ZS: Well, when you have children, you're certainly challenged in this belief. I always remind myself that Sartre and de Beauvoir didn't have children. And when you don't have children, it might be easier to believe that the child doesn't come with something.

GS: And especially if you have two children, like you do.

ZS: Right. Then you really see it.

GS: [*laughs*] In terms of that quote, I think it depends on what you define as "inside of" you. I hear that to mean "your essential tendencies." One example from my life, that it took me far too long to learn, is this: I'm a control freak. I'm defensive. And I'm an egomaniac. That's true about me.

ZS: You're a writer. I could have told you all that.

GS: You should have told me when I was ten. Of course, you weren't born yet. But that's what's "within" me. I take cheer from that quote from the Gospels because it means: Whatever is within you, don't worry about it. Don't blame yourself. Just laugh at it or urge it out into the sun. All these traits are like coins. Two-sided. All those traits—which we might want to label as "negative"—can have positive aspects, can be applied to something, can be used for something.

ZS: But 150 years ago in Dickens's time—and this may be sentimental—at least those coins could be more easily "cashed in." There was at least a sense of craft. So some of the things people had inside of them, they had the possibility of expressing in the making of things—even in a daily way with their clothes or their food. People made a good deal of both themselves. Now our daily lives are almost all consumption. Craft plays a tiny role. And today, writing seems to me like an incredible luxury, almost a perversity, something which hardly exists in the world anymore, where you get to see the fruits of your actions in a daily way.

GS: I agree with that. I haven't written for the past three or four months, and I can feel myself getting more materialistic, more conceptual and more shallow, less generous. I think you're right. I think when you get to export your creative impulse into something, it kind of lessens that busy energy that can be so confrontational and pissy. And it's funny that, at the same time, we've invented this internet thingy that takes those very traits and super-sizes them. You take somebody who has no creative outlet and then you agitate them. And there you are.

ZS: A lot of your early stories now feel prophetic. Take the recent election. Historians in 100 years might write about it as being the first internet election, in which what happened was actually an expression in the real world of a virtual reality. And you've been writing about that subject for a while.

GS: To me, it's interesting to think of this as the culmination of materialism. And by that I don't necessarily just mean gathering stuff, but the belief in the pragmatic . . . in shareholder value, that which can be demonstrated. Distrust of ambiguity. And that way of thinking somehow bleeds over into a disrespect for truth and a suspicion of intellectual activity and so on. Curiosity understood as a sign of weakness. I think that's what we're seeing. But what's really baffling to me is the way that the technology has risen up to help us become more materialistic.

ZS: What is your relation to technology?

GS: I'm starting to withdraw from it as much as I can. I don't do much of the social media stuff. Like, if I'm on Facebook, it changes my relation to the real world in a way that makes me feel sick—almost like I've had too much sugar or something. Also, I don't mind being criticized intelligently; although I don't love it. But social media sometimes feels like a vehicle for one-dimensional sniping, more than true criticism. When I wrote that piece in the *New Yorker* on Trump, I got so many online reproaches.

ZS: That was a wonderful piece. But of course you would have. When I see my friends engaging in a Twitter war for an afternoon, I think that would destroy me for a month. I know to argue against our online lives seems like the argument of the grumpy, old Luddite novelist, but I really always try to make the argument from the perspective of personal pleasure. Like, is this making you happy today? If it is, cool. If not, why not?

GS: The internet kind of feels like happiness sometimes, however. It feels like stimulation.

ZS: But there has to be a break. Addiction also feels fun while you're doing it. But after a while, you form an accommodation with it. You make it a corner of your life, not your whole life. But I think smart kids already might be doing this.

GS: I think the wave of social media rejection is coming. I think there will be a big reaction against it. It's just like sugar—[I] mean, I loved it as a kid . . .

ZS: Right. And if I were still watching TV the way I did when I was eight, we wouldn't be talking right now because I'd be watching nine and a half hours of television today. As an adult, I decided that wasn't the best option for me.

GS: But that's what's unsettling about the current culture war. I'm from a pretty working-class background, and I really worked hard in my life to eradicate those parts of myself that were stupidly trapped in that world. Those of us who come up that way made a series of choices to benefit ourselves and make ourselves more generous and open. And I see *that* being looked at askance as a form of elitism now, which is really scary. When I wrote that Trump piece, I had this uncomfortable experience of sensing a lot of things that were nascent, that I couldn't quite articulate. And one of them was this move toward anti-intellectualism. An anti-love move, even . . . To understand any plea for further consideration of a group you don't know anything about to be some form of, quote, political correctness. These things are bubbling right under us.

ZS: That's why I found the last page of your book so overwhelming. I cried. That doesn't happen to me very often. It was exactly this restatement of something so simple. You have this final image of—it's going to sound crazy to people who haven't read the book—a black man inside Lincoln riding on a horse. And for a moment, he's also inside the horse. It's a radical metaphor, made real. I read this book recently called *Grief Is the Thing with Feathers* by Max Porter. And on the last page, a character says: "I LOVE YOU I LOVE YOU I LOVE YOU." And I realized reading it that the whole book, with all its swirls and difficulty, may have been an excuse to say those words, which are basically unsayable in fiction. You can't say "I love you, I love you." It's ridiculous. And it's like the end of your book, it has an insane and simple power that I wouldn't have listened to in any other presentation.

GS: But it's interesting, when you think about it. In real life, when you have an emotional experience, it's never just because of the thing that's been said. There's the backstory. It's like Hemingway's iceberg theory—the current emotional moment is the tip of the iceberg and all of the past is the seven-eighths of the iceberg that's underwater. So when somebody you've known for twenty years, and with whom you have a full context, winks at you or whatever, it can be huge. I think in a sense what you're trying to re-create in fiction is that.

ZS: I have a final question for you. There's a quote by Kafka: "There's an infinite amount of hope but not for us."

GS: But not for us.

ZS: I don't mean to push the point, but it does seem to me from the stuff I've written, it hasn't done me any good. I never feel any better. I don't feel wise. I don't make better decisions. It's the same horseshit my life always has been. [*Saunders laughs*] The writing doesn't help *me*. I think most writers feel this way. But when I talk to other writers about you, I find they think of you as the exception to this rule. They always say, "George seems happy. George has it all figured out." I want to know if they're right. Does the practice of writing help you?

GS: Well, the first answer that came to mind is that it helps me in the sense that I really *wanted* it. I really wanted to be allowed to the table. So it makes me happy to be at the table. It sounds a little shallow, but if I imagine the shadow life, where I didn't get that chance, and all the ways my negative inclinations would have bloomed if I hadn't gotten the attention, but also the creative outlet . . . I'm not actually that happy. I mean, like you, I have multiplicities. My happiness blooms and it wilts. And there are things that are shadow sides of the creative energy that are negative and all that kind of stuff. The only thing that I say to myself is, in the spirit of that quote from the Gnostic Gospels: Writing is a way to let all that stuff out into the sun. Even if something within me is ugly, writing is a pretty good place to play with that thing and to begin to really see it. The other thing I've discovered that is a help is that there isn't a simple virtue or a simple vice. They're always connected. If you have Tendency A that you loathe, you can almost be sure that Tendency B, which you love, is somehow connected to it.

ZS: But you never feel writing these books . . . That's what I have to confess, I often feel, "What's the point? Why am I doing this?"

GS: Oh, no, I totally feel that. I think part of the reason I do it is because while I'm doing it, I don't feel it.

ZS: Yeah, that's maybe the only time I don't feel it.

GS: But I think that's okay. I don't think that's a failing. I think it's just a feature. Like, a feature of oneself. It's almost like those boats that sit really low in the water; they look kind of ugly. And then you get one of them up to eighty miles an hour and the hull comes up, and it's a beautiful thing. I'm okay with that for myself. I have to be, because I know it's true. Like when I'm not writing, I tend to get depressed and a little bit surly. And then when I'm writing, suddenly I feel enlivened. Now the only thing as I'm getting older that I notice is that it's a pattern. It's like drugs. I'm always nice when

I do drugs. [*laughs*] But, you know, I'm nicer on the drug called "writing." But honestly, the choice is: I can be a cheerful person, more awake to correction, more of a force for good . . . when I'm writing. Or I can be the opposite of all those things, when I'm not writing.

ZS: I said that was going to be my final question, but I have one more about posterity. It's that Woody Allen quote: "I don't want to achieve immortality through my work. I want to achieve it through not dying. I don't want to live on in the hearts of my countrymen. I want to live on in my apartment."

GS: The other one he has is: "It's not that I'm afraid to die, I just don't want to be there when it happens."

ZS: Right. Now all these famous people have died recently. Something about famous people dying causes an interesting mass reaction. [*Saunders laughs*] And some of the people who died were kind of epitomes of a certain effect. Like George Michael and Bowie and Prince, for example; they had this communication with so many other minds. It's not something they're present for in a weird sense. Prince can't really know how "Darling Nikki" is fused with my teenage memories. But it's a communication from which I hugely benefited, even if Prince gets nothing out of it (except money and fame). How do you feel about the idea that you've had a communication with all these minds? Is it something you can think about at all?

GS: No, it helps a lot. I love it. I was thinking the other day about the idea that you have a reader and a writer, and they're different and they're flawed and they're fucked-up, each in their own way. And most times they're in the middle percentile of human goodness. They're just who they are. Then, in the moment of reading, the writer comes up to the surface and the reader comes up to the surface and they kiss, like two fish. That actually does happen. We know that happens. They're both briefly their best selves, or at least better selves. A flawed human being writes something and sixty years later a reader picks up the book and something in them rises to meet it. And I believe that, when this happens and the reader goes out into the world the next day, there's some alteration that might possibly inflect the person positively.

ZS: I remember Wallace telling me once when I said something along those same lines, "Stop talking that John Gardner shit." [*laughs*]

GS: Oh, but he was such a believer in that too, though. And moving toward it, I think, too, in his work.

ZS: The older I get, the more I feel strongly about this: that that little nudge of the moral, if that's what it is, which cannot be measured and you can never be sure of, is a far smaller thing than the personal relation that you have with humans in the world. I can't put writing anywhere above that. There are too many of these totally awful writers, who destroyed their loved ones for their work. The idea that their writing is an excuse or an explanation or a defense for the rest of their behavior is to me obscene.

GS: Yeah, I reject that. Especially because you see young people sometimes trying to enact the assholery even before they do the work. But I think if someone could demonstrate to me that fiction did no good, I would still do it, because I think it does good *for me.* I don't know about transformation. But scientifically you *can* say: Well, it doesn't seem to hurt anybody. Personally I've been cheered by books at really critical moments. That much I believe. You were talking about the last page of that book and [the] idea that fiction sometimes is an elaborate kind of support for a fairly simple idea. One of the revelations in that book for me was this idea about citizenship. Even that word—*citizenship*—for someone my age, it makes me cringe. But, to me, the political space we're in now argues for a reboot of fairly simple ideas and the examination of the way that Americans have not been living into them. The idea of inclusion has become kind of a stone that we've passed our hand over so many times that it doesn't mean anything. But while writing this book, it occurred to me, you either believe in the Constitution or you don't. If you do, it's intense in what it wants of us.

ZS: But George, isn't there the worrying reality, particularly in America, that you could believe in something entirely—all men are created equal— and then run a system of actual human slavery alongside it and contain those two ideas in your mind?

GS: Yes. But that's been the great American demon from day one, that we've had those two ideas, and said the first so pithily while we so energetically pursued the second. It's so ironic that you often hear these right-wing people talking about the Constitution. And yet, as you were saying, this huge contradiction is manifesting itself every day in murders and injustices towards people of color. And I would say one thing writing this book did for me was underscore the fact that this issue has never been properly addressed and it hasn't gone away.

ZS: And yet there are so many people who feel like it's already been touched on enough. I heard someone on the radio being interviewed about slavery in a Southern town saying, "Oh, we don't want to hear any more about that. It was hundreds of years ago." And it hurt to hear that! It was like a physical pain in me. It was as if you brought up a traumatized or raped child and somebody said, "Oh, well, that happened when they were six."

GS: Oh, that happened to them last Thursday.

ZS: I couldn't believe that somebody I was sharing a land with would say such a thing.

GS: Yes. And this is more elitist talk, but it's partly a failure of education. Because people in my generation don't really know the reality of it. I learned when I was doing research for this Lincoln book that it was not unusual for the Northern soldiers to rape the former slave girls. There's a whole unwritten history of this. And even the written history is poorly understood by most people.

ZS: Right. Like reading Colson [Whitehead]'s book [*The Underground Railroad*], I learned things that I really should know. I'm forty-one years old. When I was reading it, I thought, this is too extreme, you know? As if all this misery is in bad aesthetic taste. And then you realize this is a daily reality for millions of people for hundreds of years.

GS: And even when it was reported by progressives of that time, it was so cleaned up. It was reshaped into oppression narratives that they were familiar with. Because the actual things that were going on were so unspeakable that they didn't have the language for them. And this is the kind of lame-ass realization that people like me have late in life. But working through that material, the finger points to white sloth, basically. We have not been energetic enough—white people haven't—in pursuing racial equity. That people, and even progressive people, have actually said a form of what that guy said, which is, "Well, that was a long time ago." And then you see a form of passivity that I, a white guy, have certainly been guilty of. I'm really sickened by it in myself now. It's like as if there's an epidemic sweeping the country and you just said, "Well, that is really terrible. I'm glad that it won't come up here."

ZS: I feel that it's also an allergic reaction to self-accusation. A lot of people seem to feel it's pathological that anyone would feel any kind of guilt about anything. [*Saunders laughs*] Often my characters are quite filled with guilt and regret, and I get letters from people saying things like: "Are you depressed? Why would anyone think about themselves this way?" But didn't guilt and regret used to be pretty normal aspects of human experience? Everyone's always saying, "Just do you." But that's not universally good advice. You don't want to tell young Adolf, "Hey, just do you."

GS: Also I think people have come to expect that in artistic representation; that every work of art should be a work of extravagant hope.

ZS: Self-promotion and hope, yeah.

GS: We watched a bunch of kids' movies this Christmas. I was kind of joking with our family by asking, "Is anyone allowed to die in a kids' movie anymore?"

ZS: No, never.

GS: I've had that my whole career. People were always hedging around the question of: Why are you so dark? What happened to you?

George Saunders, The Art of Fiction No. 245

Benjamin Nugent / 2019

My first meeting with George Saunders took place in his home of ten years, a ranch house in the Catskills. The house stood on fifteen acres of hilly woods, crisscrossed by narrow paths that he and his wife, the novelist Paula Saunders, had cleared over many afternoons, following mornings spent writing.

The Saunderses had lived in upstate New York for three decades; they raised their two daughters in Rochester and Syracuse, two of the region's Rust Belt cities, and Saunders's first three story collections, *CivilWarLand in Bad Decline* (1996), *Pastoralia* (2000), and *In Persuasion Nation* (2006), are marked by the experience of bringing up children and holding down jobs in a postindustrial economy. But the stories aren't constrained by the conventions of gritty realism. There are ghosts, zombies, prosthetic foreheads, and memories uploaded onto computers straight from human brains. Many of the stories are extremely funny, many have endings of great emotional power, and most are written in a style that's spare, vernacular, and very catchy. Appearing in the *New Yorker* since 1992, they won Saunders a MacArthur Fellowship in 2006 and have exerted an enormous influence on contemporary American fiction. The many writers who love Saunders often complain that it takes great effort not to imitate him.

In recent years, Saunders, too, has worked to write less like Saunders. *Tenth of December* (2013), shortlisted for a National Book Award, found him experimenting with new voices; in one story, "Escape from Spiderhead," the narrator imbibes a drug that causes him to compose sentences in the style of Henry James. Saunders followed that book with his first novel, *Lincoln in the Bardo* (2017), set in nineteenth-century Washington, far from the futuristic office parks and theme parks of his early work. It debuted at the top of the *New York Times* best-seller list and won that year's Man Booker Prize.

Saunders and I spoke in his kitchen over mugs of strong coffee. Furniture was sparse, because he and Paula were moving. They'd decided to sell the place and live full-time in their house outside Santa Cruz, California. But the shed where he wrote *Tenth of December* and *Lincoln* was still as it had been when he was working on those books. His desk, flanked by bookshelves, faced a table displaying perhaps ten framed photos of Buddhist teachers in robes.

Our two subsequent conversations took place in Saunders's office at Syracuse University. He's been a professor of creative writing at Syracuse for twenty years, although he's taught mostly short intensive courses since his move to the West Coast. The centerpiece of the room is a scuffed wooden desk, stained with coffee rings, that once belonged to Delmore Schwartz. The window looks out on a statue of Lincoln that presents the savior of the republic as a sad young man, clean-shaven, frowning, his head bowed. It's rumored, falsely, that the sculptor intended to depict Lincoln mourning Ann Rutledge, a woman thought by some historians to be his first sweetheart, after her death from typhoid fever in 1835.

When we finished our last session, Saunders and I drove around Syracuse. It was late autumn, and the lawns were sprinkled with fallen leaves. He showed me the bucolic parkside street where he set his story "Victory Lap" and, nearby, the squalid house where David Foster Wallace wrote *Infinite Jest*. The door to the basement apartment where Wallace lived was bright red, peeling, marked with a crooked numeral i, and lit from above by a harsh bulb. "Someone should have done this kind of interview with Dave," he said.

Saunders is easy to interview. He's chatty, kind, quick to shoot down any glib analysis of his work, and free with an anecdote, often casting himself as a blunderer whose illusions land him in hot water. Back in his twenties, he played guitar in a country band, and at sixty he looks like a veteran Nashville sideman, with a tight beard and long red hair combed back from his forehead. His accent is working-class Chicagoan, slightly lilting. He often substitutes *ya* for *you*. The effect is that when he does say you, as he did when he told me, "You have to let evil have broad shoulders," it commands attention.

Benjamin Nugent: When you were a teenager, you worked in your dad's restaurant, Chicken Unlimited. What was that like?

George Saunders: I loved it. We were this upstart franchise in competition with KFC. I was the delivery boy, and after school I'd go right over—never did any homework—and the place would be full of people I knew and loved. My parents both worked there, my sisters, aunts, friends from school. Like a party every night. We had these tricked-out 1977 Chevy vans that were carpeted inside, even the walls and ceilings, and had stoves and mini fridges so we could cater weddings and bar mitzvahs and carnivals, and, on the sides, our sort of Zen motto—CHICKEN UNLIMITED DOESN'T STOP AT CHICKEN. I was sixteen and had just gotten my license, so this was a dream job. I'd drive around Midlothian, Oak Forest, Harvey, and Markham, Illinois, four or five hours a night, cranking the Allman Brothers on the eight-track—a great job for a future writer. There'd always be a few minutes in the foyer while the family went to get their money, when you were artificially part of a household that wasn't aware it was being observed. You had access to that particular house's smell and weird decor, and maybe a gaping pet would step out of the guest bathroom or you'd hear some shouting from somewhere in the house. There was this one guy who'd always greet me with, "You married yet?" And I'd say, "I'm sixteen, sir, so . . . no."

Good! he'd say. Promise me you'll never get married. It *destroys* you. And then his wife would drift out from the kitchen, this sweet older woman, smiling . . .

And so on.

At that age I had a certain vision of the world, this very tidy, control-freak, Khalil Gibran-reading idea of nobility, like the way to be a good person was to hover righteously above all those weak, dopey sinners down there. Sort of a purity obsession. To go out in the Chicken Van every night was to constantly have that view undercut. Because the whole world was crazy and erratic and sinful. But the people I met were also sweet and weird and endearing. You'd get all of that in one night.

BN: The "Khalil Gibran-reading idea of nobility" comes up in "Sea Oak," when Angela Silveri sends the narrator a copy of *The Prophet*.

GS: Right, exactly, that was me. Very, uh, high-minded. I loved Gibran, Robert Pirsig, Ayn Rand . . . I think I understood literature to be about "how to live correctly," rather than "life—it's complicated."

At that time—I started high school in '73—there was a lot of mayhem, drinking and partying and drugs and all that. And I reacted against it. I'd go to a party and see everybody wasted and think, Why would I want to *do* that? It's so undignified. I was sort of a young old man. Even at that age, I had this feeling that America was a fallen, decadent place, and I couldn't succumb, I had to stay above the fray or I'd get stuck in a life I didn't want. That was my form of rebellion, to try to be really, really good.

BN: Chicago, as it appears in your story "Isabelle," is very violent. Did you see that kind of thing?

GS: Not really, not in person. There were probably more fistfights in our suburb than in most other suburbs. And I did a little bit of early macho-kid fighting. But "Isabelle" is more a rendering of the Chicago that came to me through family lore. My grandparents lived at Fifty-Fifth and California, in Gage Park, and my dad's stories from his childhood in that neighborhood gave me a sense of a kind of mythic Chicago—old ladies who'd had their speakeasies closed down by Al Capone, Roosevelt's motorcade passing by on Fifty-Fifth, on the way in from Midway. And just about every family was an immigrant family, within a generation or two. You really felt the old Chicago everywhere.

For example, my grandfather was in high school, and he and a friend were walking down the street. A nice, new car pulls up and the driver guy says, "Hey, does either of you kids know how to drive? You want to drive this car?" And my grandfather's like, "Hmm, seems weird." The guy jumps out and runs off down the alley, but my grandfather's friend hops in. Then this other car comes up the street and machine-guns the car, and my grandfather's friend dies. Or, my grandfather and his brother go into their, like, gang clubhouse, in an abandoned meat warehouse. And they find that their gang pals have hung up a rival gang member on a meat hook. He's still alive and my grandfather and his brother somehow persuade the other guys to let him down. Or, my dad gets beaten unconscious by another, circa 1953 gang and spends the night knocked out in a vacant lot.

So "Isabelle" came out of *that* Chicago. There was a lot of racism and race paranoia in the air—this very us-versus-them mentality. One of my earliest memories is my dad driving us through a riot in Gage Park—protests against Dr. King's visit—seeing this crazy-faced white guy up in a tree, waving a flare around. It was the sixties and all that sixties craziness felt near at hand.

BN: What was the transition to the suburbs like?

GS: I was six when we moved from the city out to Oak Forest. I remember getting lost in the new house because it seemed so palatial—just rooms opening into other rooms and *stairs* and all that. It was actually just a nice suburban house, but coming from our apartment it seemed like a country estate, like a mod country estate. It had an intercom system and the kitchen had these globe lights that were very James Bond, I thought. I really loved living there. It was, yes, a suburb, but looked at from this distance, it was really just a small town, and it was wonderful to know so many people and be able to track the changes in their lives, and also nice to get to know that strange suburban ecosystem intimately—creeks and culverts and half-built houses and stormwater sewers you could hide out in and so on.

My mom and dad always gave us a feeling of being loved and well taken care of. My mom was, is, just this font of unconditional love. My dad hadn't finished college at that point—he went back years later—but he always had money. A very charming, flamboyant guy, great storyteller, good salesman. He would give Mom these extravagant Christmas presents. One year he gave her a new Camaro—sent her to the window and it was parked out in the driveway with a big bow on it—that kind of thing.

BN: In your family, did people try to be funny?

GS: Oh yeah. Being funny was a way of being powerful. If you were an attention-needing little kid, and was I ever, you could get a lot of cred from verbal performance. If you got good grades in school, that was nice. But if you could joke at a high level, hold your own in a conversation, that was better. And this was nonstop, on both sides of my family. I just understood it as a way of being a person, like a confident person—a way of giving comfort, or demonstrating positive energy.

BN: Your dad's side was from Chicago, and your mom's was from Texas. They must have had different ways of joking around.

GS: Yes. I talk the way Chicago people talk: fast, staccato, nasal. At a Chicago family party there would be five people loudly riffing at once. Lots of teasing, wisecracks, all of that.

On the Texas side, the humor was drier. I had a couple of uncles on my mom's side who were really good mimics. They would create these funny personas and stay in character. I was fascinated by what they did to a room just by walking in—people were so happy to see them. They were doing improv, I can see now—reading the room, adjusting their performances accordingly. And that aspiration's definitely in my writing—trying to entertain an imaginary audience and lift them up a little in order to be admired by them.

I once heard someone say that writers tend to come out of families in which it is understood that language is powerful. And that was definitely the case for me, coming from both sides of the family.

BN: Some of the things you write about—the Civil War, slavery, places haunted by the past—are traditionally the domains of Southern literature.

GS: I had periods as a kid during which I identified as a Texan in exile—I was born there and we'd go to Amarillo every summer to visit my grandparents. I saw myself as, like, a future cowboy who, unfortunately, lived on the South Side and had a nasal Chicago accent. So that summer trip was like returning to the motherland or something.

But I think it's mysterious, what we end up writing about. I don't have any big intellectual agenda regarding the Civil War. I just kind of switch on when I write about it. And my feeling is, if something fascinates you, you just should go there—you have to. I don't think you have to necessarily understand why. We're looking for language-rich zones, places that get us revved up, places that feel bountiful. You can dress the process up afterward, theoretically and explanatorily, but really we're looking for a place of excitement and potential, a place that feels language-rich—it takes a lot of words to write a book and a lot of words are going to have to be taken out. So you need a deep reservoir of generative interest. One of the indicators that you've chosen a good topic is that you have strong opinions about everything that's going on in the prose—the language, the form, all of it.

When you play guitar, certain keys turn out to be more productive. You can tell that Neil Young had a period during which D was a key that was really speaking to him—D minor, or a sort of modal D. Now, why was that? I doubt even he could answer that. And yet "Cowgirl in the Sand" and "Old Man" and a bunch of other great songs came out of that period during which, for some reason, his hands were naturally gravitating toward D and knew what to do once they got there.

The biggest thing I've learned about writing is that we tend to underestimate and marginalize the irrational, intuitive aspects of it. The difference between a so-so writer and a good one, or a good one and a great one, is in the quality of the intuitive decisions she's able to make at speed.

BN: When did you know you wanted to be a writer?

GS: In high school, there was a teacher named Sheri Williams who was beautiful and funny. She would show these filmstrips of famous writers and talk about them with real admiration.

Once we were studying Hawthorne and there was a cartoon image of him, leaning against a barn or something, looking groovy, and she said something like, This is a person who is now dead, but when he was alive he went out and looked at the world with wide-open eyes and, in the process, changed it. That really appealed to me—this idea that our love of the world could get put into permanent form and then get shared with future generations. And it seemed to me that writing would be a way of forcing you to live a big life.

BN: But you weren't planning to study writing. You had a band.

GS: Right. I'd gotten into this band during my senior year, and the plan was to skip college and just, you know, go on tour. Then, over Christmas break, I went on this Chicagoland version of a ski trip, up to Wilmot Mountain in Wisconsin—fifteen minutes on the lift, two minutes coming down—and on the way back home I was reading *Atlas Shrugged*. I didn't recognize that it was a stupid novel. To me, it was just, you know, a novel, and I was reading it—the first book I'd read in years. It pulled me in with the old novelistic tricks—language and settings and people moving around and talking passionately and so forth. And it was *long*. I was really proud to be reading such a long-ass book. And in that mood of artistic exaltation, it suddenly hit me, Hey, I could go to college. I *could*. *I* could. This corny, instantaneous fantasy image came up of me at the center of a group of kids, walking through a campus, talking philosophy, and that group included, yes, some admiring girls, and we were all wearing what I thought of as "college sweaters," with big old capital letters on the chest or something, and we were, maybe, carrying those cheerleader megaphones. I had never really thought of going to college before, and the actuality of it, the idea that I might actually be able to do it, hit me hard and, well, propelled me out of the band.

I'd failed chemistry and possibly algebra, but had pretty good ACT scores. And I asked another teacher I admired, our geology teacher, Joe Lindbloom, where he'd go to college if he could do it all over. He said the Colorado School of Mines. And then he *called* them on my behalf. It was a simpler time. He said something like, "Smart kid, hasn't applied himself, maybe worth a shot?" And they said they'd consider me if I went to community college over the summer and took, like, eighteen hours of math and chemistry and kept a 2.5 GPA. And I did it. I took over the dining room table as my study area and missed all the post-senior-year fun and . . . got into college.

BN: What was the band like?

GS: Pretty good, actually. The lead guitar player, Rick Hollowell, had long hair, past his waist, and wore these fringed leather jackets. He was amazing, a really fast, rapid-fire player. Great taste, very precise. And he knew people in the business. He somehow had a connection to someone who knew the Eagles, and the idea was, if we got our shit together, we might be able to open for the opener of the opener, or something like that. It all sounds unlikely now, but I remember we went to a music store and Rick bought a PA with a $10,000 check he'd gotten from United Artists. Anyway, then I went on that ski trip and, under the unholy influence of Ayn Rand, quit the band. I knew I was letting the other guys down. But this was one of a small handful of times when this smarter part of me overruled the habitual me, as if that smarter part had a long-term plan to protect "us."

BN: Did you think about writing while you were attending the Colorado School of Mines?

GS: Yes. In the same way that, when I lived in Chicago, I wasn't actually a Chicagoan but a Texan in absentia, when I was in engineering school I wasn't an engineer but a writer waiting to happen. I thought about it, a lot. I just didn't do much of it. Mostly, I thought about how cool it would be *to have done it*—to be a person who had a thin, beautiful book out that everyone was talking about. I was still reading Khalil Gibran and Ayn Rand, and then I found a section of the Mines library—they had this tiny, antiquated literature section upstairs that stopped around 1941. So I got into Faulkner and Hemingway and Steinbeck and Dos Passos and Thomas Wolfe. I still remember that musty smell—the smell of the thirties, I thought—and the view of the Front Range out this little window and that feeling of having a new old book in my hands and the quiet, sweet dream of someday holding my *own* book in my hands.

Thomas Wolfe really spoke to me at that time, because he was so poetic and epic and autobiographical—sort of a link between the Gibran and the Rand and real literature—lots of exalted feeling, expressed singingly, I guess. I remember once stealing a day from my "real" studies to read Maupassant down by Clear Creek, in this tiny, ancient edition. I was doing some very emotive writing in my journal at that time and published a Gibran knockoff or two in the school lit mag. I also remember sacrificing a whole Sunday to read *For Whom the Bell Tolls* and this intense desire I had, walking home that night, to quit school and just get going—find a war and get involved in some kind of tragedy, nothing too bad, wounded but not killed, please, and then come home and write about it—a feeling of wanting to see if, to use a Hem-ism, I "had what it took." But I also felt like I didn't want to let my parents down, or disappoint those two high school teachers who'd helped me get this far, and also—I wasn't writing much, really, or reading enough to have acquired any useful opinions.

There was a sort of immaturity about the whole thing. I refused to read any contemporary fiction. A writer could be comfortably great only if he or she was already dead. I couldn't get my head around the notion that someone alive right now, writing about this fallen, stupid 1978 world, might be able to do something beautiful. I didn't like irreverence, at least not in literature. Shit was earnest, shit was real. So, no jokes—in literature. Everywhere else—jokes, of course. I lived in my self-made, earnest, circa 1935 aesthetic bubble, wrote lots of poems beginning with the utterance "O"— "O mountain, how you loom / over my toilsome labors of study!" I really regret that now, that timidity. Why didn't I just read everything and throw myself into it fearlessly?

BN: Why did you apply to the MFA at Syracuse?

GS: Well, that was years later—I was in my late twenties, working as a groundsman at an apartment complex across from this strip club in Texas. And I got invited to one of their parties, which turned into this crazy, drunken, albeit somewhat sexy, brawl. Being me, I drifted into a corner and picked up this copy of *People*. And there was an article about Syracuse that mentioned Jay McInerney and Raymond Carver. I'd never heard of either one of them before, didn't even know there was such a thing as a creative writing program or that you could get paid for going to school to learn to write.

At that time, there was a general aversion to MFA programs. The feeling was, if you were a real writer, you wouldn't need to stoop so low. We all said some version of that once we got to Syracuse. I'm not really an MFA kind of person. I'm more authentic and real world and out of control than that. It was like, "Why am I not in Paris? Why am I not on a ranch somewhere?" I must be defective, to be an academic. But once we got working, I could see how much I had to learn and was really grateful to be there.

BN: That was the eighties, and you studied with Tobias Wolff and Douglas Unger.

GS: Yes, and what a privilege. I remember that Doug didn't like the first wave of stories we first-year students turned in. So, during workshop, right before the break, he said, "When we come back, we're going to go around the room and you're each going to *tell* a story."

Horrors! I think he knew that, in that setting—among a new peer group, no time to "compose" a proper story, serious performance anxiety—the anti-flop instinct would kick in. We'd leave behind the pretentious and imitative and "edgy" stuff we'd been writing and bring our best stuff forward, in the name of survival. And he was right. We each told a story that was more compelling and more like the real "us" than anything we'd submitted for workshop.

The story that I told that night wasn't good short fiction, but it was a good, lively anecdote. It got laughs and there were a few quiet moments when everyone was really listening. And I realized—or, I should say, I started to realize—that the way you're going to be charming on the page is going to have some resemblance to the way you're charming in person. What else do you *have* but that? You've learned, over your life, to charm people—to seduce and persuade and get yourself out of trouble—and your writing is likely going to have some overlap with those skills. How weird would it be if the charm you had on the page had no relation to your real-life charm? They're not identical, but they are related.

BN: It's the cliché, have integrity, don't worry about the reception, turned on its head. You can produce something with more integrity if you let the entertainment instinct come out.

GS: For me, that's exactly right. It's not true for everybody, but for me it's true. When I'm writing, I'm feeling something like, I want to entertain you for twenty pages. I want you to keep reading. Actually, I want you to not be able to stop reading.

If I just concentrate on those ideas, the end result is deeper and smarter and weirder and funnier and more honest than if I'd planned it all out. The controlling part of myself drops away, thank God, the part that knows its theme and has developed a political stance and all that, and something else takes over. I don't really understand it but it has to do with instinct and iteration—honoring the impulse of the moment, over and over.

When I finally wrote a whole story out of that instinct, it was just . . . *fun.* It seemed so much easier than the laborious Hemingway or Joyce imitations I'd been doing. I had strong opinions about my prose, I knew what to do. I'd always worshipped Carlin and Pryor and Steve Martin and Monty Python. I knew what entertainment felt like on the receiving end. I'd had an incredible experience with *Jaws*, for example. I saw it like ten times in the theater, had it pretty much memorized, and the fun was all about those big, emotional, surprising, thrilling moments. The last time I saw it, I was by myself, seated between a really old man and a pregnant woman, and just before the first time the shark appears I was thinking, We're either going to lose one or gain one.

But that's why I'd been drawn to art in the first place—to make big effects and get people riled up—but somehow I'd gotten sidetracked into thinking that there was something "higher" than that—like, being intellectual, or serious, or inscrutable was somehow more important than "kicking ass."

Kicking ass, properly defined, contains all of those *and* you can't stop reading, and what you are reading seems to speak directly to that which is most intensely concerning you.

BN: You and David Foster Wallace sometimes talked about fiction. I think part of Wallace's aesthetic as a fiction writer was, entertainment is the problem. You have to control your impulse to be liked. It's interesting that the two of you wrote funny jokes and penetrating insights through opposite-sounding means.

GS: I thought one of the ways that he was entertaining in person was that he didn't care if you liked him. Whatever he said to you, that's what he really thought. Which is entertaining and also terrifying. And clarifying. You suddenly become aware of your own shit—of the things you're slightly lying about, or stepping around, or being hyperbolic about. And he was, of course, a vastly entertaining writer, and for the same reason. You feel he's writing in pursuit of some truth and is going to say it no matter what it is or how complex his diction has to be to get him there.

But here's what I find interesting. There's something that happens in the moment of creation of a good sentence, or a good swath of sentences, that feels like the dropping away of self. Somebody else shows up and that person is better than the normal, everyday you. I'm guessing that the various approaches to writing are ultimately all about getting to that moment, that moment of spontaneity and self-negation. It's going to feel different for each writer and he or she will describe it differently, but basically there's one holy fountain and we're all trying to get to it through the same woods.

Dave felt, then, that his need to be liked caused him to write in a way he didn't like. For me, writing in a way that ignores the fact that I like to be liked causes me to write in a way I don't like. To him, being audience-aware felt like pandering, maybe—to me, it feels like the path to intimate communication.

BN: Your prose style is incredibly distinctive. Far more than with most writers, you can isolate a paragraph and read it aloud to an informed literary person and they can say, "That's George Saunders."

GS: Aw, thanks. That's something that's really important to me. I want to do that which only I can do. I can live with someone thinking my stuff is juvenile or . . . well, whatever they think. As long as they concede that it is distinctive or original.

My view of myself is that I came in through the basement window of literature. I'm not well educated or well read enough to do things correctly, and when I write what seems to me a "correct" story, it's got low energy and isn't true to my experience. Somehow the story and the language have to be a little messy or low. I love the idea of pushing an idea through a too-small linguistic opening—that feeling of overflow. I love the idea that the passion contained in a story is so great that it fucks up the form and makes it unseemly and impolite.

I saw a lot of that growing up in Chicago. People who were essentially speaking in poetry, by expressing great universal longings through a somewhat restricted diction.

BN: Was there a moment when you said to yourself, I think I found a prose style?

GS: The answer is a little complicated because I found it, lost it, had to find it again seven years later.

I applied to Syracuse with a story called "A Lack of Order in the Floating Object Room," which I wrote back when I was in Amarillo. I had this dream and just semi-transcribed it, and the resulting story was very strange, different from anything I'd ever done before—and it got published right away. It was a total departure for me—telegraphic and sci-fi. It could easily have gone into *CivilWarLand*, in terms of its tone and style.

But I didn't understand it enough or believe in it enough to duplicate it. It was just a three- or four-page stroke of beginner's luck, really. Then I went to Syracuse and somehow felt like I had to "get serious." I disavowed that story and the way I'd written it. No more funny sci-fi for me. I was going to be a real writer now. I had plenty of time, and good instruction, but I couldn't seem to write anything that had any life in it. After I got out I wrote this big realist novel, never published, set in Mexico, 700 pages long, *La Boda de Eduardo*, aka *Ed's Wedding*.

So, after grad school I was in this state where I was just like, "Dang, I used to be good, for like three weeks, but I'm obviously too stupid to do this."

Then one day, at work, during this conference call, I wrote these seven or eight goofy, Seussian poems and illustrated them—just for fun, out of the corner of my eye. And I brought them home and Paula, my wife, really liked them. I could hear her laughing in the next room, not at them but with them. And this switch got thrown in my head. It goes back to that idea of entertainment. She didn't keep reading those poems because she had to, or in order to submit to my big intellectual plan—she just found them funny. There was more power in those poems than in anything I'd written during grad school. That was painful, but it was also liberating. There had been zero intentionality behind those poems, except maybe, "Kill time until this stupid conference call is over." And yet . . . they *meant* something. And they didn't mean too neatly. You couldn't quite say what they meant. The meaning was in the experience of reading them and had somehow come out of a shift in my intention from "teach the world something" to "refuse to be boring."

So I went into work the next day and wrote a knockoff of "Lack of Order"—used the same story arc and tried to approximate the same voice, but set it in a different theme park and wrote it the way I'd written those poems. Try to be funny, don't let the reader tune out, don't suck. That story became "The Wavemaker Falters."

I found that I could undercut my "Hemingway boner" by setting stories in theme parks. If you're "doing" Hemingway, but in a theme park—it's auto-ironic. *I turn the dial. Jefferson Davis overheats, spewing oil out his top hat. Hank will be mad. Hank hates Oil Cleanup.* And the resulting tone felt right for describing the life I was actually living—that working-class American life, in which it feels like the culture dislikes you and is bent on humiliating you. I was working as a tech writer, for a company called Radian, in a complex called Corporate Woods, not making much money, had a receding hairline *and* a weird, semi-rebellious ponytail. We had two kids by then and things were beautiful and fraught and . . . scary. We were renting an apartment and the job was iffy and it wasn't entirely clear how things were going to turn out for us money-wise.

BN: After "The Wavemaker Falters," which story did you write next?

GS: "Downtrodden Mary's Failed Campaign of Terror." And then "CivilWarLand in Bad Decline" was third, I think. I had a period of revising stories on the bus, on the way home. I'd print out a clean copy before I left and snag one of those really great red felt-tip pens. Bliss! There was something about revising on the bus, with nothing else to do and a limited amount of time ahead—the ride was around fifty minutes—that changed the way I edited. It was like the time constraint handed me a finer microscope, which brought my attention down to the phrase level. I was almost exclusively micro-tweaking individual phrases to taste, not thinking about plot or story or theme. It was all about the way the words looked on the page. The decisions were playful and instinctive and even self-indulgent. Kind of like, I want it that way because I *want* it that way. And working obsessively on the phrase level started to produce plot. Once you had micro-specified the state of affairs by revising, it became clear what might want to happen next. Something like that. Very pleasurable and fun.

And it turned out that working this way produced more sophisticated stories than I'd been able to write before—weirder things were happening, things that seemed to have political implications. I cared more about the people. Every day the theme park got more complex. The CivilWarLand I had in my mind was so big and detailed and it revealed itself . . . line by line. I can still sort of go there.

BN: When did that place first come to you?

GS: My officemate and good friend asked me to play guitar at her wedding. She was getting married at the Genessee Country Museum, near Rochester. It's a beautiful nineteenth-century theme park. It's done so meticulously—no power lines, all the plants curated to be period-authentic, well-informed reenactors.

So we went there one afternoon for the rehearsal. We got to roam around—it was totally empty except for us. There were moments when we could've been back in 1862. Just us and these nineteenth-century buildings and the breeze in the trees. Magical. And that night I came home with the idea of setting a story in that place, or someplace like it. The writing of the story spanned the first Gulf War. And this idea started to leach in, from that war—a virtuous intervention loses its mooring and becomes evil. But again—not by design. It just got in there, via all those micro-changes that I was making by ear, on the bus, while concentrating, mostly, on the functional details of the theme park itself.

And I discovered that I could make a fairly ambitious story via fragments. I didn't have to have a through line or a plan, didn't have to know where it was going. I could basically write a few paragraphs a day and then micro-examine those the next day and cut parts and move things around and add a few new lines. If you trimmed all the fat out of a bit, it would start to thrum with meaning—and then, all of a sudden, it would have something it wanted to cause. So there would be these, like, vital bits on the page, not linked to anything yet. And then structure became just linking up those vital bits, looking for the simplest way to connect them.

So, if you cut all the lazy shit out of a story, what's left will tell you what structure to put in place so that none of those good bits need to be lost. And then you are trying to arrange them so that they are in causal relation to one another. Does A cause B or does B cause A? It's hard to explain. But all of these decisions were now being made intuitively and quickly and on the level of common sense, answering questions like, Does this change create more energy? What's the quickest way to get to the moment of meaningful action? How can this joke be made funnier?

It was liberating. I'd been told that you couldn't write a book while working full-time because there was no time for concentration. I was finding out that, for me, anyway, concentration was always available. I could work in small bursts. Even ten minutes was enough to improve a few sentences, which meant you had moved your story that much closer to being good. Progress! And this feeling of artistic patience came over me. Like, I can do this. It may take me ten years, but if I publish a six-page story a year, I can sell the resulting book.

BN: So, style grew out of circumstances, to some degree.

GS: A hundred percent. I got an increase in attentiveness that was related to shortage of time. I'd been driving myself crazy with questions like, "What do I believe about structure?" and, "What is my theory about character development?" and, "Well, what *is* a story, anyway?" This new mode's whole idea was to put those questions aside. Just keep the reader reading, and all questions will be answered. And suddenly, as a bonus, I was blurting out things about my position in the world that I hadn't even known until I blurted them out.

BN: The story will accumulate if each line is surprising and funny and true.

GS: Yes. And conversely, if a line is a honker, the reader pulls out of it, and the story . . . stops.

Bill Buford, at the *New Yorker*, summed up this approach perfectly, years later, when we were working on "Sea Oak." He was kind of ripping it apart—cutting scenes and proposing new ones and so on. Feeling insecure, fishing for a compliment, I said, in this whiny voice, "Bill, what do you *like* about this story?"

And there was this long thoughtful silence and he said, "Well, I read a line, and I like it . . . enough to read the next."

And that was it, his entire short story aesthetic. And it's perfect. A story is a linear, temporal thing, and we have to keep being pulled into it for it to do its work.

For me, anyway, as a bear of little brain, I was, and still am, comforted by the knowledge that you don't have to have a big theory about fiction. We don't have to ask anything but, "Would a reasonable person, reading line four, get a little jolt and go on to read line five?"

BN: In a lot of your early work, like *CivilWarLand*, the stories are very kind and generous, but some of the particulars are very mean.

GS: Amazingly mean. I just read *CivilWarLand* on audiobook, and, wow. Mean, yes. The sarcastic impulse is strong in me. I find it easier to disapprove than to approve—I'll go into a situation and what's wrong with it will strike me sooner and harder than what's right with it. I've come to see this as just a tendency. It's not right or wrong, but it's who I am or, at any rate, it's what I started with—kind of a snarky, negative mind. But then there's another side of me that's completely the opposite—more tender and hopeful and Pollyannaish, which hates hurting anyone's feelings and has warm feelings toward people and feels that the point of this life, when you boil it all down, is to become more loving—but that part will also ignore and tolerate things that are actually quite negative and evil, in the name of not making a fuss, i.e., is a little reactionary.

So I think I toggle between those two tendencies, in my writing and also in my life. That's one way of looking at craft—we develop a storytelling style that accommodates the different people who exist inside of us.

I like that Flannery O'Connor quote—a writer can choose what he *writes* but he can't choose what he makes *live*. For me, what was tending to come alive on the page in those early days was the darker stuff. So, I had a knee-jerk edgy tendency, with some insecurity behind it. When in doubt, shock. Or, When in doubt, oppose conventional thinking. A feeling that the most sophisticated take on something was the most negative, or the most skeptical, or the naughtiest. At the time I was writing *CivilWarLand*, I was desperately trying to get some attention from the world. I just wanted to get a story in a magazine, you know? And I could feel that when I let my mind drift over to what was wrong, and funnily wrong, about American life, more power got into the language, and the stories went lurching off in weird directions that also felt new. They were just *better*—more lively, more considerable.

Did I approve of what they were saying? Well, yes, actually. But they were like friends who were suddenly speaking too frankly. They kind of shocked me. I sometimes felt, "Well, you're rude, but I have to, mostly, agree with your conclusions, and wow, you are pretty exciting, but also, you're embarrassing me." It was as if I'd bought a dog, for all of the usual reasons, and then the dog started preaching these very hard-edged, truthful sermons. Do you bless the dog or resent it? My moral rationalization for those stories now is that, if you're going to make a scale model of good and evil, you have to let evil have broad shoulders. It has to be real evil. Then you've got a real and valid fight going on and the results matter.

But at the time I was just standing there with my prose energy meter, measuring the output, trying to retain the bits that were giving off energy, without worrying too much what I thought of their moral-ethical content.

My goal has always been to write stories in which the beauty of life is fairly represented—the goodness in people and nature, and the love and the hope—but in which the other side is also fairly represented—the incredible cruelty of people and of the universe itself. It's all true! And all happening at once! But I think that representing positive virtues is harder, technically.

BN: It seems like you've always approached fiction as a moral-ethical undertaking.

GS: Yes. My first job, unpaid, was as a reader of the Epistle, at church. It was a great job for a natural ham like me. A microphone, a great text, a captive audience. But there were these moments where the truth of what I was reading and the language in which it had been expressed and the instantaneous reaction of the audience—an increase in the quality of silence, you might call it—came together. So, that was a moral-ethical experience that was also an artistic experience.

There was a period during which I tried to engage any writer I admired—David Foster Wallace and Jonathan Franzen and Ben Marcus and Zadie Smith, to name-drop a bit—into conversations about, generally, How do we get out of Snarkville? It seemed like fiction was becoming a tool, primarily, for rejecting everything. It had lost its celebratory tonality. I certainly participated in that, and fair enough, this country can be incredibly violent and corporate and stupid. But I'd started feeling that, in my own work, certain modes had been disabled, or disqualified—could there ever be a happy marriage, or a CEO who wasn't diabolical?—that sort of thing. Our family life was so warm and caring, and the corporation where I worked was full of all sorts of people, people doing favors for one another and coming to work in the midst of real personal hardships and so on, but somehow I felt I didn't have the technical chops to get those more positive traces into my stories.

I remember going for a walk with Franzen in New York after *The Corrections* came out. I asked him, "What is it like to have a book that is so good and so artistically daring be so successful? What is there left to do, after that?" And he said, "Well, I don't think that book is as kind as I feel." I thought that was really beautiful and insightful. A lovely aspiration, to be kind—which he really is—and try to write a book as kind as you are.

BN: Do you think you'd be a different writer if you hadn't had children?

GS: For sure. I'm not sure I would have ever published anything. Before we had our kids, I was a decent person, kind of habitually, but nothing felt morally urgent. Then the kids came, and everything suddenly mattered. The world had a moral charge. If I love these guys so much, it stands to reason that every other person in the world has somebody who loves them just as much—or they *should have* someone who loves them as much. The world was full of consequence. That which helps what you love is good, that which hurts it is bad, and even a small hurt is significant. You see somebody come into the world, tiny and brand new and blameless, and you're like, "That person deserves the best." So, by implication, everybody deserves the best.

It made work meaningful. I had a job as a tech writer, and it was a hard job, a combination of dull and demanding. Not exactly the life I'd dreamed of. And yet suddenly, it was an interesting place to write about, full, as it was, of people who had once been somebody's kids and were often there for the same reason I was, to provide for their families.

I know other writers might feel that kids would impede them. And, depending on how you're wired and so on, that can definitely be true. But for me, it lit the world right up. And in the stories, you can see that. If a character of mine is insufficiently motivated, I just . . . give him a kid. Suddenly, they're not working that stupid job for themselves.

BN: You're known to spend a great deal of time on each story.

GS: It ranges from a day, with a story like "Sticks," which is just a few paragraphs, to fourteen years, on "The Semplica Girl Diaries." Typically it's . . . eight months? The one I'm working on now has taken over a year. I tend to get locked up at certain points. A student of mine once quoted Einstein as having said, "No worthy problem is ever solved in the plane of its original conception." I can't find any proof that Einstein ever said this, exactly, but I hope he did, because it's exactly right. When a story locks up and you get stuck, that's its way of saying, "Hey, dummy, you are trying to solve me in the plane of your original conception."

I learned at a certain point to stop running a timer. When I was younger, I'd think, I've been working on this story for four months. It *has* to be done. How can it *not* be? But soon enough, I found out that my stories don't work that way. Back in the day there was this wine commercial in which Orson Welles says, in that stentorian voice, "No wine before its time." I love that idea. To write a decent story is such a huge and unlikely accomplishment that we shouldn't care how long it takes. How much time would you be willing to spend to create something that lasts forever?

BN: When you were writing "The Semplica Girl Diaries" over fourteen years, did you leave it alone for long periods of time and go back to it?

GS: Yes, definitely. There were times when it sat there for three or four months while I did other things. Then I'd come back, have a little burst of progress, get stuck again.

So that's another tricky thing about writing—there's no reliable method. At least I haven't found one. The tricks that you discovered writing the last story don't work for this new one, and so on. It's like being a plumber but every time you show up, the pipes are made of different materials and transport different types of liquid and you're given weird new tools. And you're drunk. Part of the job, then, is to be cool with that—with the notion that you are never going to "master" writing. The only mastery is getting increasingly comfortable with the idea that you are never going to be a master—you are going to be a perennial clueless beginner with every new story, really, for sure. You'd better be, or you'll turn into a hack.

BN: How much did "Semplica" change between the earliest drafts and the final?

GS: The first half stayed mostly the same for many years. That was one of the frustrating things. I'd read the first half and think, I know this is good. And then I'd get to a certain place—I could show you just where it is in the text—and couldn't get past it. I'd write the next ten, or twenty, or thirty pages and polish those up, but then when I reread it from the beginning, the energy would always drop at that same place. I was basically repeating beats—good text, nothing new happening. A movie producer once told me that every structural unit of a story has to do two things—be entertaining in its own right and advance the story in a nontrivial way.

So it was a period of generating and then polishing sections that I later put in the garbage. I have about 200 pages of discards. They're all good, funny enough, polished to about the same quality as the rest of the story. But they didn't move the story forward in a significant way.

I'm having anxiety flashbacks just thinking about this.

BN: Do you ever wind up with nothing left from the early drafts?

GS: No—there's usually something of the very first draft in there, if only in the shape, or a few lines. But there's a lot of changes happening from draft to draft. It usually goes something like this. I type a page or two and then start revising that—kind of adjusting the phrases to where I can live with them, cutting out stuff that feels like padding, or like the conventional way of saying something. Then, part of it . . . is good. The word that always comes to mind is *undeniable.* A feeling like, Any reasonable reader is going to like this. And you've made one of those "vital bits" I referred to earlier. It starts to feel like there's something happening that's nontrivial. A character wants something, or something's at stake, or there's just some obvious next thing that wants to happen, or a bit of dialogue that has power. And then I'm in it. I make a sort of declaration of faith. You are still a mess, dear story, but I believe in you. The feeling goes from, This is probably a piece of crap, to, This will have value eventually if I just persist.

It's maybe not so different from a relationship. If you're somebody who breaks up with somebody every time you have a fight, then that's as deep as you're ever going to go—you're a first-fight guy. You'll never find out what might have happened if you'd gone past that first fight, i.e., what a little faith might have gotten you. But if you say, "I'm not breaking up with you, no matter what," then you're going to get through the fight, and there's going to be something on the other side that you couldn't have anticipated. So, learning to revise has an aspect of faith, I guess—you've slogged through the Field of Shit enough to believe that the, uh, Field of Not-Shit is on the other side.

BN: "Sea Oak" was another one where there were hundreds of pages of drafts, right?

GS: Yes, and I can tell you exactly where I got stuck on that one, too. It's right after the funeral. I wrote scene after scene after that and "finished" the story four or five times.

I remember taking a shower and thinking to myself, "Jeez, it's a really good story up to that moment right after the funeral. Why can't you finish this thing? Are you a professional or what?" Very self-flagellating—I was, yes, self-flagellating in the shower. And I thought, "You know, it's obvious that Aunt Bernie is the most interesting thing in the story, so she has to come back." Which I'd known for months. I had her coming back in dream sequences and flashbacks and all that. But after I thought, "She has to come back," this other little voice in my head blurted out, "From *the grave*." It literally just completed the phrase like that. And then I finished the story in, like, two weeks or something. Really easy. I'd seen a million zombie movies, so I knew how to take it from there.

So, to me, there's something really interesting about this notion that there is a below-the-surface part of the mind participating in the writing of a story, and that what we call "process" is about getting out of the way of that part of the mind, so it can assert itself more freely.

BN: That makes me wonder about "Bohemians." It has such a great twist, with Mrs. Hopanlitski turning out to be a fraud. Did you know that was coming, early on?

GS: No, not at all. I'd written up to the point where she was engaging with the kids for the first time—on page 185 of the book. There's this speech that I'd written for her that always struck me, on rereading, as false—the kind of speech a youngish writer, like me, at the time, would write for an Eastern European lady. It had this mock-Isaac Babel tone. I would always feel my reading energy flag slightly at that point, at the falseness of it. But if I cut that speech, the whole story fell apart. It felt like a vital bridge to the unwritten rest of the story.

So, at one point, I was reading that passage and, self-flagellating at my desk this time, thought something like, "Why are you such a bullshitter?

You know this whole passage is false." And this inner voice shot back, "I'm not a liar. She is." That is, the reason her speech felt false was that . . . it was. She'd been lying all along about having been a refugee.

Sometimes there's a defect in your prose. If you attribute it to yourself, well, you're just a bad writer. But if you say, "Hey, I'm just a ventriloquist here, that's the character talking, which is why the prose is so shaky"—well, then you're a good writer, making a character.

And for someone like me, who is spottily educated, this is a really powerful thing, because the very real defects in my way of expressing myself can be converted into assets.

Let's say you have a mailman in your story, and you have in mind that he's a good guy, the hero of the story, but in one of his speeches he's coming off as a little simple—he keeps repeating himself. And he's doing that because you, the writer, just wrote some repetitious text. Well, you could go in and fix it, cut out the repetitious bits, and most times you should definitely do that. But let's say that, on rereading, there's something you like about his particular style of repetition. You could say, "Hmm, why is this guy repeating himself? And then you start working with that. What is at the heart of his urge to repeat himself? How is his repetitiousness central to who he is as a person? How does his repetitiousness affect his relationships with other people?" Suddenly a "defect" in your prose has become an indicator of character.

BN: It's so interesting to hear you say that. Because I think so often what happens in your work is that we're in a character's stream of consciousness, and the moment it starts to sound bullshitty is the moment where things start to take off.

GS: That's right. The character tells me something I didn't know, through his "off" diction, which is sometimes legitimately my "off" diction, or through some odd belief he suddenly blurts out, or a patch where he or she falls out of voice. That's the story saying, through the character, Don't fence me in. I appreciate your starting me off, but I have some thoughts of my own. And that's exciting, because, at some level, that means there can be no mistakes. There are only changes of plan, and our job is to be alert to changes in the plan.

My mind—my everyday mind—is predictable and mundane and reductive. If we sat here and brainstormed story ideas, all of mine would be obvious. So, this way of writing we're discussing lets me sidestep that predictable, everyday mind, via technique.

BN: Whom do you show new stories to first?

GS: To Paula. But kind of late in the game—like, when I'm sure I've done all I can and feel good about it.

BN: Do you change your stories a lot in response to Paula's edits?

GS: Yes. She's a great reader for me—if it doesn't move her emotionally, then there's something wrong with it. She really knows me—knows the forms of my falseness, I guess you could say. She knows my cheap tricks and isn't buying them. She can always tell when I'm phoning something in or faking it or trying to sneak a clumsy patch by her.

I really trust her first, emotional reaction. If she reads something and goes, "Yeah, it's kind of good" . . . that's a defeat. I usually piss and moan for a few days, like, "Why did I even *show* it to her?" And then it's back to the drawing board. It's a blessing, truly, to have someone who knows you that well.

But if she reacts genuinely and emotionally, I know I have something.

After it passes the Paula Test, I send it to Deborah Treisman, my editor at the *New Yorker*. Deborah and I have worked together for about fifteen years now. And again I really trust her. She's incredibly protective of her writers. She told me once that part of her job, especially with writers who are more established, is to make sure they're not repeating themselves, to make sure that each new story represents real progress for them. That's a beautiful thing, to know that somebody's looking out for you in that way. I love working with her. It's like an adventure we go off on together, to see how much more light we can get the story to give off through the revision process.

When I first sent Andy Ward at Random House the Lincoln book, that was a big, scary day. I had to imagine that it wasn't what he expected my next book to be. To get back a letter that was 80 percent yes, love it, let's do it— that was amazingly empowering. He has that superpower of seeing what a book could be and endorsing it with his faith. And then the book grows into it. His faith makes the close work that comes afterward much easier to do.

When I was first starting out and was working with editors from smaller magazines, I found that there could sometimes be too much ego present in the edits. Like, the editor had to prevail, had to kind of assert himself over you. These great editors, like Andy and Deborah, have much more confidence. They realize that praising what's praiseworthy is a legitimate part of editing. And that to edit precisely is a form of praise—it means the editor is inside the story with you, rooting for it just like you are, but also really in touch with its strengths and weaknesses.

BN: You're fairly unusual in that you didn't write a novel for a really long time. Did you feel pressure during the first twenty-five years of your career to change?

GS: I really didn't. I felt a little pressure from *me*, because I'd grown up in a world that said a novel was a serious intellectual badge and stories were what you did to get ready. Once I started writing stories, I realized how wrong that is. Stories are hard, the hardest form, I think. There are a lot of sloppy novels that can't stand up to a single story by Yates. I was really lucky, because my agent, Esther Newberg, never pressured me. One thing she told me early on was if you get a story in the *New Yorker*, that's as difficult as publishing a first novel. She was really supportive of the idea that the short story is not an inferior form. *CivilWarLand* made a nice little splash and made a career possible. So I never felt any pressure at all. Except, as I say, from myself.

A couple of times, with "Jon" and "Semplica Girls," I had a moment of feeling, "Ah, this could be it. This could be my *novel!*" But then, once I'd conceptualized the piece as a novel, I'd make the mistake of setting aside all my internalized, hard-won rules about pace and cause and effect. And the thing would sprawl, and be a mess, until I went, "Ah, right, sorry, you are a story after all." So by the time I was writing *Tenth of December*, I was like, "Okay, George, you've had a really nice life just from writing stories, so don't be an ingrate. Double down, make yourself a less talented Alice Munro. Just write stories all the time." And that was a nice feeling—it gave me permission to experiment even more, to say, "This form is going to be my whole artistic life."

BN: And then you wrote a novel.

GS: And then I wrote a novel.

But I'm not even sure it's a novel, really. There's a lot of white space in that baby. I don't know what that book is, other than that which I needed to tell that particular story in a way that seemed exciting.

I had to change my ideas about style a bit—had to consent to let in some language that was a little less flamboyant, more normal. And in the ghost voices, I let myself be a bit derivative, to pay stylistic homage to, let's say, Faulkner, to Joyce. The way I thought of it was, If there are going to be this many voices, I can't always sound like myself. I can't always sound like someone trying to be stylistically distinctive. Sometimes I'm going to have to sound like a regular person, speaking. I was sampling historical texts and nineteenth-century letters and then started inventing some, and it became clear pretty quickly that those invented texts were going to need to blend with the real ones, and not stand out from them, which meant that "style" was suddenly equal to "whatever is needed," even when that meant dialing back the fireworks. After all those years of priding myself on having a distinctive style—and after the long struggle to find a voice at all—it felt risky to give that up. But also exciting, to say to yourself, "Okay, that's worked pretty well for you—now what else have you got?" I saw somewhere that the first thing they do at Juilliard is train the young actors out of their regional accents. They teach a sort of flat American English, so that the actors can layer in dialect and accents on top of that. Writing the novel felt something like that, like, to attain the real, collective voice of the book, and become a channel for all of these disparate voices, I was going to have to sacrifice "my" voice.

BN: In *Lincoln*, and in "Mother's Day," there's a moment before someone dies, during the transition into death, in which they must willingly let go of the self before death forcibly tears the self away from them. Why is that choice important?

GS: I'm not sure. I think, in both cases, the character is realizing, at the eleventh hour, that this thing he has been calling "himself" is, and always was, just a temporary construction—the self is a thing he has made with his thoughts. And now the time has come to say goodbye to that false construction. Those characters just have that realization shortly before it's forced on them by reality, that is, by death itself. I'm guessing I owe that move to stories like "Snows of Kilimanjaro" and, especially, some of Tolstoy's stories, like "Master and Man," and *The Death of Ivan Ilyich*, and "Alyosha the Pot"— in which those last moments, and then some, are narrated.

BN: When did you get into Tolstoy and the other Russians?

GS: After I finished *CivilWarLand*, I was feeling trapped inside the voice I'd used in that book—that terse, first-person, present-tense voice. I wanted to read myself out of it. So I just read for six months, and it was mostly the Russians.

The Russians of that period were taking on the big questions and using sophisticated artistic strategies to get answers that weren't programmatic. In their work, you get the sense that good comes out of evil and vice versa— it's a continuum, not a binary. And while I felt then, and still feel, that it's important to critique the way we live, because America is a really frightening construct that's eating people every day, I also think that any sort of us-versus-them critique is going to come up short. The ultimate form of critique is to really look at the way things are—How do they actually happen? What are the mixed impulses in a given person? and so on—to work toward a kind of holy ambiguity, a feeling of earned confusion. So, a story, at its highest level, is not saying, This is wrong, but, Thus it is. It is showing the multiplicity of reality, and with, even, a touch of affection.

Can we let a bunch of contradictory ideas resonate together, without denying the truth of any of them? What would *that* look like, in the context of a story? And how would exposure to that system of contradictions inform our moral positioning, and our actions?

BN: Has your sense of your role as a writer changed at all since the election in 2016?

GS: Right now I'm writing an essay about Nikolai Gogol's great story "The Overcoat." There's never going to be a more beautifully political story than that. Anyone reading that story will get their affection for the underdog rejuvenated. And what's more political than that? But Gogol wasn't "taking on" the czar. He was doing something bigger and more timeless than that—he was, I guess you could say, "taking on the inner czar that we all have inside us." I have a very limited gift and the essence of that gift, as I've come to understand it, is that I can sometimes produce a moment or two of increased empathy in a reader. And I'm grateful for that gift and understand it as, fundamentally, political.

BN: It's a fairly rare thing for people to be as loyal to the short story form as you are. Do you worry about the torch being passed?

GS: No. It's a beautiful form and people find it. Or it finds them. And the form will change with the times. It has to, it should. One of the things I love about teaching at Syracuse is that you meet class after class of talented young people, and it makes you an optimist. And you get to give that kind of student a sort of lineage advice—you get to pass on to them ideas like, Yes, you are responsible for every single line. You are. No one else will be.

I remember years ago, working at Radian, writing *CivilWarLand*, thinking, "Wow, I've been working on this same paragraph for five days. Is that normal?" And then that wise little voice in my head asked, "Well, is it getting better? If so, then yes. It may not be normal, per se, but obviously it's what you have to do." And this light went on, like, "It's going to be as hard as it needs to be, and my job is to not chicken out."

So, you're sitting there in a conference with a student and it's the moment when you get to lightly affirm a realization she is just starting to have about that. You see that she's at that point in her work. And, with writers as talented as ours, you don't have to say much. It's just lightly blessing their good instincts, subtly reassuring them. Yes, it actually does take that long, the story form does reward that level of care. Yes, it is your job to imprint every single line with your artistic view. Writers that good, when they hear that, they're relieved, because they suspected all along that it was that way.

Index

About the Editor

Michael O'Connell is associate professor of humanities at Siena Heights University in Adrian, Michigan, where his scholarly interests focus primarily on the intersections of religion, particularly Catholicism, and contemporary literature. His critical essays appear in *Christianity and Literature, Renascence, American Catholic Studies, Religion and the Arts,* and the *Journal of David Foster Wallace Studies.* He is the editor of *Conversations with George Saunders,* and is currently working on a study of violence in contemporary American Catholic fiction.

www.ingramcontent.com/pod-product-compliance
Lightning Source LLC
Chambersburg PA
CBHW030111030726
47498CB00007B/2332

* 9 7 8 1 4 9 6 8 4 0 3 0 1 *